*e*Directives: Guide to European Union Law on E-Commerce

# Law and Electronic Commerce

## Volume 14

*The titles published in this series are listed at the end of this volume.*

# *e*Directives:
# Guide to European Union Law on E-Commerce

Commentary on the Directives
on Distance Selling, Electronic Signatures,
Electronic Commerce, Copyright in the
Information Society, and Data Protection

Edited by

Arno R. Lodder

Henrik W.K. Kaspersen

KLUWER LAW INTERNATIONAL

THE HAGUE / LONDON / NEW YORK

Library of Congress Cataloging-in-Publication Data

ISBN 90-411-1752-0

Published by Kluwer Law International,
P.O. Box 85889, 2508 CN The Hague, The Netherlands.

Sold and distributed in North, Central and South America
by Kluwer Law International,
101 Philip Drive, Norwell, MA 02061, U.S.A.
kluwerlaw@wkap.com

In all other countries, sold and distributed
by Kluwer Law International, Distribution Centre,
P.O. Box 322, 3300 AH Dordrecht, The Netherlands.

*Printed on acid-free paper*

# Preface

In literature still no consensus has been reached about the question whether *e-commerce* and *newconomy* should be qualified as a *hype* or that indeed a new age has come with serious opportunities for further economic growth. In the short term the former may be true but in the long term the latter will prove to be true too, as is at least the opinion of the editors. It should be admitted that the initial expectations of enterprises and the stock market for a prosperous growth were not met, but the tokens are there that it is a matter of time before enterprises and consumers will fully discover the advantages of doing business electronically. In the mean time, in fact all business enterprises make use of the World-Wide Web to provide information about their products and services. It is quite clear that those websites already fulfil a very important function in (e-)commerce, and will only become more important in the future. The Web is the easy window to the global market.

So far for the economic prospects. From a legal point of view the fact that business is done electronically brings a need for review of the laws concerned. Horace characterised his co-citizens by means of the adagium '*Si possi recte, si non quocumque modo rem*' (make money by right means, if you can, if not by any means). The safeguards already present in the law should at least also apply to the electronic environment. Moreover, since e-commerce will involve many international transactions, there is also a need for international harmonisation of the national laws.

In Europe, it is self-evident that the European Union should take legal initiatives on behalf of its Member States in order to coordinate the legislative process concerning e-commerce activities, and it did. Since the Ministerial Conference in Bonn in July 1997 e-commerce is a key issue on the Commission's agenda, and a number of Directives were launched since then or will be shortly.

This book differs from other books on law & e-commerce. Its aim is not to provide just an overview of the relevant issues. Rather a number of important EU Directives regarding the regulation of e-commerce are brought together and discussed. The book deals with topics like electronic contracting, electronic signatures, copyright and also with data protection aspects of e-commerce. For the reader's convenience the text of the Directives, as well as the preceding recitals are placed in appendices. Each author discusses one Directive in his field of expertise. As an additional service, Directives and related legal documents will be published on the website:

http://www.rechten.vu.nl/~lodder/ecommerce

This book is meant as comprehensive legal source of e-commerce legislation for both academics (LL.M-students and academic staff) and practitioners (attorneys, company lawyers, consultants). It is not only of interest for readers in the EU Member States (because their national law is or is about to be adapted to the Directives), but also for readers in aspirant Member States of the EU, as well as for readers in other countries where e-commerce has emerged, like the Unites States of America.

The editors in particular wish to thank Ms Celine Suen, assistant-researcher at the Computer/Law Institute, for her skilful and dedicated assistance in the editing of the texts.

Amsterdam, September 2001

Arno R. Lodder
Henrik W.K. Kaspersen

# Summary of contents

# Detailed table of contents

# Chapter 1

# Introduction

## Arno R. Lodder

It is hard to imagine that the application that turned the Internet into such a popular medium, the World Wide Web, was not around at the beginning of the 1990s.[1] The first online stores started to appear halfway the 1990s, e.g. Amazon.com opened its 'doors' in the summer of 1995. The economic expectations of doing business online were high, it would turn the traditional economy into a new economy. The emerging electronic market has given rise to all kind of legal questions concerning various topics, such as online contracting, means of identification in an electronic environment, copyright on the Internet, etc. The European Union has been interested in electronic commerce, for reasons of expected economic impact, at least since 1997. In April that year the European Commission presented a communication titled 'A European Initiative in Electronic Commerce'.[2] Four key areas were identified:

- Widespread affordable access to the infrastructure;
- Creation of a legal framework;
- Raising awareness;
- International cooperation.

Regarding the first area the main initiative, following the general EU telecom policy, has been the liberalisation of the telecommunication market. The last two areas deal with making the public aware of the opportunities of electronic commerce and the cooperation with third countries, in particular with the United States. It is the second mentioned area this book focuses on: the creation of a legal framework for electronic commerce. Four Directives central to the regulation of electronic commerce in the European Union (EU) are provided with article-by-article comments, viz. 97/7/EC on distance selling, 1999/93/EC on electronic signatures, 2000/31/EC on electronic commerce, and 2001/29/EC on copyright in the information society. Moreover, data protection and electronic commerce is addressed in the final chapter.

The Commission indicated in their 1997 e-commerce initiative that, in order for the European Union to profit fully from the new economy, realisation of the initiatives had to take place by 2000. In January 2000 the first *pure* e-commerce Directive

---

[1] The WWW was made public in 1991, but only after the first browser Mosaic appeared in 1993 its popularity rapidly increased. See, T. Berners-Lee & M. Fischetti (1999), *Weaving the Web The original design and ultimate destiny of the World Wide Web, by its inventor*, San Fransisco: Harper.

[2] COM (97) 157 final.

1

*A.R. Lodder and H.W.K. Kaspersen (eds.),*
*eDirectives: Guide to European Union Law on E-Commerce*, 1–9.
© 2002 *Kluwer Law International. Printed in the Netherlands.*

entered into force,[3] viz. the Directive 1999/93/EC on electronic signatures. Around the same time, on March 23/24 2000, the European Council (held in Lisbon) declared that the EU had to strive to become 'the most competitive and dynamic economy in the world.' The adopted plan was given the name *e*Europe (an Information Society for all). The three main objectives of the *e*Europe 2002 plan were:
1.   A cheaper, faster, and secure Internet;
2.   Investing in people and skills;
3.   Stimulate the use of Internet.

A way to stimulate the use of Internet is by *accelerating e-commerce*, which appeared to mean that all remaining electronic commerce legislation had to be pushed through by the end of that year, to try to help the European Union to catch up with the US. Ironically, also in the spring of 2000, the e-commerce market collapsed, the NASDAQ[4] dropped significantly. As a consequence, the then existing unrealistic expectations about the success of e-commerce were put into perspective. No longer merely fancy ideas for an Internet company, without any business plan illustrating how to make profit, were financially supported. From now on investments should be based on a solid business plan, so the economics of electronic business do follow the same rules as traditional businesses. This does not imply, however, that the volume and growth of business over the Internet as such should be underestimated. Undeniably, the Internet provides unprecedented opportunities, in particular for the exchange and dissemination of information, but also for online banks, travel agencies, bookstores, CD shops, and auction sites, to mention just some of the most popular e-commerce applications.

This introductory chapter pays attention to EU initiatives relevant for the regulation of e-commerce that are not discussed in detail in the other chapters. But first follows a brief exploration of the term e-commerce.

## 1.1   What is e-commerce?

Electronic commerce is often interpreted as being just Internet commerce, for example in the following definition Patricia Buckley gives in a US government document on the digital economy:[5]
'(...) electronic commerce (i.e., business processes which shift transactions to the Internet or some other non-proprietary, Web-based system). Electronic commerce is a means of conducting transactions that, prior to the evolution of the Internet as a business tool in 1995, would have been completed in more traditional ways–by

---

[3]   One could argue that this already happened in 1997 with the publication of Directive 97/7/EC on distance selling. However, although the main area of application of this Directive is e-commerce, it has not been drafted for that purpose (see also section 2.1).
[4]   Index for technology related stocks, see <www.nasdaq.com>.
[5]   See <www.e-commerce.gov/ede/chapter1.html>.

telephone, mail, facsimile, proprietary electronic data interchange systems, or face-to-face contact.'

Interestingly, the 'traditional ways' refer also to electronic means (fax, EDI). So, commercial activities performed with these means are actually part of electronic commerce. Not only the US government, also the European Union sees e-commerce largely as Internet-based. The term that is often used by the EU in this context, the Information Society, refers mainly (or, as some people say solely) to Internet applications.

A pure definition of electronic commerce is one by Roger Clarke, who has been working on electronic commerce related topics already since the late 1980s. He claims that electronic commerce is usually defined as:[6]

'the conduct of commerce in goods and services, with the assistance of telecommunications and telecommunications-based tools'

The renown UNCITRAL Model Law on Electronic Commerce focuses on the shift from paper-based to electronic communication:[7]

'Noting that an increasing number of transactions in international trade are carried out by means of electronic data interchange and other means of communication, commonly referred to as "electronic commerce", which involve the use of alternatives to paper-based methods of communication and storage of information,'

Summarising, the basic notions of electronic commerce are:
- commercial context;
- goods and services;
- (tele)communication;
- business transactions.

On the basis of these concepts I would like to propose the following definition of e-commerce:

*Any business transaction concerning goods and services, including relating commercial activities, where participants are not at the same physical location and communicate through electronic means.*

## 1.2 Types of electronic commerce

A taxonomy of types of electronic commerce can be based on either the parties involved (businesses, administrations/governments, and consumers) or the commercial activities explored (e.g., webvertisement, orders of physical goods via electronic means, electronic delivery of digital goods, electronic information

---

[6] See <http://www.anu.edu.au/people/Roger.Clarke/EC/ECDefns.html#EC>.
[7] See <http://www.uncitral.org/english/texts/electcom/ml-ec.htm>.

services). The involved parties are Businesses (B), Consumers (C), and Administrations/Governments[8] (A/G). The following relations can be identified:

- B2B (Business to business; still by far the most successful);
- B2C (Business to consumer; as will appear in the remainder of this book, electronic commerce regulation is especially concerned with this type);
- B2A/G (Business to administration; this type contributed significantly to the success of electronic commerce in the USA);
- C2C (Consumer to consumer; quite popular on the Internet, for example auction sites like eBay.com);
- C2B (Consumer to business; for example joint purchases: Letsbuyit.com)
- C2A/G (Consumer to administration; I know of no examples yet);
- A/G2B/C/A/G (also known as E-government; transformation of the administration (government) from paper organisations to virtual organisations.)

The various commercial activities can be headed under what is often referred to as services of the Information Society (see section 4.2.2). These information society services include both the selling of products and deliverance of services. The reason to use a general term is that the border between selling a product and rendering a service is no longer always a clear one.[9]

## 1.3    The EU and e-commerce regulation

An often mentioned reason for the drafting of e-commerce regulation is the raising of confidence at the side of the seller of online goods and services, and, in particular on the side of the buyer/consumer.[10] However, even without the rise of electronic commerce the information society brought a need for review of the laws, because current legislation was drafted in a mainly paper-based society.

These days, it is hard to identify a legal domain that does have some connection with e-commerce. However, some legal issues more related to doing business electronically than others. The most important issues are addressed in the Directives that are discussed in the remaining chapters, e.g., online consumer protection, electronic contracting, electronic signatures, copyright, data protection (for more details, see section 1.4). In this section some other EU initiatives that deal with e-commerce are briefly discussed. A complete overview is not aimed at, if possible at all in this rapidly changing field. Merely, the aim of this section is to point out

---

[8]   One could question whether A/G is an electronic *commerce* party. However, if the term is not interpreted in a strict sense, services of administration/governments are usually included.

[9]   For example, downloaded software can be considered a product as well as a delivered service (see section 2.6).

[10]  See also the Council Resolution of 19 January 1999 'The Consumer Dimension of the Information Society', *OJ* C 23, 28.1.1999.

initiatives and refer to the relevant texts on those initiatives. In addition to this overview, new developments and initiatives in the field of law & e-commerce can be found at the Law & Electronic commerce site.[11]

### 1.3.1 E-money and financial services

Most internet payments are still done by credit card. Electronic money, as its name suggests, is an alternative more suited for payment over the internet. These days almost all banks offer the possibility for the account holder to check his account via the internet. However, these bank services as well as any account-based debit or credit card, are not examples of electronic money. Rather, electronic money is a surrogate for bank notes and coins, a value stored on a chip card or on the computer hard disk of the owner of the money. On electronic payment systems in general, the Commission issued the non-binding Recommendation 97/489/EC concerning transactions by electronic payment instruments and in particular the relationship between issuer and holder.[12] The recommendation mainly addresses the issue of liability in case of loss, theft or irregularities. The voluntary implementation of this recommendation remains restricted to national banking codes, and as such commercial issuers of electronic money not being banking institutions are not affected by this recommendation. In order to regulate the issuance of electronic money, the European Union has created two Directives.

The first is Directive 2000/28/EC of 18 September 2000 amending Directive 2000/12/EC relating to the taking up and pursuit of the business of credit institutions.[13] By this Directive the issuance of electronic money is brought within the scope of (parts of) the general Directive 2000/12/EC for credit institutions. As a consequence, the same regulation is applicable to both banks and non-banks that issue electronic money.

The second is Directive 2000/46/EC of the European Parliament and of the Council of 18 September 2000 on the taking up, pursuit of and prudential supervision of the business of electronic money institutions.[14] This Directive is also applicable to both banks and non-banks, and introduces, according to recital 5 'a technology-neutral legal framework that harmonises the prudential supervision of electronic money institutions to the extent necessary for ensuring their sound and prudent operation and their financial integrity in particular.'

Finally, the working documents on *Payment card charge back when paying over Internet*, and *Payment by e-purse over the internet*[15] should be mentioned.

---

[11] See <http://www.rechten.vu.nl/~lodder/ecommerce>.

[12] *OJ* L 208/52, 2.8.97.

[13] *OJ* L 275/37, 27.10.2000.

[14] *OJ* L 275/39, 27.10.2000.

[15] European Commission, DG Internal Market, MARKT/173/2000, 12 July 2000, and MARKT/174/2000, 24th April 2001.

Particularly targeted at consumer protection is the Directive concerning the distance marketing of consumer financial services and amending Directives 97/7/EC and 98/27/EC. This Directive on 'financial services' (insurance, banking and investment services) supplements Directive 97/7/EC on distance selling (see chapter 2), and regulates similar issues as Directive 97/7/EC. After the Commission proposal in October 1998, and the amended proposal in July 1999, not much has happened. On December 7 1999 the Internal Market Council was asked by the Consumer Affairs Council to conclude the discussion. Amongst others the following conclusion was adopted: 'The Council stresses the importance of the proposal (...) and the urgency of its adoption.' Nonetheless, another one and half year later during the Council meeting Internal Market/Consumer Affairs/Tourism, on 30-31 May 2001, only what rules should apply to financial service providers during the transposition period of the Directive was discussed (and no agreement was reached). In the autumn of 2001 this Directive still is not final. However ... at the moment this text was on the point of being sent to the publisher, rather unexpectedly political agreement was reached (27 September 2001). So, if not by the end of 2001, probably at the beginning of 2002 this Directive will enter into force.

## 1.3.2    E-Tax[16]

The 1998 EU Commission's Communication on E-commerce and Indirect Taxation did not result in much concrete proposals yet.[17] Notably, there is hardly a topic more difficult to regulate than tax in general in the EU, in particular online value-added taxes (VAT). In December 2000 the Parliament rejected a (controversial) proposal for a Directive amending Directive 77/388/EEC with a view to simplifying, modernising and harmonising the conditions laid down for invoicing in respect of value added tax.[18] According to this proposal, online sellers from all over the world had to collect VAT from EU customers of digital products and services. In the summer of 2001 a new proposal on this issue was supported by the Commission and all Member States, except the UK that declared: 'this approach would give rise to inequality of treatment for non-EU suppliers compared to EU suppliers, imposing additional compliance burdens on the former; be difficult for non-EU operators to comply with and near impossible for Member States to enforce, entail a complex distribution system, expensive to implement and difficult to monitor; and, not explicitly be an interim measure.' The UK proposed to exempt online VAT regarding consumers on the short term, and cooperate with the OECD that develops initiatives on this issue. Obviously the final word has not been said on this subject.

---

[16]   See on this topic <http://www.ecommercetax.com/>.
[17]   COM (1998) 374 final.
[18]   *OJ* C 337 E 65, 28.11.2000.

### 1.3.3 Jurisdiction

The Brussels convention on jurisdiction was concluded in 1968.[19] As a general rule, jurisdiction is exercised by the Member State in which the defendant is domiciled. The consumer is protected, under certain circumstances he can sue the other party in his home state. In the Council regulation that replaces the Brussels convention,[20] a new Article 15 and 16 extend the protection of consumers that contract over the Internet.[21] No longer the place where the contract is concluded is decisive, but for any conflict about a product or service ordered from a website the consumer can sue the service provider in its home country (see also section 4.2.2). As regards the applicable law, the Rome convention on law applicable to contract law from 1980[22] is under revision. The Commission plans to present a Green Paper at the beginning of 2002,[23] in which the law applicable to e-commerce contracts should be taken into account, including protection of the online consumer. Another initiative is the so-called Rome II convention, on law applicable to non-contractual obligations. On this topic the Commission plans to present a proposal before the end of 2001.[24]

### 1.3.4 Miscellany

This section enumerates in chronological order some other initiatives relevant for e-commerce, and, as far as not self-explanatory, provide them with a brief explanation:

- Directive 98/48/EC amending Directive 98/34/EC laying down a procedure for the provision of information in the field of technical standards and regulations.[25] This Directive extends the scope of Directive 83/189 (recently amended by Directive 98/34/EC), which covers national rules affecting the free movement of goods, to include rules on Information Society services;
- Directive 98/84/EC on the legal protection of services based on, or consisting of, conditional access. Examples of these services are pay-TV, video-on-demand, music-on-demand, and electronic publishing;[26]
- Council Resolution of 19 January 1999 on the Consumer Dimension of the Information Society;[27]
- Council Decision of 22 December 2000 adopting a multiannual Community programme to stimulate the development and use of European digital content on

---

[19] A consolidated version of the Convention was published in 1998, *OJ* C 27, 26.01.1998.

[20] Council Regulation (EC) No 44/2001 of 22 December 2000 on jurisdiction and the recognition and enforcement of judgments in civil and commercial matters, *OJ L* 12/1, 16.1.2001.

[21] M.D. Powell & P.M. Turner-Kerr, 'Issues in e-commerce – European Union, Putting the E- in Brussels and Rome', *Computer Law & Security Report* 2000, Vol. 16, no. 1, p. 23-27.

[22] A consolidated version of the Convention was also published in 1998, *OJ* C 27, 26.01.1998.

[23] Communication of the Commission, COM (2001) 278 final, 23.05.2001.

[24] Ibid.

[25] *OJ* L 217, 5.8.1998.

[26] *OJ* L 320/54, 28.11.1998.

[27] *OJ* C 23/1, 28.01.1999.

the global networks and to promote linguistic diversity in the information society;[28]

• Initiatives on the out-of-court settlement of disputes, including online dispute resolution, e.g. the Extra Judicial Network, and the financial counterpart FIN-NET (see section 2.9.3 and 4.7.2), and recently the Commission Recommendation on the principles for out-of-court bodies involved in the consensual resolution of consumer disputes.[29]

## 1.4    Structure of the book

EU directives are directed towards the Member States of the European Union. The Member States are under an obligation to amend their law according to the EU directives. As a consequence, national law of the Member States is influenced by EU directives. This is in particular true for information society services (e-commerce). Although the field of e-commerce is rapidly changing, the discussion of the Directives in this book remains valuable over time.[30] After the implementation of the discussed Directives, the changes to national (civil) law of the Member States are far-reaching.

The four central e-commerce Directives are discussed in chronological order:
• Chapter 2 – Directive 97/7/EC on the Protection of Consumers in respect of Distance Contracts;
• Chapter 3 – Directive 1999/93/EC on a Community framework for electronic signatures;
• Chapter 4 – Directive 2000/31/EC on certain legal aspects of information society services, in particular electronic commerce, in the Internal Market;
• Chapter 5 – Directive 2001/29/EC on the harmonisation of certain aspects of copyright and related Rights in the information society.

Although the style of each chapter varies depending on the author, the commonality of the chapters is far more obvious. Explanatory notes address all Articles of the Directives in a clear and profound manner. The Directives discussed in chapters 2-5 can be found in the appendices 1-4, respectively. Finally, Chapter 6 discusses EU initiatives, in particular Directive 95/46/EC and 97/66/EC on data protection as far as relevant for e-commerce. Since the final chapter is not devoted to a single Directive,

---

[28]  *OJ* L 14/32 , 18.01.2001.

[29]  *OJ* L 109/56 , 19.04.2001.

[30]  In this respect the approach of this book differs from other books in the domain of law & e-commerce, in which the starting point is the issues rather than the regulation dealing with those issues. See, for example, T.R. Broderick, *Regulation of Information Technology in the European Union*, Kluwer Law International 2000, D Tunkel & S York (eds.), *E-commerce: A Guide to the Law of Electronic Business*, Butterworths 2000, M. Chissick & A. Kelman, *Electronic Commerce: Law and practice*, London: Sweet & Maxwell 2000, and S. Singleton, *E-Commerce: A Guide to the Law*, Gower Publishing 2001.

and given its scope not all Articles are addressed, the source material of this chapter is not included in the appendix. However, the text of all directives, as well as various other documents referred to in this book, can be downloaded from:

http://www.rechten.vu.nl/~lodder/ecommerce

# Chapter 2

# Directive 97/7/EC on the protection of consumers in respect of distance contracts

## Julia Hörnle, Gavin Sutter, Ian Walden

Important dates regarding the Directive 97/7/EC of the European Parliament and of the Council of 20 May 1997 on the protection of consumers in respect of distance contracts are in chronological order:

- **1992, April 7** – Proposal adopted by the Commission;[1]
- **1993, May 26** – Proposal approved by the European Parliament, subject to amendments;[2]
- **1993, October 7** – Amended proposal adopted by Commission;[3]
- **1995, June 29** – Common position adopted by the Council;[4]
- **1996, November 27** – Decision Conciliation Commission;
- **1997, January 16** – Approval by the European Parliament;[5]
- **1997, May 20** – Signed by the European Parliament and the Council;
- **1997, June 4** – Publication in the Official Journal;[6]
- **2000, June 4** – Directive should be implemented by the Member States.

## 2.1    Introduction

By their very nature, commercial activities carried out over the Internet are carried out at a distance; i.e. the vendor and purchaser are not at the same physical location. From a public policy perspective, governments are concerned that in such an environment consumers are more vulnerable and therefore need the protection of law. Directive 97/7/EC, the 'Distance-selling Directive', is a direct response to such concerns and is therefore a critical component of the emerging regulatory framework for electronic commerce in Europe. However, the paradox is that the Directive was never designed with Internet-based commerce in mind. It pre-dates the idea of the Internet as *the* commercial environment for the 21<sup>st</sup> Century, and as a consequence

---

[1]   *OJ* C 156/14, 23.6.1992.
[2]   *OJ* C 176/85, 28.6.1993.
[3]   *OJ* C 308/18, 15.11.1993.
[4]   *OJ* C 288/1, 30.10.1995.
[5]   *OJ* C 33/76, 3.2.1997.
[6]   *OJ* L 144/19, 4.6.1997.

*A.R. Lodder and H.W.K. Kaspersen (eds.),*
*eDirectives: Guide to European Union Law on E-Commerce,* 11–31.
© 2002 *Kluwer Law International. Printed in the Netherlands.*

has been labelled as an example of the limitations of legislators trying to regulate in a rapidly developing environment.

Although the Distance-selling directive was only adopted four years ago, the initial Commission proposal dates back to 1992.[7] This proposal was the Commission's response to a 1989 Council Resolution on consumer protection policy, which identified 'new technologies involving teleshopping' as an area worthy of further study.[8] Such is the nature of the European legislative process that once introduced, the proposal gained a momentum of its own which carried it through to its eventual adoption relatively unaltered. When considering the provisions of the Distance-selling directive, it is therefore always important to bear in mind its history: essentially pre-Internet.

## 2.2    Article 2 – Definitions

To qualify as a contractual arrangement subject to the Distance-selling directive, four criteria have to be met. First, the parties to the contract are not simultaneously physically present, therefore the supplier 'makes exclusive use of one or more means of distance communication.' Second, such distance is only relevant in respect of the period up to and including the moment the contract is concluded. The subsequent performance of the contract, whether physically or at a distance, is an ancillary issue. Third, the contract is between a 'supplier' and a 'consumer.' Business to business electronic commerce, such as web-exchanges, is not subject to the Directive. Fourth, the supplier must be using 'an organised distance sale or service-provision scheme', which would seem to exclude the ad hoc provision of goods and services in response to specific consumer requests.

In terms of 'means of distance communications', Annex I provides an indicative list, since 'the constant development of those means of communication does not allow an exhaustive list to be compiled' (recital 9). As a consequence, the list is unchanged from that originally proposed by the Commission in 1992. The only reference to an Internet-based service is electronic mail. The rest are predominantly traditional mechanisms, paper and telephony-based. The list provides an interesting historical insight into perceptions of which technologies would come to the fore, such as 'videophone (telephone with screen)', but which are still in their infancy some nine years later.

As well as 'suppliers', the Directive also singles out the 'operator of a means of communication' for special attention: e.g. the telecommunications operator, the

---

[7]   Proposal for a Council Directive on the protection of consumers in respect of contracts negotiated at a distance; *OJ* C 156/14, 23.6.1992.

[8]   Council Resolution on future priorities for relaunching consumer protection policy; *OJ* C 294/1, 22.11.1989.

broadcaster or the postal services. Two of the subsequent references to 'operators' are designed to exclude the application of the Directive's provision: Article 3(1) and Article 5(2). However, Article 11(3)(b) calls upon Member States to take measures to ensure the 'operators' 'cease practices which do not comply' with the provisions of the Directive. Such measures could, for example, potentially include a requirement upon operators to monitor the usage of their services by 'suppliers' to ensure compliance with the terms of the Directive. We are not aware that any Member States have implemented any such obligations; although such provisions would now be limited under Article 15 of Directive 2000/31/EC on electronic commerce, which prohibits any general obligation to monitor (see section 4.6.4). 'Operators' may, however, impose contractual obligations upon their customers to comply with the relevant national implementing measure.

## 2.3 Article 3 – Exemptions

Article 3 details two categories of exemption: complete exemption from the Directive and exemptions from specified provisions. The sales of financial services at a distance are exempt, although the Commission has put forward a separate proposal to encompass such activities, which is being considered by the Council and Parliament.[9]

Automated vending machines and automated commercial premises, such as cash machines, are exempt. However, the latter term would seem problematic in an Internet environment. It is unclear why a web site does not fall within the concept of an 'automated commercial premise.' No definition is given of a 'commercial premise', such as requiring the person to be simultaneously present at the premises, which is the obvious implication. A web server will be located within some form of commercial premise, simply at a remove from the consumer. Such questions clearly challenge the validity of the Directive in its current form.

The construction and sale of immovable property is exempt from the Directive, a category of transactions which Member States may also exempt in respect of the validity of electronic contracts under Article 9(2) of Directive 2000/31/EC on electronic commerce (see section 4.5.1).

Auctions are also excluded due to the special nature of their legal arrangements. It is perhaps ironic that one of the great success stories of the Internet as a commercial environment has been in the area of online auctions, with companies such as eBay. However, in terms of consumer disputes, the credit card company Visa reported in 1999 that one of the major grounds for disputed payments in Europe concerned goods bought through Internet-based auction services.

---

[9] Proposal for a Directive of the European Parliament and of the Council concerning the distance marketing of consumer financial services and amending Council Directive 90/619/EEC and Directives 97/7/EC and 98/27/EC; *OJ* C 385/10, 11.12.1998.

The delivery of consumables, such as food and drink, are exempt from Articles 4 (requirement to provide prior information); 5 (written confirmation of information); 6 (right of withdrawal) and 7(1) (performance). In an era of Tesco Direct and other online supermarket services, the exemption from the information requirements seems unnecessary and inappropriate. Again, use of the phrase 'regular roundsmen' was clearly intended to limit application to traditional service suppliers, such as milk and bread, but the terminology lacks clarity of scope and application.

## 2.4 Articles 4 and 5 – Transparency rights of the consumer

### 2.4.1 The reason for the transparency provisions

Articles 4 and 5 impose an obligation on the supplier to give the consumer certain information. The purpose of these provisions is to ensure that the consumer makes a well-informed purchasing decision, which is in the interests of both consumer protection and competition policy. Also, transparency is to create trust in the relatively new sector of distance communication commerce, as stated in recital 11:
'whereas the means of distance communication must not lead to a reduction in the information provided to the consumer'

Before examining the details of the two provisions it is worthwhile to briefly recall the specific information problems. For web-based electronic commerce, there is an opportunity to describe the goods or services in great detail, in addition using visual aids such as photographs and graphs. On the other hand, because of the intangible nature of web sites, the identity and geographical location of the supplier will often be unclear. Furthermore, where goods are purchased, the consumer will be unable to physically examine them, for example as to quality, feel, colour and size. These issues are further compounded in the case of telephone sales where there are no visual aids. For these reasons it was considered necessary to establish minimum information requirements.
It should also be pointed out that the information requirements contained in the Distance-selling directive overlap and supplement with those contained in Articles 5, 6 and 10 of the Directive on electronic commerce.[10]

### 2.4.2 The point at which the information must be given

The first question, then, is when must this information be given? The Directive makes a distinction between 'prior information' in Article 4, which must be given 'in good time prior to the conclusion of any distance contract' (Article 4(1)), and 'written confirmation of information' in Article 5, which must be given 'in good time during the performance of the contract For goods, the supplier must provide this written confirmation, at the latest when the goods are delivered to the consumer.

---

[10]  See further Section 4.3.2.

Thus Article 4 contains the information which must be provided at the outset. Article 5 contains the information to be given sometime during performance of the contract.

### 2.4.3 The manner in which the information must be given

The next question is, how must this information be provided? This question has provoked some controversy and consequently, the wording in the Directive is not entirely clear.

Unsurprisingly, the Article 4 information to be provided at the outset must be clear and comprehensible (Article 4(2)). This would exclude information in very small print hidden away deep inside a web site or contradictory or misleading information. However, it should not affect the language used, since 'the languages used for distance contracts are a matter for the Member States' (recital 8). Furthermore, it must be clear that the information is a commercial communication (Article 4(2)).

Article 4(2) then goes on to say that the information must be provided in a manner 'appropriate to the means of distance communication used'. This provision probably means that the information can be given in the same manner as the distance communication method used, i.e. in the case of a phone call, orally and in the case of a web site, electronically on that web site.

However, the subsequent Article 5 confirmation has to be provided to the consumer in writing or in 'another durable medium available and accessible to him'. Such confirmation need not be provided where the consumer has already received the information in writing (e.g. in an advertisement leaflet or a catalogue) or in 'another durable medium'.

It is not entirely clear what the formulation 'on a durable medium' means. Recital 13 states that 'whereas information disseminated by certain electronic technologies is often ephemeral in nature insofar as it is not received on a permanent medium; whereas the consumer must therefore receive written notice....' Thus, durable medium means a permanent medium. Presumably a permanent medium is one that can either be stored or printed out. Therefore confirmation by e-mail and fax would probably meet this requirement, which seems to be the position of the UK government:

'We consider that confirmation by electronic mail would meet the definition of confirmation in "another durable medium available and accessible to [the consumer]", where the order has been made by means of e-mail. We have not however specified this in the Draft Regulations since the Directive is not specific on the point, and only a court can determine the meaning of the wording.'[11]

---

[11] DTI Publication, *Distance Selling Directive – Implementation in the UK*, November 1999, at para. 3.9. See also DTI Publication, *New Regulations for Business to Consumer Distance Selling - A Guide for Business*, October 2000, p.17.

The final implementing Regulations do not clarify this point. However, it is questionable whether a distinction can be made between an email, which is sent to the consumer by the supplier, from a web site, which requires the consumer to initiate the process of obtaining the information. Arguably few consumers would bother to download/save the information on the web site, since this might take too long especially where the consumer is using a slow dial-up connection. However ultimately this issue has not been decided yet.

### 2.4.4    Prior information-information to be given at the outset

The following information must be given before the contract is concluded:

- the supplier's name (and in the case of advance payment also his address), (Article 4(1)(a));
- the main characteristics of the goods or services, i.e. essentially a description of the goods or services (Article 4(1)(b));
- the price including all taxes (VAT) and all delivery costs (Article 4(1)(c) and (d));
- the arrangements for payment, delivery or performance of services (Article 4(1)(e));
- the existence of a right of withdrawal, unless the sale is exempted from that right (Article 4(1)(f));
- if the consumer is to use a premium rate telephone number the cost of the call must be specified (Article 4(1)(g));
- how long the offer or the price remains valid (Article 4(1)(h));
- where there is a continuous supply (e.g. mobile phone, cable/satellite TV, gas or electricity) or where there is a recurring supply (e.g. a monthly book or CD club) the minimum duration of the contract (Article 4(1)(i)).

In the case of telephone selling, the caller must ensure that at the beginning of the conversation he informs the consumer about the supplier he represents and the commercial purpose of the call (Article 4(3)).

### 2.4.5    Information which must be confirmed

With the exception of the last three items (premium rate, duration of the offer and minimum duration of ongoing contract), the information must be confirmed in writing or in another durable medium unless it has been given in writing or another durable medium from the outset. Thus, the information items in Article 4 (1) (a)-(f) must be confirmed in writing or another durable medium. In addition, the following information must be included in this confirmation:

- the details about when and how the consumer can exercise the right to cancel;
- a geographical address to which the consumer can address any complaints;
- if the supplier provides any after-sales services or guarantees, the details of such services and guarantees;

- if the contract is for a service with no specific end date or for a period longer than a year (e.g. mobile phone, satellite/cable TV, gas or electricity), the supplier must provide details on how to cancel the contract (Article 5(1)).

There is one exception: no confirmation need be provided where the service is provided through the means of distance communication and invoiced by the operator of the distance communication (e.g. premium rate telephone services). However, even for such services the consumer must be able to obtain the geographical address of the supplier to address any complaints (Article 5(2)).

## 2.5 Article 6 – Right of withdrawal

Recital 14 of the Distance-selling directive raises the fact that in respect of a distance contract, 'the consumer is not able actually to see the product or ascertain the nature of the service provided before concluding the contract...' It is for this reason that, in respect of contracts to which the Directive applies (see above, Article 3), Article 6(1) provides the consumer with a right to withdraw from a distance contract. The consumer does not have to give any reason for such a withdrawal, and the right may be exercised without penalty. This right is to be made available to consumers for a period of 'at least seven working days'; it can be available for as long as up to three months, depending upon the circumstances.

Essentially this right is designed to provide the consumer who purchases goods or services at a distance the same opportunity to inspect what is on offer at close quarters that a consumer making such a purchase in a traditional 'bricks and mortar' shopping environment will have. It enables the purchaser to make a fully informed choice before the sale is regarded as completely finalised and binding upon the consumer. While the Directive does not mention electronic commerce directly, its potential significance for Internet-based consumer sales is clear. Electronic commerce continues to develop rapidly in terms of the amount of money it generates each year, however, the variety of products that are popularly bought online is still limited. Books, CDs, theatre and airline tickets are commonly purchased over the Internet. Buying basic groceries online from a large supermarket company is beginning to become more popular in the UK, for example, but remains a minority activity. Retailers of many other consumer products remain unable to take full advantage of electronic commerce methods as potential purchasers are reluctant to buy without first inspecting the product, especially if it is a new product or service and/or the company offering the same is not one with which the consumer is familiar. A right of withdrawal, however, means that a potential consumer can take full advantage of the benefits of shopping online (lower price, home delivery, etc.) knowing that if the product or service is not to his liking, he can withdraw from the contract without penalty or need of any justification.

Article 6(1) also makes provision for calculating the timeframe in which the right is available. Regarding contracts for the sale of goods, providing that the Article 5 obligations on written confirmation of relevant information (see above) have been met, the period during which the right of withdrawal may be exercised begins on the day that the goods are received by the consumer. If, on the other hand, the information required by Article 5 has not been provided, the period for exercise of the right to withdraw from the contract is to be three months. Again this period is to begin on the day that the consumer receives the goods. However, should the supplier provide the required information at any time within these three months, the exercise of the right is limited to the seven working day period referred to above. This period begins on the same day as the information is provided: i.e. '[the withdrawal period] shall begin as from that moment' (Article 6(1)).

In respect of distance contracts for the provision of services, the period for the exercise of the right of withdrawal is calculated differently. Where the Article 5 obligations are met, the seven working day period begins on the day of *conclusion of the contract*. If the Article 5 obligations are not met until after the contract has been concluded, the period for exercise of the right begins on the day that these are fulfilled ('as from that moment') – providing that this does not exceed three months from the day of conclusion of the contract. Where the Article 5 obligations are not met, the period is to be three months from the day of conclusion of the contract. As is the case with distance contracts in respect of goods, if the information obligations are met within these three months, the period becomes seven working days from the moment of fulfilment of Article 5.

The limitations of time put upon the exercise of the right of withdrawal by the Directive are not absolutes per se, rather, they offer a minimum standard. Some Member States have implemented the minimum periods given in the Directive;[12] whilst others have chosen to extend these periods further. The German Distance Selling Act sets the basic withdrawal period at two weeks, also raising the maximum from the three months in the Directive to four months, while the Italian Distance Contracts Decree 1999 retains the upper limit of three months where the information requirements are not complied with, but sets the standard period at 'ten working days'.[13]

Another way in which the withdrawal period varies is in relation to instances in which the Article 5 obligations are not met before goods are received or a contract for services is concluded. It is to be presumed from the wording of Article 6(1) that if the Article 5 obligations are met on the last day of the three month period the

---

[12] See, for example, UK Consumer Protection (Distance Selling) Regulations 2000, SI 2000/2334, at Regulation 11 and 12; the Belgian Trade Practices and Consumer Protection and Information (Amendment) Act, at Article 20; the Austrian Distance Contracts Act 1999, at Article 5(e).

[13] [2000] 1 C.L.E. 462, at Article 5(1).

withdrawal period will extend a further seven days, making the total period in such a case three months and seven days.

Member States have approached these provisions differently. For example, under the UK Consumer Protection (Distance Selling) Regulations, in respect of contracts for goods, where the Article 5 information has not been provided, the period is three months. Should the information be provided during these three months, then the withdrawal period will end on the expiry of the seven working day period, beginning on the day *after* the day on which the consumer receives the information (not the same day as in the Directive). The three months is not given as an absolute limit, thus should the information be given on the last day of the three months, the cancellation period will run for a further seven working days. Where the information is not provided at all, the cancellation period runs for three months plus a further seven working days.[14] The additional seven days atop the three month period where the information is not provided at all confirms the prima facie interpretation of the Regulations that the period can extend beyond the three months where the relevant information is provided on the last day of the three months. The UK Regulations make the same provisions with respect to contracts for services, except that the cancellation period is calculated from the 'day after the day on which the contract is concluded.'[15]

In Germany, the Distance Selling Act provides that the withdrawal period ends unconditionally with the expiry of the four months which is sets as the upper period, irrespective of whether the information has arrived on the last day of that period. The Italian Distance Contracts Decree adopts the same approach as the German Act, the three month upper limit being an absolute cut off point (Article 5(1)(a) & (b)). The Austrian Distance Contracts Act broadly repeats the ambiguous phrasing of the Directive.[16] This jumble of differing periods presents a challenge where a consumer in one Member State has contracted with a company in another; while as a general matter of law at Community level, the consumer cannot be 'short-changed' by being expected to abide by a shorter withdrawal period than he would be entitled to under the law of his own jurisdiction, this poses a potential problem for online retailers who may have to be aware of several different periods set by different Member States where their customers might be located. Certainly this is an obstacle in the way of the harmonisation, which the European Union sought to bring about with the introduction of the Distance-selling directive (see, for instance, recitals 1 to 4).

There lies a further potential problem with the way in which these withdrawal periods are calculated under the Directive. Clearly the point in time at which the contract is concluded is very distinct from that in which goods may be delivered; it is unlikely that this will often be on the same day. This is not a problem until we come

---

[14]  UK Regulations, supra n. 13, at regulation 11.
[15]  Ibid., at regulation 12.
[16]  [2000] 1 C.L.E. 141, at Article 5(e).

to consider the position where it is unclear whether a specific contract is a contract for goods or a contract for services. Specifically, it is unclear whether software which is purchased online and delivered as a digital download – an increasingly common occurrence – is to be treated as goods or services. Clearly the same program purchased on a physical medium is classified as goods, even though what is of value is the information itself rather than the medium via which it is delivered. However, while arguably the mode of delivery in and of itself makes little or no difference to the consumer, the supply of the information for digital download renders a contract concerning software open to interpretation as a contract for services. Clearly a program designed on a bespoke basis to fulfil the needs of a specific consumer would qualify as a service contract, but it would seem illogical that a standardised package should be classified differently purely on the basis of the means of delivery employed. However, the OECD has argued that for purposes of VAT and customs duties, software delivered via digital download should be treated as services.[17] The question of classification remains very much open – when one considers other similar situations, such as the online delivery of music, or pay per view streaming video, and so on, it becomes apparent that this issue of classification may have very wide reaching consequences.

Article 6(2) sets out what is required of the supplier where the right of withdrawal is properly exercised. The crux of the requirement is to promptly refund all money paid out by the consumer, without charge. This reimbursement must be carried out within thirty days, as soon as is possible. The supplier is permitted to charge the 'direct cost of returning the goods' to the consumer. The limitation of charges which may be made to the consumer exercising the right to withdraw to 'the direct costs for returning the goods' is given as a matter of principle in recital 14. While it may be most properly considered to be designed to assist the general aims of the Directive in providing appropriate protection for the consumer in relation to distance contracts, it may also be considered that it serves to place a fair limit on the expenses for which the supplier will be liable. Where defective goods, or goods which the customer did not order, have been supplied, it is right and proper that the supplier of these should foot the bill for their return. However, where the right of withdrawal is exercised, there is no question that the goods or services are in any way defective, simply that the consumer has now had the appropriate opportunity to inspect them and has decided not to accept them. If the consumer elects to return goods or withdraw from a contract for services when the quality of neither is in question, it seems entirely reasonable for him to be expected to meet the cost of return. Of course, a supplier who wishes, as a matter of marketing strategy, to offer a 'no cost trial', with a 'free-post' return arrangement for goods which a consumer has decided not to keep, is not prohibited from assuming this extra responsibility.

---

[17]   OECD News Release of 13 October 1998, at note 7.

Article 6(3) places further limitations upon the right of withdrawal. The right may not be exercised in respect of certain limited contracts; note, however, that these exceptions are not absolute: the contracting parties may agree otherwise. Again, while these limitations are practical, common-sense measures, a supplier who wishes to assume the extra responsibility for reasons of commercial strategy may do so. Those contracts which Article 6(3) lists as exempted from the right of withdrawal are the following six.

1.   Contracts for the supply of services where the performance of the contract has, with the agreement of the consumer, already begun prior to the end of the seven working-day 'cooling off' period referred to in Article 6(1).

This would prevent an unscrupulous consumer from benefiting to a certain degree from the provision of a service before withdrawing from the contract in an attempt to avoid payment. In any case, unlike a contract for goods which can be easily identified and returned, services cannot be returned to the degree in which they have already been performed, thus the concept of a right of withdrawal is not appropriate.

2.   Contracts for the supply of goods or services the price of which may vary due to financial market conditions beyond the control of the supplier.

This exception prevents a consumer from pulling out of a contract with a supplier where outside market factors have acted to raise the cost to the consumer, rendering it higher than they are prepared to pay. The chief effect of this exception will be that it will give some reasonable certainty to the supplier that he will not be prevented from passing on such an additional cost to the consumer where this would eliminate any appropriate economic benefit from the contract (i.e. in terms of cost-effectiveness, it costs him more than it is now worth to perform his end of the contract).

3.   Contracts for the supply of goods made to the consumer's specification or clearly personalised, or due to the nature of goods cannot be returned or are liable to deteriorate or expire rapidly.

It seems reasonable that, where there is no question that the quality is in any way substandard, a consumer should not be able to reject goods made to his own specification. Where the Directive's provisions will require further clarification at the national level – most likely through case law – is in the limitations to be placed upon this exception. Where does 'clearly personalised' stop and mere choice of stock options begin? For example, if a consumer purchases a car online, requesting a specific colour, this will clearly be a standard product. But what if a custom colour, to be mixed to the individual consumer's specification, is offered, along with other significant cosmetic and/or other alterations to the standard model, many of which will not be reversible without considerable expenditure? Is this enough to qualify for the exception? In most cases it is likely that the line between stock options and personalised will be obvious, but there are potential grey areas that will fall to be decided by the courts.

No guidance is given as to what might be covered by goods '…which, by reason of their nature, cannot be returned'; Member States' national provisions by and large repeat this form of words. To some degree this provision has the ring of a catch-all, however, it is most likely applicable to cases in which return of delivered goods is significantly impractical for the consumer. For instance, a consumer who purchases a new car online may find it prohibitively expensive to arrange the transport for return; to pass this expense on to the supplier runs contrary to the general provision of the Directive as regards return costs where the right to withdraw has been exercised.

Goods which 'are liable to deteriorate or expire rapidly' are, by contrast, readily identifiable. Perhaps the best expression of this is to be found in the Austrian Distance Contracts Act 1999, Article 5(f): 'perishable goods and goods with a sell-by date.' The main product groupings covered by this will be flowers and food products: flowers will, if not 'dead', certainly be withered and unsuitable for resale well within seven working days, while food is subject to strict regulations concerning dates after which it cannot be sold. It is no injustice to the consumer to exempt such sales from the right to withdraw as any single such item is unlikely to be of great expense (and in any case the cost of return would probably render it non-cost-effective). On the other hand, the return of such goods to the supplier, were this to happen on a wide scale, could result in considerable cost being accrued if the goods have perished (as in the case of fresh fruit and vegetables, flowers, etc) or cannot be resold (canned foods which have passed their sell-by date). In any case, unless there is something wrong with a supply of such goods, such as delivery of the wrong items or not meeting quality standards, where an appropriate remedy will always be available to the consumer, it is highly unlikely that a consumer ordering basic groceries from an online supermarket web site for delivery would want to return them.

4.  Contracts for the supply of audio/video recordings or computer software which has been unsealed by the customer

It has become increasingly the norm in recent years for film, music and computer software sold on physical media to be sold shrink-wrapped or with a physical seal of some sort which must be broken in order to access the information contained on the disc / tape. Suppliers often adopt a policy that a refund will only be offered in respect of such goods returned for reasons other than defectiveness providing that this seal remains intact. This is a simple but nonetheless reasonably effective means of ensuring that a consumer cannot take a copy of the content and return the original, thereby acquiring the information without paying the proper charge.

Where information is sold online and supplied via digitised download, it is highly likely that a consumer who exercises his right to cancel the contract will already have exercised the information, and may well have retained a copy of it. How does a supplier replicate the concept of 'unsealed' in an online environment? In the UK, the government suggested that 'the term "unsealed" refers to the user's indicating assent to the terms of the End-User Licence Agreement.'[18] However, such an interpretation is not present in the implementing regulations and will ultimately lie with the discretion of a court. Given that the Internet is increasingly being used as a means of delivery of information for sale to customers, this gap in the Distance-selling directive is likely to increase in significance.

5. Contracts for the supply of newspapers, periodicals and magazines

Newspapers, periodicals etc. are generally of value only while they remain current. To permit the consumer to withdraw from the contract and return such goods to the supplier would mean, in many instances, burdening the supplier with goods which were no longer saleable, and which the consumer may already have gained the benefit of.

6. Contracts for the supply of gaming and lottery facilities

This final exception is self-explanatory.

Article 6(4) places an obligation upon all Member States to ensure that their legislation provides that where all or part of the price of goods or services in the contract is paid by credit, that credit agreement is to be cancelled without penalty where the consumer has properly exercised the right to withdraw. This is clearly an important provision in the context of distance contracts made on the Internet. Electronic cash has yet to achieve any significant usage by consumers – the traditional credit card, with its familiarity and ease of making payments across currencies, is still the standard way of making Internet payments. The provision that a penalty charge should not be levied against the consumer is significant insofar as the charge made to a supplier by a credit card company in relation to accepting a card payment cannot then be passed on to the consumer who elects to exercise his right of withdrawal.

The rules on the cancellation process for credit agreements are left up to the Member States individually: 'Member States shall determine the detailed rules for cancellation of the credit agreement' (Article 6(4)). Similarly, Article 6 does not set out any procedural rules for the valid exercise of the right of withdrawal in general, again, leaving this up to individual national legislatures, albeit implied rather than in any such explicit provision. The technical rules are thus varied across the Member States. In Germany, for instance, in order to validly withdraw from a contract, under the Distance Selling Act the consumer must either send back the purchased goods or provide the supplier with written notice of the withdrawal in a 'durable medium.' Unless, of course, the supplier of goods ordered from a product catalogue has included terms in the contract of sale which provide in place of the right to withdraw the alternative right to return the goods, which may only be exercised by actually returning the goods themselves.

---

[18] DTI Consultation supra n. 16, at para. 4.5.

The UK Consumer Protection (Distance Selling) Regulations provide that the contract is cancelled when the consumer provides a notice of cancellation to the supplier (Regulation 10(1)); Regulation 17 makes it clear that this event is generally considered to precede the return of the goods. This notice of cancellation must be 'in writing or in another durable medium available and accessible to the supplier' (Regulation 10(3)); post, facsimile and email are all sufficient to satisfy this requirement (Regulation 10(4)). The Italian Distance Contracts Decree, on the other hand, requires a 'written notice to the geographical address of the place of business of the supplier by registered post and acknowledged receipt.' The notice may also be sent 'by telegram, telex and facsimile' – it is unclear whether this is to include email, although it might be applied by analogy – 'on the condition that it is confirmed by registered post with acknowledgement of receipt within 48 hours thereof.' (Article 5(4)) Thus, while a consumer to whom the UK jurisdiction applies can exercise the right of withdrawal in relation to an Internet contract merely by sending an email to 'the business electronic mail address last known to the consumer' (Regulation 5(4)); a consumer bound by the Italian rules must comply with much stricter regulations. This presents a potential problem for suppliers of goods and services over the Internet, as they will require to be aware of the requirements of each Member State, and ensure that they are in compliance with their corresponding obligations. The harmonisation aims expressed in the preamble to the Directive (see recitals 1-4) are certainly not assisted by this state of affairs.

## 2.6    Article 7 – Performance

In line with the preamble's recognition of the '[necessity] to provide a time limit for performance of the contract if this is not specified at the time of ordering' (recital 15), Article 7(1) places an obligation upon the supplier to execute the customer's order inside a maximum period of 30 days following the day on which the customer forwarded the order in question to the supplier. The supplier may provide otherwise, thus allowing for goods or services which may require longer to produce, as well as those suppliers who may wish, as a matter of market strategy, to commit themselves to performance within a much shorter time period – 'next day delivery' and so on.

Where the supplier fails to perform his end of the contract due to unavailability of the goods or services which have been ordered, Article 7(2) obliges him both to inform the consumer and to return any payment made by the consumer as soon as is possible within a thirty day maximum period. This provision ensures that where a contract cannot be fulfilled for reasons of unavailability, speedy repayment is made to the consumer. This requirement is similar in spirit to the obligation to perform the contract where such is possible (and no agreement to do otherwise has been made) within the same period of time – in neither case the consumer is to be out of pocket, without either delivery of the ordered goods or services or return of any payment made, for any longer than is necessary.

Article 7(3) places some limitations around the supplier's obligations under Article 7(2). The supplier is not always obliged to provide a refund: where 'goods or services of equivalent quality and price' are available, the supplier may elect to substitute these for the ordered goods. Note, however, that this may only be done where it has been agreed with the consumer prior to the conclusion of the contract that this course of action may be taken in these circumstances. The provision of substitute goods is common in Internet contracts for groceries from supermarkets and other low value purchases where the choice of one brand or similar product over another is of no great significance. As the value of the goods in question rises, it becomes less likely that substitute goods will be acceptable to the consumer: the more expensive the item, generally speaking, the more likely it is that the consumer wants that specific item for a specific reason, not any similar item which the supplier may have access to. It is likely that the kinds of goods in relation to which substitute products will be offered will be established as a matter of relevant industry practices rather than legal regulation.

The information given to the consumer regarding the potential delivery of substitute goods must be 'clear and comprehensible'. As a matter of general contract law, to be enforceable, provision that substitute goods of equivalent quality and price must, inter alia, be validly incorporated into the contract. There are no technical requirements laid out in the Directive as to how this might be done. However, a hyperlink on the order page to clear terms and conditions is likely to suffice, especially if the order form is constructed such that the consumer has to fill in a 'tick-box' to the effect that he has read and understood the terms and conditions of sale before the software will permit continuation of the order process. Of course, this is no guarantee that the consumer will have actually read the terms of the contract, however, as long as the term concerning provision of substitute goods is clearly expressed with the appropriate attention drawn to it within those terms and conditions linked to, it may be presumed that the supplier has done enough to comply with the Directive.

The cost of returning substitute goods is to be met by the supplier, and the consumer must be informed of this. It is fair that the supplier pay for the return of substitute products as such goods are ultimately not what the consumer ordered, thus the consumer should not be responsible to meet the cost of their return if they do not suit. Equally, an obligation to pay for the return of substitute goods which are not acceptable to the consumer provides an impetus for the supplier to ensure that all such goods are indeed a reasonable alternative of the same quality and price.

Article 7(3) makes it clear that where substitute goods or services have been provided, this supply is not inertia selling, an activity which is prohibited by Article 9. Inertia selling is, essentially, where the supplier sends goods which have not been requested to a consumer, requiring either payment or return of the goods (see section

2.8 below). This is rightly to be distinguished from the supply of substitute goods, as under Article 7(2) the consumer has been fully informed of the possibility of substitute goods, and has agreed to the potential receipt of same. Article 7(3) and Article 7(2)'s requirement that the supplier pay the cost of returning substitute goods where these are not accepted by the consumer together provide a satisfactory balance between the interests of the consumer and of the supplier.

## 2.7    Article 8 – Payment by card

The Distance-selling directive obliges Member States to facilitate the consumer in the following situations:
- Consumer requesting that a payment be cancelled where his / her payment card has been fraudulently used in relation to a distance contract which falls under the ambit of the Directive;
- Where a consumer's payment card has been used fraudulently, the consumer must be able to be recredited with money paid out or to have it returned.

Again, by leaving the legal regime designed to offer these protections to the customer up to the Member States, there will inevitably be barriers to the harmonisation that the Directive seeks. There may also be further difficulty due to Article 8's limited scope. The Article applies only in relation to 'payment cards'. Clearly this will include traditional credit and debit cards, as well as newer smart card technologies. However, the protection offered by Article 8 is worded such that it effectively excludes payment systems which do not feature a physical payment card. Card-based systems still virtually monopolise Internet payments, however, other, software-based forms of electronic payments have been developed. Use and further development of e-money is unlikely to occur at any significant level unless such protection is offered; those few consumers who do use e-money risk losing out under a de facto two-tier protection system. Some protection for consumers party to distance contracts, intending to pay using software based payment, may be offered by various EU initiatives relating specifically to e-money, however, it would seem eminently sensible to offer full protection to consumers on a non-technology specific basis.

## 2.8    Articles 9 and 10 – Unsolicited supply and contact

Article 9 obliges Member States to take measures against the unsolicited supply of goods and services, where the consumer has not placed an order and the supply involves a demand for payment. In a number of Member States, such practices were already subject to regulatory control.

In the UK, for example, the relevant legislation is the Unsolicited Goods and Services Act 1971. However, despite existing legislation, implementation of this provision has required elaboration, partly due to the different legal nature of goods and services.[19] Under UK implementing regulations, the recipient of unsolicited goods has the right to dispose of the goods 'as if they were an unconditional gift to him' and the rights of the sender to the goods are extinguished. A criminal offence is committed where a demand for payment for unsolicited goods or services is made, e.g. through the sending of an invoice; whilst an offence of greater seriousness arises where legal proceedings are threatened against the recipient or some form of default is registered against him.

Article 10 of the Distance-selling directive is concerned with the use by suppliers of communications technologies to engage in unsolicited contact with potential customers. This provision shows a particular concern of public policy makers with the use of telecommunications systems to make unsolicited contact. Article 10(1) specifies that the use of automated calling systems and facsimile machines requires the 'prior consent of the customer'. By contrast, other forms of communication may be used provided that there is 'no clear objection from the consumer' (10(2)). The former requires the supplier to positively seek the consumers consent, whilst the latter enables such practices to continue until an objection has been made.

Unsolicited contact using telecommunications systems has also been subject to specific legislative treatment under Directive 97/66/EC on data protection and telecommunications[20] and Directive 2000/31/EC on electronic commerce. Directive 97/66/EC echoes the protection granted under the Distance-selling directive, but extends such protection to 'subscribers' and other legal persons who may not be consumers (Article 12(1) and (3)). The Commission has proposed extending such protection to all forms of electronic communication.[21] The Electronic Commerce directive does not restrict the use of such techniques, but regulates their form and imposes an obligation to consult 'opt-out registers' on service providers (Article 7).[22]

## 2.9 Articles 11, 12 and 17 – Access to justice, enforcement and consumer redress

### 2.9.1 Enforcement

Member States are put under a general obligation to ensure that there are measures to ensure compliance with the provisions of the Directive (Article 11(1)). Furthermore Member States are under an obligation to take measures to ensure that suppliers and

---

[19] UK Regulations, supra n. 16, at regulation 24.
[20] Directive 97/66/EC of the European Parliament and of the Council concerning the processing of personal data and the protection of privacy in the telecommunications sector, *OJ* L 24/1, 30.1.1998.
[21] See Proposal for a Directive of the European Parliament and Council concerning the processing of personal data and the protection of privacy in the electronic communications sector, COM (2000) 385, 12 July 2000.
[22] See further Chapter 4.

operators of distance communication means cease practices conflicting with the terms of the Directive (Article 11(3)(b)). Thus, as usual under European law, the Directive leaves it to the discretion of the Member States how to enforce the implementation legislation (e.g. by providing for administrative or criminal sanctions, contractual rights of consumers, by providing that a conflicting term in a contract is void, by providing for supervisory bodies etc.).

In the UK, for example, the Regulations provide that the Office of Fair Trading and the Local Authority Trading Standards have a duty to consider complaints. They also have a power to apply to the courts for an injunction against offending suppliers.[23] It has been debated whether this rather cumbersome procedure is effective. The original draft of the Regulations issued by the Department of Trade and Industry (DTI) provided for criminal sanctions, which were then omitted from the Regulations under pressure from industry, with the exception of criminal sanctions for inertia selling. However the DTI has announced that it will keep this issue under review.[24] Furthermore any term which is inconsistent with the Regulations will be void.[25]

### 2.9.2    Standing for consumer organisations?

The problem with the enforcement of consumer rights generally is that often large-scale infringement of rights result in a large number of small value claims, where each individual consumer is unable or sufficiently motivated to pursue an individual claim for damages or other remedy.

To address this problem, the Directive provides for locus standi before the courts or before the competent administrative authorities for public consumer bodies, consumer organisations and professional organisations with a legitimate interest in acting (Article 11(2)). Recital 20 explains with regard to this provision:
'Whereas non-compliance with this Directive may harm not only consumers but also competitors; whereas provisions may therefore be laid down enabling public bodies or their representatives or consumer organisations which under national legislation have a legitimate interest in consumer protection or professional organisations which have a legitimate interest in taking action to monitor the application thereof.'

The difficulty of implementing this provision of the Directive into national law is that it presupposes the existence of established structures which allows recognised consumer bodies to take action before the courts or authorities. Not all Member States currently have such structures involving independent consumer organisations

---

[23]  UK Regulations, supra n. 13, at 26 and 27. See also DTI Business Guide, supra n. 12, at p. 24

[24]  See Youngerwood, A. and S. Mann, 'Extra Armoury for Consumers: The New Distance Selling Regulations', *Journal of Information Law & Technology* 2000, Issue 3: <http://elj.warwick.ac.uk/jilt>, at p.7.

[25]  Supra n. 13, at regulation 25.

or bodies. However, such structures are being established under the Injunctions directive, which applies to the Distance-selling directive.[26]

The Injunctions directive grants a 'qualified entity', including 'organisations whose purpose is to protect the interests' of consumers, the right to bring an action before the courts or administrative authorities.[27] In the UK, the government, in its consultation on the implementation of the Distance-selling directive, initially proposed that the Consumer Association be granted such a status;[28] although this was absent in the final regulations.

### 2.9.3 Access to justice, out of court settlement and EEJ-net

Furthermore the Directive envisages the establishment of out-of-court dispute settlement systems (Article 17). As provided for in this Article the Commission has issued a report in March 2000[29] dealing with the feasibility of establishing effective means to deal with consumers' cross border complaints in respect of distance selling (and comparative advertising). In May 2000, the Commission jointly with the Portuguese Presidency launched a network of national out-of-court settlement schemes called EEJ-Net (European Extra-Judicial Network).[30] The background to Article 17 and this initiative is the increase in cross-border electronic commerce and the concomitant rise in cross-border consumer disputes. Because of the excessive costs of cross-border litigation, which effectively denies most consumers with small value claims access to the ordinary courts, cross-border out-of-court settlement procedures are crucial. The idea is to create a network of general application covering all disputes over goods and services intended to ensure that consumers can enforce their rights through access to low cost, simple and effective means of solving cross-border disputes.

Member States have committed themselves to providing a single contact point in their Member State (so-called 'Clearing Houses'). The consumer can complain to the 'Clearing House' in his Member State for information and support with a view to resolving the dispute by an out-of-court dispute resolution system at the place where the business is located. The Council Resolution on the Adoption of an EEJ-Net of 13 April 2000 by the Consumer Council called on the Member States to put in place the appropriate structures.[31] This is, of course, only the starting point for working out the

---

[26] Directive 98/27/EC of the European Parliament and of the Council of 19 May 1998 on injunctions for the protection of consumers' interests; *OJ* L 166/51, 11.6.1998, at Article 1 and Annex.

[27] Ibid., at Article 3(b).

[28] DTI Consultation, supra n.12, at Schedule 6 of the draft regulations.

[29] COM (2000) 127 final.

[30] See the Commission Document on the EEJ-Net at:
<europa.eu.int/comm/consumers/policy/developments/acce_just/acce_just07_en.html>.

[31] Council Resolution of 25 May 2000 on a Community-wide network of national bodies for the extra-judicial settlement of consumer disputes; *OJ* C 155/1, 6.6.2000.

necessary structures. The main problem is language barriers.[32] Another problem is, as mentioned with respect to the issue of locus standi for consumer organisations, that not all Member States have one single consumer complaints body, such as a consumer ombudsman. For example, in the UK there are 20 different bodies, all of which only cover particular sectors.[33]

### 2.9.4    Burden of proof

The Member States may, but need not provide for a reversal of the burden of proof (Article 11(3)(a)). If Member States take this option the supplier would have to show that he complied with the information and confirmation requirements, time limits and consumer consent. The reason for this provision can be found in recital 22: the use of the means of communication is not under the consumer's control, therefore the supplier should prove that the communication has 'reached' the consumer.

### 2.9.5    Contracting-out

Article 12 of the Directive provides that consumers cannot waive their rights under the implementation legislation of the Member States. Furthermore the Directive provides that consumers must not lose these rights by a choice of law clause used by the supplier and stipulating the law of a non-Member State (Article 12(2)).

## 2.10    Articles 13 and 14 – Lex specialis and higher consumer protection standards

Where there is a conflict between different Community laws, the more specific Community law shall prevail. Article 13 states expressly that the Directive only applies insofar there are no particular provisions in Community law which deal with specific types of distance contracts.

Article 14 provides that the Directive establishes minimum standards. It is not intended to prevent the introduction of more stringent rules by the Member States to ensure a higher level of consumer protection. However such measures must be compatible with general EC law and in particular the rules on freedom of movement of goods and the freedom to provide services in Articles 28 and 49 of the EC Treaty.

## 2.11    Articles 15 and 18 – Entry into force and implementation deadline

The Directive entered into force with its publication in the Official Journal, 4. June 1997, Article 18. The deadline for implementation passed on 4 June 2000.

---

[32]  See the Commission Document at:
     <europa.eu.int/comm/consumers/policy/developments/acce_just/acce_just07_en.html>.
[33]  See the Commission Document at:
     <europa.eu.int/comm/consumers/policy/developments/acce_just/acce_just07_over_en.html>.

## 2.12 Concluding remarks

When establishing a web-based commercial presence, the Distance-selling directive is one of the key pieces of legislation with which organisations have to comply. It directly impacts on the way in which a web site is designed. It provides consumers with a high level of protection, combined with enforcement mechanisms, however underdeveloped at the current time.

This review has highlighted numerous provisions that create legal uncertainty and difficult compliance issues for organisations. However, the majority of these issues reflect the fact that the Directive was drafted in a pre-electronic commerce environment. As part of the Commission's objective to establish a comprehensive framework for electronic commerce in Europe, consideration should be given to the need to revise this critical piece of the framework.

# Chapter 3

# Directive 1999/93/EC on a Community framework for electronic signatures

## Jos Dumortier

Important dates regarding the Directive 1999/93//EC of the European Parliament and of the Council of 13 December 1999 on a on a Community framework for electronic signatures are in chronological order:

- **1998, May 13** – Proposal adopted by the Commission;[1]
- **1999, January 13** – Proposal approved by the European Parliament, subject to amendments;[2]
- **1999, April 29** – Amended proposal adopted by the Commission;[3]
- **1999, June 28** – Common position adopted by the Council;[4]
- **1999, October 27** – Approval by the European Parliament;[5]
- **1999, December 13** – Signed by the European Parliament and the Council;
- **2000, January 19** – Publication in the Official Journal;[6]
- **2001, July 19** – Directive should be implemented by the Member States.

## 3.1    Introduction

### 3.1.1    Terminology

The European Directive 1999/93/EC of 13 December 1999[7] deals with *electronic* signatures in the widest sense of that term. However, nobody can deny that most of its provisions are dealing with one particular type of e-signatures: those based on public key cryptography, or commonly called 'digital signatures'. A digital signature is a technique by which it is possible to secure electronic information in such a way

---

[1]  *OJ* C 325/5, 23.10.1998.

[2]  *OJ* C 104/49, 14.4.1999.

[3]  COM (1999) 195 final.

[4]  *OJ* C 243/33, 27.8.1999.

[5]  *OJ* C 154/51, 5.6.2000.

[6]  *OJ* L 13/12, 19.1.2000.

[7]  Directive 1999/93/EC of the European Parliament and of the Council of 13 December 1999 on a Community framework for electronic signatures, *OJ* L 13, p. 12, see also <http://europa.eu.int/comm/internal_market/en/media/sign/Dir99-93-ecEN.pdf>.

33

*A.R. Lodder and H.W.K. Kaspersen (eds.),*
*eDirectives: Guide to European Union Law on E-Commerce, 33–65.*
© 2002 *Kluwer Law International. Printed in the Netherlands.*

that the originator of the information, as well as the integrity of the information, can be verified. This procedure of guaranteeing the origin and the integrity of the information is also called: authentication.

The digital signature technique makes use of so-called public key cryptography. The basic nature of digital signatures is that the author of electronic information can sign this information by using a secret cryptographic key. This key must be kept private at all times by the user. The signature can only be verified with the associated public key of the author. This public key is made public0.

The idea behind this authentication is the confirmation of identity by proving the possession of a secret key. The author encrypts the information or a part of it with his secret key. The recipient of the information can check the identity of the author by decrypting the information with the public key of the presumed author. If the decryption is not successful, the recipient will not validate the message. This process of authentication relies on the public keys of the users that are accessible to all the communication partners and on a trusted relationship between the identity of the users and their public key.

The authentication procedure is based on the presumption that the public key really belongs to the signer. This presumption is, however, not self-evident. The risk exists that somebody creates a key-pair, places the public key in a public directory under somebody else's name and thus signs electronic messages in the name of somebody else. Furthermore, a public and private key pair has no inherent association with any identity because it is simply a pair of numbers. Therefore, the assurance should exist that the public key really belongs to the claimed identity.

The answer is to rely on third parties to certify public keys. A third party must guarantee the relationship between the identity and the public key. This association is achieved in a digital certificate that binds the public key to an identity. These third parties are known as certification authorities and must be accepted by all users as impartial and trustworthy.

Although the European Directive deals mainly – according to some writers even exclusively – with the use of digital signatures as a substitute for hand-written signatures produced by natural persons, the technique of digital signatures has many other applications. It can actually be used in all circumstances where the origin and the integrity of computer data have to be secured.

### 3.1.2    Cryptography policy

The discussion about a European regulatory initiative in the field of digital signatures entered into a new phase in 1996. Before this time, every attempt to put the theme on the political agenda collapsed at a very early stage because of the refusal by several governments to submit their cryptography policy to a discussion on the European or, even worse, on the international level. Cryptography was still very much considered a matter of state security and national defence. But as a result of the pressure of industry to adopt a more liberal viewpoint on this matter and the necessity of increasing the security of electronic commerce, the Member States gradually came to the agreement that the questions about the use of encryption for confidentiality purposes should be separated as much as possible from the use of cryptography for authentication.

This view was explicitly expressed for the first time in the draft OECD Guidelines for Cryptography Policy. In the recommendation addressed to the Member States to adopt these guidelines, it was stated 'that the use of cryptography to ensure integrity of data, including authentication and non-repudiation mechanisms, is distinct from its use to ensure confidentiality of data, and that each of these uses presents different issues.'[8]

Already before the final version of the OECD Guidelines was adopted, the European Parliament invited the Commission in 1996 to prepare as soon as possible legal provisions concerning information security and digital identification[9] and shortly afterwards, the Council of Ministers requested the Member States and the European Commission 'to prepare consistent measures to ensure the integrity and authenticity of electronically transmitted documents.'[10]

On October 15, 1996, a call for tender concerning a study on the legal aspects of digital signatures was launched. The aim of the study was to provide the Commission with an 'overview of national policies, EU policies, existing and envisaged rules and regulations, as well as (de facto) practice including export controls, concerning digital signatures in the Member States as well as in the EU's main trading partners.'[11]

On July 8, 1997, concluding the European Ministerial Conference on 'Global Information Networks: Realising the Potential', ministers of 29 European countries adopted the 'Bonn Declaration'[12] setting out a number of key principles to pave the way for a rapid growth in Europe of the use of global information networks. In the section on digital signatures, the ministers emphasised the need for a legal and technical framework at European and International level, called upon industry and international standards organisations to develop technical and infrastructure standards for digital signatures and expressed their will to initiate the necessary steps

---

[8] OECD Guidelines for Cryptography Policy, available at <http://www.oecd.org/dsti/sti/it/secur/prod/e-crypto.htm>.

[9] European Parliament Resolution A4-244/96 of 19.9.96, *OJ* C 320 of 28.10.96, p.164.

[10] Council Resolution Nr. 96/C 376/01 of 21 November 1996 on new policy-priorities regarding the information society, *OJ* C 376 of 12.12.96.

[11] This study was awarded to the Interdisciplinary Center for Law and IT of the K.U.Leuven, Belgium. The results have been published in J. Dumortier & P. Van Eecke, *The Legal Aspects of Digital Signatures*, 6 volumes, 566 pages, Gent, Mys & Breesch, 1999, see <http://www.law.kuleuven.ac.be/icri/projects/digsigbook.htm>.

[12] European Ministerial Conference, Bonn 6-8.7.97; the final declaration is available at <http://europa.eu.int/ISPO/bonn/Min_declaration/i_finalen.html>.

to remove barriers to the use of digital signature in law, business and public administration and to provide legal and mutual recognition of certificates.

One of the barriers for a generalised use of digital signatures was, from the beginning, the lack of generally recognised standards in this area. This led consequently to the involvement of the standardisation bodies. At the European level the challenge was first taken up by ETSI with a first report on the requirements for trusted third parties in 1997.[13] The standardisation process was also taking place at the global level, for example in the framework of the ITU[14] and the Internet Engineering Task Force.[15]

### 3.1.3   First national legislative initiatives

Meanwhile draft national legislation on digital signatures was introduced in some EU Member States. The German Bundestag approved on 22 July 1997 the so-called *Signaturgesetz*.[16] The purpose of the law was to 'create general conditions under which digital signatures are deemed secure and forgeries of digital signatures or manipulation of signed data can be reliably ascertained.' The law offered an administrative framework within which people could make use of digital signatures in a secure manner. Everybody remained free, however, to make use of this framework or not.

The law defined a 'digital signature' as 'a seal affixed to digital data which is generated by a private signature key and establishes the owner of the signature key and the integrity of the data with the help of an associated public key provided with a signature key certificate of a certification authority (...).' For the purposes of the *Signaturgesetz*, a digital signature was consequently always a signature generated by making use of asymmetric cryptography and with a public key provided with a certificate.

The *Signaturgesetz* established a very detailed framework, which was further developed in an ordinance of 8 October 1997. At the top of this framework the German supervisory authority for the telecommunications sector[17] granted licenses to certification authorities wishing to operate under the legal framework, after an examination of their application file including a security concept in accordance with

---

[13]   ETSI 201 057 v.1.1.2 (1997-07), Telecommunications Security; Trusted Third Parties; Requirements for TTP Services, available at <http://pda.etsi.org/exchangefolder/eg_201057v010102p.pdf>; The document describes the general requirements for TTP services taking into account legal and commercial imperatives and without going into technical detail.

[14]   The main result of the ITU standardization effort has been the acceptance of the recommendation X.509; the current version (03/2000) is available via <http://www.itu.int/itudoc/itu-t/rec/x/x500up/x509.html>.

[15]   In the framework of IETF the PKIX working group was established in 1995 with the intent of developing Internet standards needed to support an X.509-based PKI; see further at <http://www.ietf.org/html.charters/pkix-charter.html>.

[16]   Bundesgesetzblatt, I, 1997, p. 1870.

[17]   Regulierungbehörde für Telekommunikation und Post (RegTP), see <http://www.regtp.de>

the security requirements of the law and after a check of the implementation of that security concept by a body recognised by the supervisory authority.

Around the same period, legislation on digital signatures was also enacted in Italy. A law of 15 March 1997 established the principle of the recognition of instruments, data and documents constituted by the public service and by private individuals using computers or telecommunications, contracts stipulated in such form, and their archiving and transmission using computer instruments, 'for all legal purposes'.[18]

This principle was further developed in a decree of the President of the Republic approved by the Council of Ministers on 31 October 1997. This decree stated that a digital signature would not be legally valid unless an officially accredited certification authority had certified the public key.[19]

### 3.1.4    The preparation of the Directive

It is evident that, as soon as the first drafts of the national laws in Germany and Italy became public, the European Commission started to seriously worry about the internal market effects of these legislative initiatives. In its April 1997 adopted communication 'A European Initiative in Electronic Commerce'[20] the European Commission announced for the first time its intention to come forward with a specific initiative on digital signatures. This initiative was aimed at ensuring a common legal framework encompassing the legal recognition of digital signatures in the Single Market, setting up minimum criteria for certification authorities, as well as pursuing world wide agreements. In its communication the European Commission expressed the need for a sound and flexible regulatory framework generating confidence for both business and consumers and ensuring full and unlimited access to the Single Market.[21]

On October 8, 1997, the Commission adopted the communication 'Ensuring security and trust in electronic communication: Towards a European framework for digital signatures and encryption'.[22] The Commission believed that a common framework

---

[18] Law 59 of 15 March 1997, Supplemento Ordinario alla Gazzetta Ufficiale della Republica Italiana n.63 del 17 March 1997.

[19] For a brief presentation of the Italian law of 1997, see the presentation of dr. Giovanni Buonomo at <http://www.oecd.org/dsti/sti/it/secur/act/emef21.pdf>.

[20] European Commission, Communication to the European Parliament, the Council, the Economic and Social Committee and the Committee of the Regions, *A European Initiative in Electronic Commerce*, 15.4.97, COM (97) 157, par. 51; . The text of the communication is available at <http://www.cordis.lu/esprit/src/ecomcom.htm>.

[21] COM (97) 157, p. 13.

[22] COM (97) 503 'Ensuring Security And Trust In Electronic Communication: Towards a European framework for Digital Signatures and encryption'; The text can be found at <http://www.swiss.ai.mit.edu/6805/articles/crypto/eu-october-8-97.html>, <http://www.datenschutz-berlin.de/sonstige/dokument/com97.htm>, or <http://www.cyber-rights.org/documents/97503.htm>; see also the report of the European Parliament, Committee on Legal Affairs and Citizens' Rights, of 20 May 1998, available at <http://www.infosociety.gr/infosoc/policies/digital/docs/598IP0189_EN.pdf>.

for digital signatures and encryption, both crucial instruments to make electronic commerce on the Internet more secure, was urgently needed. As far as digital signatures are concerned, the communication confirmed the Commission's intention to present a draft directive with the following objectives:

- to define common requirements for the establishment of certification authorities;
- to stimulate and coordinate measures of Member States aiming at the legal recognition of digital signatures.
- to ensure that appropriate regulation will contribute substantially to the rapid take-up of this authentication instrument crucial for secure communication on open networks.

The Commission emphasised that the regulation should be flexible enough to react to new technical developments. The communication stresses that it is important that regulation does not restrict, neither *de iure* nor *de facto* the contractual freedom of parties and that it will for the same reason also be crucial that regulated and unregulated digital signature schemes can co-exist and are interoperable.

In the meeting of the Council of the Telecommunications Ministers of 1 December 1997 the plan of the European Commission was favourably accepted. In the conclusions of the meeting the Council 'calls upon the Commission to proceed according to the time-table laid down in the communication, in particular to propose as soon as possible a Directive on digital signatures.'[23]

Consequently the European Commission started to draft a proposal for such a Directive. To support this work the Commission, together with the Danish presidency, organised an expert hearing in Copenhagen on 23-24 April 1998.[24] During this meeting, the Commission reported about its drafting work, but an official version of the draft directive was not put forward before 13 May 1998. The press release mentioned as the main elements of the draft directive the following:[25]

- Essential requirements for electronic signature certificates and certification services;
- Establish minimum liability rules for service providers;
- Legal recognition of electronic signatures;
- A technology-neutral framework;
- Scope: public networks, not closed user groups;
- Certification services without prior authorisation, voluntary accreditation schemes;
- Cooperation with third countries on mutual recognition of certificates.

---

[23] The text of the conclusions of the Council meeting is available at
<http://europa.eu.int/comm/internal_market/en/media/sign/teleconc.htm>.

[24] The report of this hearing is available at <http://www.fsk.dk/fsk/div/hearing/index.html>.

[25] <http://europa.eu.int/comm/internal_market/en/media/infso/sign.htm>.

As far as the negotiation procedure in the Council is concerned, a first attempt to achieve a political agreement collapsed in the Telecommunications Council of 27 November 1998. Some Member States argued that the Directive should provide a framework for secure electronic signatures and that the level of security should be defined at a high level, comparable with the approach of the German *Signaturgesetz*. Others were more in favour of a lower security level because they were afraid that strict requirements might constitute an obstacle for the widespread use of electronic signatures. The disagreement was largely due to a misunderstanding about the concept of digital signatures, about the difference between legal rules and standards and about the basic principles behind the German *Signaturgesetz*.[26]

On 13 January 1999 the European Parliament issued its opinion in first reading about the proposed directive.[27] The Council came to a common position on 22 April 1999.[28] To achieve a compromise, a distinction was introduced between obligatory requirements (Annex I to III) and recommendations (Annex IV). The recommendation for second reading of the European Parliament was delivered on 14 October 1999.[29] The Directive was finally signed on 13 December 1999 and published in the Official Journal of 19 January 2000. Starting from that date, the Member States had 18 months time to transpose the Directive into their national law.

### 3.1.5 Standardisation

The Electronic Signatures directive was the first example of 'co-regulation' at the European level. Only the general principles are defined in the Directive itself. These principles have to be further specified by self-regulatory mechanisms, mainly in the form of technical standardisation.

At the end of 1998 the European Commission issued a mandate to the European standardisation bodies – CEN/ISSS, CENELEC and ETSI, within the framework of the European ICT Standardisation Board – to analyse the future needs for standardisation activities in support of essential legal requirements as stated in the draft directive in relation to electronic signatures products. The assessment of available standards and current initiatives at global and regional level, both in formal standardisation bodies and industry consortia, should identify gaps and the need for any additional standardisation initiatives in all relevant forms, such as standards, specifications, agreements, workshops or any other form of consensus building. On the basis of this analysis, a work programme had to be proposed.

---

[26] The confusion among the negotiators in the Council is explained in J. Dumortier & P. Van Eecke, 'Electronic Signatures. The European Draft Directive on a common framework for electronic signatures', *Computer Law & Security Report* 1999 15(2):106-112.

[27] *OJ* C 104 of 14.4.1999, p. 49,; see also the report of the Committee on legal affairs and citizens' rights (rapporteur: Wolfgang Ullman) of 16 December 1998.

[28] See <http://europa.eu.int/comm/internal_market/en/media/sign/composen.htm>. The text of the amended proposal – COM 1999 (95) final - is available at <http://europa.eu.int/comm/internal_market/en/media/sign/signamen.pdf>.

[29] The EP reference of this document is A5-0034/1999.

To meet the requirements of the Commission mandate, the ICTSB launched the European Electronic Signature Standardisation Initiative (EESSI).[30] The first result of this initiative was the publication in July 1999 of an expert report about future standardisation requirements at the European level.[31] On the basis of this report EESSI approved a work programme with a division of tasks between CEN and ETSI.[32] During the following months, intensive work has been performed in the area of standardisation of electronic signatures. An impressive first set of deliverables has been given to the European Commission on 3 April 2001.[33]

## 3.2    Article 1 – Scope of the Directive

The purpose of the Directive is 1) to facilitate the use of electronic signatures and to contribute to their legal recognition and 2) to establish a legal framework for electronic signatures and certain certification-services in order to ensure the proper functioning of the internal market. The Directive has, in other words, a dual objective.
As far as the first objective is concerned, Article 1 is formulated in a prudent manner. The Directive does not contain an overall regulation of electronic signatures but it only aims at 'facilitating' their use. Neither does the Directive intend to entirely cover the question of legal recognition of electronic signatures. It only wants to 'contribute'.

The second objective – the establishment of a legal framework – is a European reaction against the legislative initiatives in some of the Member States, mainly in Germany and Italy. The aim is to create a common European legal framework in order to avoid divergent national laws in this domain. During our analysis of the provisions of the Directive we will discover what is meant by the term 'legal framework' in this respect. The framework does not cover all kinds of certification services but only 'certain' services. We will see that the framework is in the first place regarding certificate *issuers* and much less other categories of certification service providers.

Article 1 further specifies that the Directive 'does not cover aspects related to the conclusion and validity of contracts or other legal obligations where there are requirements as regards form prescribed by national or Community law.' Recital 17 specifies that the Directive 'does not seek to harmonise national rules concerning contract law, particularly the formation and performance of contracts, or other

---

[30]  For an overview of the activities of EESSI, look at
      <http://www.ict.etsi.org/eessi/eessi-homepage.htm>.
[31]  H. Nilsson, P. Van Eecke, M. Medina, D. Pinkas & N. Pope, *European Electronic Signature Initiative (EESSI)*, Final Report of the EESSI Expert Team, 20 July 1999, available at
      <http://www.ict.etsi.fr/eessi/Final-Report.pdf>.
[32]  See <http://www.ict.etsi.org/eessi/Open-Seminar-Spring2000/EESSIworkdescr4.doc>.
[33]  A description of these deliverables is available at <http://www.ict.etsi.org/eessi/ddd.doc>.

formalities of a non-contractual nature concerning signatures. For this reason the provisions concerning the legal effect of electronic signatures should be without prejudice to requirements regarding form laid down in national law with regard to the conclusion of contracts or the rules determining where a contract is concluded.' National provisions requiring, for instance, the use of paper for certain types of contracts, are consequently not affected by the Directive.

Article 1 further provides that the Directive does not affect rules and limits, contained in national or Community law, governing the use of documents. Many provisions in the law of the Member States impose the use of particular forms, for instance for tax declarations, building permits, etc. Sometimes the law requires that documents are archived for a certain period of time. As long as these laws do not permit the use of electronic forms or electronic document archiving, electronic signatures cannot be used in these domains.

In recital 16 we can read that the Directive 'contributes to the use and legal recognition of electronic signatures within the Community; a regulatory framework is not needed for electronic signatures exclusively used within systems, which are based on voluntary agreements under private law between a specified number of participants; the freedom of parties to agree among themselves the terms and conditions under which they accept electronically signed data should be respected to the extent allowed by national law; the legal effectiveness of electronic signatures used in such systems and their admissibility as evidence in legal proceedings should be recognised.' In the explanatory memorandum of the draft directive, the Commission justifies this as follows: 'There are obvious applications of electronic signature technology in closed environments, e.g. a company's local area network, or a bank system. Certificates and electronic signatures are also used for authorisation purposes, e.g. to access a private account. Within the constraints of national law, the principle of contractual freedom enables contracting parties to agree among themselves the terms and conditions under which they do business, e.g. accept electronic signatures. In these areas, there is no evident need for regulation.'[34]

It is evident that the Directive has important consequences on the Member States' cryptography policies. One of the primary aims is to guarantee the interoperability of electronic signature products. Essential requirements specific to electronic-signature products must be met in order to ensure free movement within the internal market and to build trust in electronic signatures, but recital 5 stresses this has to be done without prejudice to Council Regulation 3381/94/EC of 19 December 1994 setting up a Community regime for the control of exports of dual-use goods and Council Decision 94/ 942/CFSP of 19 December 1994 on the joint action adopted by the Council concerning the control of exports of dual-use goods. Moreover the Electronic Signature directive does not harmonise the provision of services with

---

[34] COM (98) 297final, p. 6.

respect to the confidentiality of information where those services are covered by national provisions concerned with public policy or public security.[35]

## 3.3    Article 2 – Definitions

### 3.3.1    (Advanced) electronic signature

Before the Commission issued its first version of the draft directive in May 1998, all the European documents regarding this subject, used the term 'digital signature'. In the original draft directive of May 1998, the European Commission started to use 'electronic' signature. The definition of 'electronic signature' in the first draft was however still more or less identical with the present definition of an 'advanced' electronic signature.

In the final text the term 'electronic signature' has been given an extremely wide sense: 'data in electronic form which are attached to or logically associated with other electronic data and which serve as a method of authentication.' Recital 8 justifies this approach, stating that 'rapid technological development and the global character of the Internet necessitate an approach which is open to various technologies and services capable of authenticating data electronically.'

The definition is actually so wide that it is sufficient to simply put a name under an electronic mail to have an electronic signature. Fortunately this very wide definition does not have many legal consequences because, except in Article 5(2), all the provisions of the Directive are dealing with 'advanced' or with so-called 'qualified' electronic signatures.

An 'advanced electronic signature' is an electronic signature meeting the following four requirements:
1.  uniquely linked to the signatory;
2.  capable of identifying the signatory;
3.  created using means that the signatory can maintain under his sole control, and;
4.  linked to the data to which it relates in such a manner that any subsequent change of the data is detectable.

Everybody will notice that these requirements are formulated in a very general and technology-neutral manner. In practice the market offers today only one solution that meets these four requirements: electronic signatures based on the digital signature technique or, in other words, making use of public key cryptography. In the framework of EESSI, a format for advanced electronic signatures has been described in the ETSI Technical Specification (TS 101 733). It is based on the existing standard format that dominates the e-mail and document security market (i.e. Internet specification RFC 2630). It also specifies how time-stamping or trusted archiving services may be used to ensure that the electronic signature remains valid for long

---

[35]  See Recital 6.

periods so that it can later be presented as evidence in case of a dispute. The document defines how the Internet specification RFC 2630 cryptographic message syntax should be used for advanced electronic signatures and defines additional fields and procedures, which are compatible with this syntax, to support long term validity. The evidence provided through use of the ETSI format can prevent the signatory later attempting to deny (repudiating) having signed a document, and can be verified even after the validity of the supporting certificate expires.[36]

A 'signatory' is defined as 'a person who holds a signature-creation device and acts either on his own behalf or on behalf of the natural or legal person or entity he represents.' The European Parliament suggested here to specify that a signatory could only be a 'natural' person but this amendment was not integrated in the final text. The probable reason for this is that in some Member States, such as the United Kingdom, a document is not only considered to be 'signed' if it contains a hand-written signature by a natural person but also when it bears a company's seal, a stamp or simply a name, as long as the authentication is sufficiently clear.[37] Following current technical standards, however, only a natural person can be the holder of a 'qualified' digital certificate (see further).

Contrary to the original draft the signatory is no longer 'the person who creates an electronic signature': it is the person who holds the signature-creation device. Such a device is defined in Article 2(5) as: 'configured software or hardware used to implement the signature-creation data.' A common example of a signature-creation device is a *smart card*, but there are many other possible devices such as a *smart pen*, a mobile phone, a PDA or a computer hard disk. The signatory is the person who holds this device and who acts in order to generate a signature. The signature can be either on behalf of the signatory himself or on behalf of a natural or legal person or entity he represents.

Signature-creation data are 'unique data, such as codes or private cryptographic keys, which are used by the signatory to create an electronic signature.' The term 'signature-creation data' consequently refers to the private key, whereas 'signature-verification data' – defined as 'data, such as codes or public cryptographic keys, which are used for the purpose of verifying an electronic signature' – is used as a technology-neutral synonym for the public key. The software or hardware used to verify the public key is called 'signature-verification device'.

Signature-creation devices and signature-verification devices are both part of the more general category of 'electronic signature products'. These are defined in Article 2(12) as 'hardware or software, or relevant components thereof, which are intended to be used by a certification service provider for the provision of electronic-signature

---

[36] ETSI TS 101 733 'Electronic Signature Formats', V.1.1.2 (2000-12) is available at <http://pda.etsi.org/exchangefolder/ts_101733v010202p.pdf>.

[37] Chris Reed, 'What is a signature?', available at <http://elj.warwick.ac.uk/jilt/00-3/reed.html>.

services or are intended to be used for the creation or verification of electronic signatures.'

### 3.3.2    Certificates and certification services

Article 2(9) defines a 'certificate' as 'an electronic attestation which links signature-verification data to a person and confirms the identity of that person.' A 'qualified certificate' is 'a certificate which meets the requirements laid down in Annex I and is provided by a certification service provider who fulfils the requirements laid down in Annex II of the Directive. Annex I lists not less than ten requirements for qualified certificates. The ETSI Technical Specification (TS 101 862) defines how the X.509 public key certificate format, which dominates the public key infrastructure market, may be used to meet the requirements of Annex I of the Directive. In addition, where there is currently no defined mechanism for meeting a requirement (e.g. limits on the value of the transaction) the specification builds on the existing extension capabilities of X.509 to define the necessary optional data structures.[38]

Certification-service-providers issuing qualified certificates must meet the requirements laid down in Annex II. ETSI Technical Specification (TS 101 456) defines security management and policy requirements for certification service providers issuing qualified certificates. It defines two specific policies for: 1) CAs issuing qualified certificates to the public, and 2) CAs issuing qualified certificates to the public requiring use of a secure signature-creation device. In addition, it defines a general framework for other policies for CAs issuing qualified certificates including those applicable to closed communities.[39]

Article 2(9) of the Directive contains a very broad definition of the concept of 'certification service provider': 'an entity or a legal or natural person who issues certificates or provides other services related to electronic signatures.'[40] Recital 9 justifies this by stating that 'electronic signatures will be used in a large variety of circumstances and applications, resulting in a wide range of new services and products related to or using electronic signatures; the definition of such products and services should not be limited to the issuance and management of certificates, but should also encompass any other service and product using, or ancillary to, electronic signatures, such as registration services, time stamping services, directory services, computing services or consultancy services related to electronic signatures.'

---

[38]    ETSI TS 101 862 V.1.1.1 (2000-12) is available at
        <http://pda.etsi.org/exchangefolder/ts_101862v010101p.pdf>.

[39]    ETSI TS 101 456, V 1.1.1 (2000-12) is available at
        <http://pda.etsi.org/exchangefolder/ts_101456v010101p.pdf>.

[40]    The German electronic signature law, on the contrary, defines a certification service provider as a provider of 'qualified' certification services (§ 2,8 of the law). See A. Rossnagel, 'Auf dem Weg zu neuen Signaturregelungen', *MMR* 8/2000, p. 452.

According to recital 12 the CA has to be established in accordance with national law. Member states are free to establish a state-controlled entity as a CA. A state-controlled CA can be created in different forms depending on the administrative law of the respective Member State. In most cases of public entities, there is a choice between establishing the CA as part of the administration, as a state-controlled legal person or as a private legal person that is mainly owned by the government. The suitable form for creating this type of certification authority will depend on the extent of state control to be exercised over it.

Although it is theoretically possible for a natural person to offer certification services, the organisational and administrative efforts to be made will usually require the set up of a corporation. However, it might be possible for a natural person to act as a sub-entity of another CA, for example as a registration authority. In most cases where natural persons assume the role of a trusted third party they do not act for themselves but as representatives of another entity. For example, if a CEO of a certain company issues certificates to the employees of that company, he acts on behalf of the company and not for himself as a natural person. In the few cases in which a natural person might actually become a CA no act of incorporation is necessary.

The most common form of providing certification services, however, is through a private legal person. Regarding their organisation, CAs can also be a sub-entity of another corporation or an association consisting of other sub-entities. The available and suitable forms of corporations depend on the law of the country in which the certification authority will be established. As is the case for all businesses, the most suitable form of corporation to conduct the business has to be decided by taking into consideration a number of factors. The main factors include the applicable tax regulations and liability limitations, the size of the corporation, the available capital, etc.

## 3.4     The certification services market – Articles 3(1 –3, 7) and 4(1)

### 3.4.1     Free circulation of certification services

The main provision concerning certification services – in its widest sense – is probably Article 4(1). It provides that each Member State shall apply the national provisions which it adopts pursuant to the Directive to certification service providers established on its territory and to the services which they provide. Member States may not restrict the provision of certification-services originating in another Member State in the fields covered by this Directive.

The notion of establishment has been developed by the European Court of Justice in the context of the freedom and the right of establishment, as guaranteed in Article 43 of the European Community Treaty. In the *Gebhard* case, the Court stated that 'the concept of establishment within the meaning of the Treaty is a very broad one, allowing a Community national to participate, on a stable and continuous basis, in the economic life of a Member State other than his state of origin and to profit there from, so contributing to economic and social interpretation within the Community in the sphere of activities as self-employed persons.'[41]

The essential requirements for an establishment seem to be (i) a fixed, i.e. a stable and permanent establishment,[42] (ii) for an indefinite period, (iii) in another Member State than the state of origin, and (iv) the actual pursuit of an economic activity.[43]

The meaning of 'establishment' has to be seen in contrast with the notion of 'provision of services' of Article 49 of the European Community Treaty.[44] In essence, the difference concerns the temporary nature of the provision of services in another Member State than the state of origin. The temporary nature of the activities has to be determined in the light, not only of the duration of the provision of the service, but also of its regularity, periodicity and also its continuity.[45] The fact that the provider is equipped with some form of infrastructure does not necessarily mean that the temporary aspect of the services is lost.

If a certification service provider is only established in one Member State, he will be submitted to the legal provisions enacted in that Member State in the field of the Directive. The law of that Member State will also be applicable to services provided in other Member States. A CSP established in Belgium, for example, will remain under the supervision of the Belgian authority even if he provides the majority of his services in other Member States. The other Member States are not allowed to restrict the provision of the services of the Belgian provider, even if the Belgian legal rules in the field of the Directive are less strict.[46] If the CSP is established in more than one Member State, he will be submitted to the laws of all these Member States. It is not very clear yet whether or not this will lead to practical difficulties.

Following Article 3(7) Member States may use electronic signatures in the public sector subject to possible additional requirements. Such requirements shall be objective, transparent, proportionate and non-discriminatory and shall relate only to the specific characteristics of the application concerned. Such requirements may not constitute an obstacle to cross-border services for citizens. It is not yet very clear how the last part of this provision has to be interpreted. The possibility granted to public administrations to specify more in detail the characteristics of their public key infrastructure seems self-evident and necessary to achieve a sufficient degree of

---

[41] *Gebhard v Consiglio dell' Ordine degli Avvocati e Procuratori di Milano* ( Case C-55/94)[1995] ECR I-4165, para. 25.

[42] *INASTI v Kemmler* ( Case C-53/95) [1996] ECR I-704, para 8.

[43] *R.v Secretary of State for Transport, ex p. Factortame* ( Case C-221/89) [1991] ECR-I-3905, para 20.

[44] P. Craig, G. De Burca, *EU Law, Text, Cases and Materials*, 1998,Oxford University Press, 728.

[45] *Gebhard v Consiglio dell' Ordine degli Avvocati e Procuratori di Milano* (Case C-55/94)[1995] ECR I-4165, para. 26.

[46] It is however almost certain that the services from foreign certification service providers will be restricted because of the generalized use, in some Member States, of so-called 'accredited' electronic signatures.

interoperability. It is also understandable that the additional requirements have to be objective, transparent, proportionate and non-discriminatory. Less clear however is the provision that the additional requirements 'shall relate only to the specific characteristics of the application concerned.' The public key infrastructure set up by the governments in the Member States will evidently serve a multitude of applications. It is difficult to imagine that the requirements with regard to the PKI would have to be specified for every single e-government application.

The additional requirements specified by national, regional or local governments in the Member States will moreover almost necessarily constitute an obstacle to cross-border services. In Germany, for example, several applications in the context of e-government will probably require the use of 'accredited' electronic signatures. Residents from other Member States will therefore in practice be forced to use a German accredited certification service provider or an assimilated non-German provider.

### 3.4.2 No prior authorisation

Article 3(1) prohibits Member States to make the provision of certification services subject to prior authorisation. Recital 10 specifies that '(...) In order to stimulate the Community-wide provision of certification services over open networks, certification service providers should be free to provide their services without prior authorisation (...)' The consequence is that any certification service provider will have to be allowed to provide his services without prior authorisation. At the same time the Directive requires the EU Member States to make sure that the provisions of the European directive are adhered to by the certification service providers.[47] As a result, Member States have to ensure that certification service providers that operate on their territory offer their services in compliance with the EC-directive, but may not exercise supervision by requiring prior authorisation. Thus, national legislators have to find a way to exercise supervision without setting up a system of mandatory examination prior to the commencement of services.

### 3.4.3 Voluntary accreditation

Article 3(2) states that, without prejudice to the prohibition formulated in Article 3(1), 'Member States may introduce or maintain voluntary accreditation schemes aiming at enhanced levels of certification service provision.' Article 2(13) defines voluntary accreditation as 'any permission, setting out rights and obligations specific to the provision of certification services, to be granted upon request by the certification service provider concerned (...).'
Further, according to Article 3(2) of the Directive, 'all conditions related to such schemes must be objective, transparent, proportionate and non-discriminatory.' Recital 11 explains that 'voluntary accreditation schemes should encourage the

---

[47] See Recital 13.

development of best practices among certification service providers.' In recital 12 it is stated that 'Member States should not prohibit certification service providers from operating outside voluntary accreditation schemes' and that 'it should be ensured that such accreditation schemes do not reduce competition for certification services.'

The idea behind a voluntary accreditation scheme is that it offers an incentive for service providers to offer high quality services to meet the requirements of the accreditation scheme. The certified compliance should attract potential clients. In contrast to mandatory surveillance, voluntary accreditation schemes are supposed to have the advantage of being able to adapt more easily to developments in a quickly changing technical environment. Since accreditation schemes are regulated by market forces – i.e. the market players have to gauge if the expected rise in revenue generated by the anticipated increase of consumer trust is worth the necessary investment for complying with the security requirements of an accreditation scheme – they are assumed to be able to adapt to business needs more quickly.

The legislation efforts of the EU Member States show different approaches to the establishment of such accreditation schemes. While some countries plan to set up an accreditation scheme that is controlled by the state, others prefer a privately governed accreditation scheme.[48]

The conditions devised by the public German accreditation scheme are rather strict and provide an enhanced level of security. Meeting the criteria requires substantial investment by certification authorities.[49] This solution will be particularly welcomed by certification service providers who have already made the investments necessary under the old German Signaturgesetz to provide certificates for electronic signatures. Article 15(1) of the German law[50] provides that certification-service providers may be accredited by the competent authority upon application; the competent authority may make use of private offices for the accreditation. Accreditation is given if the certification-service provider can show that the requirements under the law are fulfilled. Accredited certification-service providers obtain a quality sign by the competent authority. This should proof the qualified electronic signatures (qualified electronic signatures with provider accreditation) based on their qualified certificates offer security that has been comprehensively tested technically and administratively. They shall be allowed to call themselves accredited certification-service providers and refer to the proven security in legal and business transactions.

The UK government originally also took powers under Part I of the Electronic Communications Act 2000 to establish a statutory voluntary approvals regime. The Alliance for Electronic Business – a consortium of industry bodies concerned with

---

[48]   Coleman/Sapte, 'E-Commerce Bill - Ireland, the Irish Electronic Commerce Bill 2000', *Computer Law & Security Report* Vol. 16 no. 4 2000, p. 249.

[49]   Emmert estimates an investment of about 380.000 Euros, see Emmert, 'Haftung der Zertifizierungsstellen', *CR* 99, 244 ff, 249.

[50]   The text of the German law, which entered into force on 22 May 2001, is available at <http://www.iid.de/iukdg/einstieg.html> (German unofficial version and an English translation).

the promotion of electronic business – has established the tScheme in response to and as an alternative to the Government implementing the powers taken under Part 1 of the ECA. The tScheme in the UK therefore exists as a non-statutory voluntary approvals regime for trust service providers. The government is working in partnership with the tScheme but it is clearly private sector-led.[51]

Besides these national accreditation schemes, a number of private organisations, such as Identrus, are developing criteria to be fulfilled by their members as well. If meeting these criteria becomes a precondition for membership in a certain organisation, the organisation functions as an accreditation scheme in the terms of the Directive from a legal point of view. To obtain the benefits of being a member of a recognised organisation, the participating companies have to meet certain standards that are devised by the organisation.

Another difference between the accreditation schemes is the required security level. The German accreditation scheme, for example, consists mainly of the requirements of the old *Signaturgesetz* of 1997 but it has been modified into a voluntary scheme whereas in the former law the accreditation was necessary to enter the market.[52] The conditions devised by the public German accreditation scheme are rather strict and provide an enhanced level of security.[53] Meeting these criteria requires substantial investment by certification authorities.[54] In other Member States, such as France or Belgium, the voluntary accreditation is aimed at giving CAs an opportunity to get an official label of 'qualified' CA. The security requirements are therefore limited to what is listed in the Annexes I to III of the Directive. France, for example, provides the possibility for CAs to be recognised as qualified by voluntary accreditation. The responsible accreditation body will be designated and the accreditation procedure will be defined in an order of the Minister of Industry. The voluntary system of accreditation has been organised in the context of the COFRAC (The French Accreditation Body). This is a system of accreditation established by the French State in 1994, according to which a public body accredits persons and institutions, which on their turn carry out quality tests and issue quality labels.[55] For reasons of efficiency France did not want to establish a specific system of accreditation for CAs. Accreditation is not a one-time event. Article 15(2) of the German law, for example, provides that the testing and approval shall be repeated after any changes that greatly affect security, and at regular intervals of time.

How can a user know if a certification service provider is accredited? In the German law the supervisory authority issues root certificates to the accredited CAs and also

---

[51]  See further <http://www.tscheme.org/>.

[52]  A. Rossnagel, 'Das neue Recht elektronischer Signaturen', *NJW* 2001, p. 1821.

[53]  The German accreditation scheme includes, for example, also prior examination of secure signature validation devices, technical components used by the CA, etc.

[54]  Emmert estimates an investment of about 380.000 Euros, see Emmert, 'Haftung der Zertifizierungsstellen', *CR* 99, 244 ff, 249.

[55]  See also: <http://www.cofrac.fr>.

keeps a public register wherein the accredited CAs are listed. Accredited CAs will consequently have a label from the supervisory authority.

In practice some Member States are creating, besides 'qualified' electronic signatures, a new category of 'accredited' electronic signatures with a higher security level. In Germany for instance, Rossnagel[56] distinguishes four differences between 'qualified' and 'accredited' electronic signatures.

The establishment of a number of different accreditation schemes may have advantages and disadvantages for certification authorities. On the one hand, divergent rules in this area might be problematic from the point of view of certification service providers since the process of application for accreditation involves a lot of financial and administrative investment by the applying CA. In most cases, reports by independent experts are required, audits are held and detailed information has to be provided. If a CA intends to offer his services in more than one European country, he might have to go through the required procedure many times to be accredited in each state. Especially accreditation schemes that are only open to service providers on the national market[57] require extensive investment by an internationally active certification service provider. If accreditation is geographically limited, the benefits of being able to refer to the compliance with an accreditation of one Member State when offering services in other Member States may be limited as well. Even if a national accreditation scheme is principally open to service providers who are established and operate in another state, it might not suffice to be accredited in only one Member State for practical reasons. Although it would be possible for a service provider to refer to a national accreditation when offering services, customers are likely to put more trust into an accreditation scheme of their own country because they are more likely to be familiar with its trustworthiness.

On the other hand, the establishment of different national accreditation schemes that are open to certification service providers of all countries will lead to an increased competition among these schemes. According to the European Electronic Signature directive, accreditation schemes may not be based on discriminatory requirements. Thus, the restriction of such a scheme to service providers established in one particular Member State as opposed to providers established in other Member States would violate the provisions of the Directive. Thus, national accreditation schemes will potentially be open to any certification authority based in Europe. As a result, only those accreditation schemes that are both accepted by users and by CAs will be successful. Which accreditation schemes will be the ones to be accepted by the market remains to be seen.

---

[56] A. Rossnagel, 'Das neue Recht elektronischer Signaturen', *NJW* 2001, p. 1821.

[57] According to Irish law, for example, only CAs who offer their service in the state have guaranteed access to the national accreditation schemes.

### 3.4.4 Supervision

Article 3(3) provides that national law has to establish appropriate systems to allow *supervision* of CAs established on its territory and issuing *qualified certificates to the public*. National law thus has to establish supervisory bodies, which see to it that CAs issuing qualified certificates comply with the requirements laid down in Annex I, II and III.

Article 3(3) is one of the most problematic provisions of the Directive, because at the same time it is prohibited to make the provision of certification services subject to prior authorisation. The said prohibition does not only extend to authorisations given by national bodies prior to the actual provision of certification services by a provider, but also includes all measures with a similar effect.

Member States may decide how to ensure the said supervision. The Directive does not preclude the establishment of private-sector-based supervision systems (recital 13). But in no case the supervision system may produce the same effect as a requirement of prior authorisation.

While interpreting the obligation to ensure the supervision of CAs, the Member States have to proceed cautiously. It is important to strike a balance between consumer and business needs (recital 14). The consumer and the public in general must have the possibility to recognise qualified certificates and must be protected against the illegal use of the designation 'qualified'. At the same time the companies must be able to offer their certification-services to the public freely and without obstacles.

Several Member States solve this problem by requiring the certification service provider established on their territory to give notification to the appropriate public authority before starting the provision of services. Such notification is, for example, mandatory in Germany, Austria and Denmark.[58]

The obligation to notify can be very similar in its practical effect to the requirement of prior authorisation. According to German law, for example, a certification service provider is only allowed to offer his services if he has demonstrated that he fulfils the requirements of the law, such as for example providing proof for having the sum of 500.000 Deutsche Mark (about 250.000 Euros) at his disposal for liability purposes (§ 12 of the German Law). At the latest with the commencement of his services he has to notify the public authority and provide proof of compliance with the signature law. If the national authority finds that the certification service provider does not fulfil the statutory requirements, it can disallow him to continue his services.[59] It should be noted, however, that the German *Signaturgesetz* only applies to issuers of

---

[58] See for example the Austrian *Signaturgesetz*, available at:
<http://www.a-sit.at/signatur/rechtsrahmen/rechtsrahmen.htm>.

[59] See § 19 III of the German law.

qualified certificates, with the result that certification authorities that do not intend to issue these types of certificates can without impediments offer their services.

In other EU Member States, such as for example Ireland or the UK,[60] CAs can provide their services without having to perform any prior actions.[61] In such countries, it is considerably less complicated and expensive for certification authorities to offer their services. Regarding the fact that Member States may not restrict the provision of certification services originating in another Member State in the fields covered by this Directive (Article 4(1)) and that qualified certificates that are issued by a CA situated in any EU-Member State will have to be given equal legal effect in any other EU-Member State, CAs might consider establishing their business in one of the states with less strict requirements.[62]

## 3.5 Electronic signature products – Articles 3(4-6) and 4(2)

### 3.5.1 Free circulation of electronic signature products

Article 4(2) of the Directive urges the Member States to ensure that electronic signature products complying with the Directive are permitted to circulate freely in the internal market. Recital 5 specifies, 'the interoperability of electronic signature products should be promoted. (...) Essential requirements specific to electronic-signature products must be met in order to ensure free movement within the internal market and to build trust in electronic signatures, without prejudice to the regulation regarding dual-use goods.'[63]
Article 3(5) provides that the Commission may, in accordance with the procedure laid down in Article 9, establish and publish reference numbers of generally recognised standards for electronic signature products in the Official Journal of the European Communities. Member States shall presume that there is compliance with the requirements laid down in Annex II, point (f), and Annex III when an electronic signature product meets those standards.

### 3.5.2 Secure signature-creation devices

These requirements for secure signature-creation devices (Annex III) ensure the functionality of advanced electronic signatures. They do not cover the entire system

---

[60] See <http://www.dti.gov.uk/cii/datasecurity/electronicsignatures/index.shtml>.

[61] See Article 29(1) of the Irish Electronic Commerce Bill. However, even if no specific authorization is required for certification service providers, an admission to commence a trade may still be required by general administrative law.

[62] At the moment of writing, the UK Government is organizing a public consultation whereby the modalities of the future supervisory regime is one of the main issues, see
<http://www.dti.gov.uk/cii/ecommerce/europeanpolicy/index.shtml>.

[63] Council Regulation (EC)No 3381/94 of 19 December 1994 setting up a Community regime for the control of exports of dual-use goods and Council Decision 94/ 942/CFSP of 19 December 1994 on the joint action adopted by the Council concerning the control of exports of dual-use goods.

environment in which such devices operate. There are no formal requirements in the Directive regarding the signature creation process and environment. However, a CEN Workshop Agreement (CWA 14170) supports the objectives of the Directive by specifying 'voluntary' security requirements for the signature creation systems which create advanced electronic signatures with the help of secure signature-creation devices and qualified certificates by means of 1) a model of a 'signature-creation environment' and a functional model of 'signature– creation systems', 2) overall requirements that apply across all of the functions identified in the functional model, and 3) security requirements for each of the functions identified in the signature-creation system, excluding the secure signature-creation device.

Two CEN Workshop Agreements (CWAs 14168 and 14169) define more specifically the security requirements for secure signature-creation devices. The security requirements are formulated in a Protection Profile following the rules and formats specified in the international standard ISO 15408.

Article 3(4) of the Directive provides that the conformity of secure signature-creation-devices with the requirements laid down in Annex III shall be determined by appropriate public or private bodies designated by Member States. In a Decision of 6 November 2000 the Commission, pursuant to the procedure laid down in Article 9, established criteria for Member States to determine whether a body should be designated.[64] Article 2 of this Decision states that, 'where a designated body is part of an organisation involved in activities other than conformance assessment of secure signature-creation-devices with the requirements laid down in Annex III to Directive 1999/93/EC it must be identifiable within that organisation' and that 'different activities must be clearly distinguished.'

Following Article 3 'the body and its staff must not engage in any activities that may conflict with their independence of judgement and integrity in relation to their task.' In particular, the body must be independent of the parties involved. Therefore, the body, its executive officer and the staff responsible for carrying out the conformance assessment tasks must not be a designer, manufacturer, supplier or installer of secure signature-creation-devices, or a certification service provider issuing certificates to the public, nor the authorised representative of any of such parties. In addition, they must be financially independent and not become directly involved in the design, construction, marketing or maintenance of secure signature-creation-devices, nor represent the parties engaged in these activities. This does not preclude the possibility of exchange of technical information between the manufacturer and the designated body.

---

[64] Commission decision 2000/709/EC of 6 November 2000 on the minimum criteria to be taken into account by Member States when designating bodies in accordance with Article 3(4) of Directive 1999/93/EC of the European Parliament and of the Council on a Community framework for electronic signatures, *OJ* L 289 of 16.11.2000, p. 42.

Article 4 of the Decision provides that the accreditation body and its personnel must be able to determine the conformity of secure signature-creation-devices with the requirements laid down in Annex III to Directive 1999/93/EC with a high degree of professional integrity, reliability and sufficient technical competence.

Following Article 5, the body has to be 'transparent in its conformity assessment practices and shall record all relevant information concerning these practices.' All interested parties must have access to the services of the body. The procedures under which the body operates must be administered in a non-discriminatory manner. Article 6 states that the body must have at its disposal the necessary staff and facilities to enable it to perform properly and swiftly the technical and administrative work associated with the task for which it has been designated. In Article 7, the Decision specifies that the personnel responsible for conformity assessment must have: 1) sound technical and vocational training, particularly in the field of electronic signature technologies and the related IT security aspects, and 2) satisfactory knowledge of the requirements of the conformity assessments they carry out and adequate experience to carry out such assessments.

Article 8 states that the impartiality of staff shall be guaranteed. Their remuneration shall not depend on the number of conformity assessments carried out, nor on the results of such conformity assessments. Following Article 9 the body must have adequate arrangements to cover liabilities arising from its activities, for example, by obtaining appropriate insurance. Article 10 provides that the body must have adequate arrangements to ensure the confidentiality of the information obtained in carrying out its tasks under Directive 1999/93/EC or any provision of national law giving effect thereto, except vis-à-vis the competent authorities of the designating Member State. Finally, following Article 11, where a designated body arranges for the carrying out of a part of the conformity assessments by another party, it must ensure and be able to demonstrate that this party is competent to perform the service in question. The designated body must take full responsibility for the work carried out under those arrangements. The final decision remains with the designated body.

A determination of conformity with the requirements laid down in Annex III made by the bodies designated by a Member State has to be recognised by all other Member States. As far as the conformity of secure signature-creation devices is concerned, an accreditation in one Member State is, in other words, sufficient for the distribution of the device in all the other Member States.

### 3.5.3   Secure signature-verification devices

According to Article 3(6), Member States and the Commission shall work together to promote the development and use of signature-verification devices in the light of the recommendations for secure signature-verification laid down in Annex IV and in the interests of the consumer. In order to fulfil this goal, a CEN Workshop Agreement (CWA 14171) contains a specification for the signature verification procedure, including both the products used for verification, and their management. The standard identifies the security requirements for the various elements of a signature verification system. Beyond the verification process itself, the standard identifies the various interfaces, i.e. Application Programme Interfaces (APIs) or Man-Machine Interfaces (MMIs) that are needed, in particular, to select the signer's document and the electronic signature to be verified, to present the signer's document with the right format, to get the signer information and the output status after signature verification, to get additional data for long term verification and to fetch information from various CSPs. The CWA identifies the data that need to be captured and archived so that they can later be used for arbitration, should a dispute occur between the signer and verifier. The document uses the concept of a signature policy as the basis for verification of an electronic signature.[65]

## 3.6 Article 5 – Legal effects of electronic signatures

Article 5 is without any doubt the most controversial provision of the Directive. Recital 20 explains: 'advanced electronic signatures which are based on a qualified certificate and which are created by a secure-signature-creation device can be regarded as legally equivalent to hand-written signatures only if the requirements for hand-written signatures are fulfilled.' Recital 21 further specifies that 'in order to contribute to the general acceptance of electronic authentication methods it has to be ensured that electronic signatures can be used as evidence in legal proceedings in all Member States' and 'the legal recognition of electronic signatures should be based upon objective criteria and not be linked to authorisation of the certification service provider involved.' In the same recital one can also read: 'national law governs the legal spheres in which electronic documents and electronic signatures may be used' and 'this Directive is without prejudice to the power of a national court to make a ruling regarding conformity with the requirements of this Directive and does not affect national rules regarding the unfettered judicial recital of evidence.'

Article 5(1) deals with 'advanced electronic signatures which are based on a qualified certificate and which are created by a secure-signature-creation device.' They are commonly called 'qualified electronic signatures'. The Directive attributes to this category of electronic signatures, in relation to electronic data, the same status as hand-written signatures have in relation to paper documents. In other words, Article 5(1) does not contain an obligation to use electronic data processing. Legal rules enforcing the use of paper documents can consequently continue to exist and they do not have to be abrogated, at least not according to this Directive.[66] But where the use of electronic data processing is legally permitted, the qualified electronic

---

[65] In ETSI TS 201 733 a 'signature policy' is defined as 'a set of rules for the creation and validation of an electronic signature, under which the signature can be determined to be valid'. See further the IETF Internet-Draft 'Electronic Signature Policies', <http://ftp.ietf.org/internet-drafts/draft-ietf-smime-espolicies-01.txt>.

[66] The progressive abrogation of such rules is, as far as electronic contracts are concerned, one of the objectives of the Electronic Commerce Directive.

signature should, in relation to these data, receive a status that is equivalent to the legal status that hand-written signatures normally have in relation to paper documents.

It is of course not contrary to Article 5(1) to replace current legislation requiring hand-written signatures by new legislation in which the use of electronic data is permitted without the use of qualified electronic signatures. It is not the objective of the Directive to require the use of qualified electronic signatures in every situation in which, up to now, the use of hand-written signatures was obligatory. On the other hand, Member States can also continue to introduce new legislation requiring additional security guarantees, above the level of qualified electronic signatures. In relation to paper documents, hand-written signatures are not the exclusive security measure either. In all cases, however, where in relation to paper documents a hand-written signature would have been sufficient, Member States have to give an equivalent status to qualified electronic signatures when they start to allow the use of electronic data processing as a substitute for the paper documents. The status of the hand-written signature in its relation to paper documents determines, in other words, the status of the qualified electronic signature in relation to electronic data. In the longer run, this solution may lose its efficiency because the hand-written signature will not forever be present as a reference point.

The second rule of Article 5(1), stating that qualified electronic signatures should be admissible as legal evidence in legal proceedings, seems superfluous. Digital data, including electronic signatures, are accepted as evidence in legal proceedings in all Member States. Only the value of such evidence varies between the Member States. Moreover the question of the acceptability of electronic signatures as evidence in legal proceedings is, in most of the Member States, dealt with on a case-by-case basis and left to be decided by the judge in each specific case. Recital 21 explicitly mentions that the Directive does not affect the role of the judge in this context.
As a general principle the Directive states in Article 5(2) that Member States may not deny the legal effect of an electronic signature or the admissibility as evidence in legal proceedings only because of the electronic form of the signature or because the requirements of the Annexes I to III are not being fulfilled.

Article 5(2) essentially states, in other words, that electronic signatures may not be denied legal effectiveness and admissibility as evidence in legal proceedings solely on the grounds that it is in electronic form or that the signature in question is not a qualified signature. The effect of Article 5(2) is that Member States may not draft or maintain regulation, or endorse or authorise private rules with a view to condemn the use of an electronic authentication tool solely by virtue of its electronic format or non-qualified nature. However, the matter to be determined is how the absence of legal validity under Article 5(2) can be paraphrased in positive terms. In other words, how must a denial be framed other than by reference to its electronic format, in such a manner that the Directive is not infringed upon?

It is fair to infer from the plain language that a denial of legal effect requires something more than a reference to its electronic format. This seems to translate into a requirement that a substantive disapproval must be involved, as such that any objection must be 'on the merits' of the particular technology involved. It is required, in other words, that any denial of an electronic signature's legal effect or admissibility would be based on an affirmative finding of, e.g., a lack of technological reliability, circumstantial impropriety, or accountability. A denial of legal effect must be fully supported by a sufficiently reasoned and rationally based evaluation, one that is individual in nature, rather than being general in design.

As to the interaction with Article 5(1), the rule in Article 5(2), pursuant to its inclusive wording, is applicable to all electronic signatures, including 'qualified signatures'. But by way of contrast, this does not mean that a non-qualified electronic signature would be equipped with the legal effect of a hand-written signature. Rather, Article 5(1) introducing universal a priori validity represents a narrow prerogative confined to technologies of preferably superior design.

## 3.7  Article 6 – Liability

In its Article 6, the Electronic Signature directive contains liability provisions for issuers of qualified certificates.[67] Providers of qualified certificates are liable for certain information contained in the certificate and the accuracy of revocation lists. Article 6 provides for a minimum of CA liability. This means that the Member States can go beyond the requirements of Article 6 in their implementation of the Directive, but they are not allowed to introduce a lesser extent of liability on CAs. For example, Member States are allowed to introduce strict liability for CAs or to introduce liability provisions that also cover CAs issuing non-qualified certificates. In this respect, the effect of Article 6 of the Directive is the enforcement of user protection. On the other hand, Article 6(3) and 6(4) foresee certain liability limitations that the Member States have to recognise. These provisions can be considered as 'CA friendly.'

### 3.7.1  Qualified certificate

Firstly, the minimum liability provisions of the Directive only apply if a certificate has been issued as a qualified certificate. Thus, whether the defective certificate is actually qualified or unqualified is irrelevant, decisive is its designation by the CA. The reason behind this condition becomes clear obvious when considering that the requirements to be fulfilled by a certificate to be qualified and by a certification service provider to fall under the definition of Annex II, are mostly set up to guarantee the security of the certification service. In the majority of cases, the signatory and the relying party do not have the means to control if a certificate is

---

[67] This chapter is based on a report drafted by Regina Rinderle, researcher at K.U.Leuven-ICRI in the context of the TIE-project. For more details about this project, see <http://www.tie.org.uk/tie_project.htm>.

actually qualified in the terms of the Directive. They rely on the designation of the certificate by the CA as qualified as it is required for qualified certificates in Annex I(a).

### 3.7.2    Issued to the public

Moreover, the certificate has to be 'issued to the public' or 'guaranteed to the public' (Article 6 (1), (2)). The meaning of this term is open to interpretation. While the expression 'issued to the public' could be understood to refer to 'a publicly accessible directory', we prefer to follow an interpretation that is primarily based on recital 16 of the Directive. According to this recital 'a regulatory framework is not needed for electronic signatures that are exclusively used within systems, which are based on voluntary agreements under private law between a specified number of participants.' The provisions of the Directive do not apply to such closed systems because 'the freedom of parties (...) should be respected to the extent allowed by national law.' Since the Directive on electronic signatures expressly refrains from regulating the rights and obligations of parties in a closed system, it seems plausible that certification service providers operating in a closed system are also excluded from the liability provisions of the Directive, since their mutual relationships enable them to set up their own contractual liability provisions. While in an open system, the relying party typically does not have any contractual relationship with the certification authority and is therefore dependent on the law to introduce an appropriate liability system, the relying party in a closed system can rely on the contractual liability of the CA.

In our opinion, the expression 'issuing to the public' can be interpreted as referring to certification services that are open to verifiers that do not have a prior relationship with the CA.

### 3.7.3    'Guaranteed to the public'

As an alternative to having issued a qualified certificate to the public, a CA can also be held liable for having 'guaranteed' a qualified certificate 'to the public'. To further qualify the situation in which a certification service provider can be considered to have 'guaranteed a certificate to the public' in the terms of Article 6, it has to be taken into account that the guaranteeing CA is equally liable to the issuing CA. To justify this extent of liability, the guarantee required will have to go beyond a simple recognition of the other CAS public key, as it is the case in cross-certification. One case of guaranteeing a certificate is mentioned in Article 7(1)(b) of the Directive. According to this provision, obtaining a guarantee from a certification service provider who is established in a EU Member State is one of the three possibilities for a non-EU certification service provider to issue qualified certificates within the EU that receive the legal recognition of Article 5 of the Electronic Signature directive.

### 3.7.4 Claimant ('relying party')

The Directive imposes a minimum of liability on the party relying on a Certification Practice Statement.[68] The recipient of an electronic signature, who relies on one or more certificates when verifying that signature, is undoubtedly a 'relying party' in the meaning of Article 6 of the Directive. As far as the signatory is concerned, however, the situation appears more ambiguous. It is not quite clear from the wording of the Article if the signatory is included.

The signatory enters into a contract with the CA regarding the issuance of the certificate. Therefore, it could be argued that liability of the CA to the signatory is governed by the terms of that contract or national contract law only and that the liability provisions of the Directive do not apply to the signatory. Considering the fact that the liability rules of the Directive do not apply to closed systems (recital 16), it could be argued that in the relationship between signatory and CA, questions of liability should also be governed by contractual stipulations.

Another possibility is to treat the liability provisions of the Directive as default law: As far as there are no prevalent contractual regulations in the CSP-signatory relationship, Article 6 of the European directive in its transformed national form applies. This approach, however, would be inconsistent with the specification of the liability provisions as 'a minimum' in Article 6 of the Directive.

Finally, Article 6 could be regarded as a minimum liability rule that the signatory cannot be deprived of by contractual terms. It could be argued that one of the aims of the Directive is to ensure the security of the certificate market through a concept of 'liability instead of supervision.'

### 3.7.5 Liability causes

According to Article 6(1) of the Directive, CAs are liable for the accuracy and completeness of all the information in the certificate, the identity of the signatory holding the signature creation data corresponding to the signature-verification data given or identified in the certificate, and the complementary usage of signature creation data and signature-verification data if the CA has created them both.

According to Article 6(2) the CA is liable for failure to register the revocation of the certificate. This provision almost exclusively applies to CAs who have not delegated the CRL services to another entity.

---

[68] A Certification Practice Statement (CPS) is a statement of the practices which a certification authority employs in issuing certificates. A model (RFC 2527) for drafters of a CPS is available at <http://www.ietf.org/rfc/rfc2527.txt>.

### 3.7.6    Reasonable reliance

Liability of CAs, according to Article 6(1) and (2) of the Electronic Signature directive, requires 'reasonable reliance' by the party who suffered the damages. The term reasonableness is rather vague and requires interpretation. Depending on the point of view, reasonable reliance could either only be excluded in cases of extreme carelessness by the relying party or it could be interpreted as a considerable liability limitation for certification authorities.

A terminological parallel could be drawn to US-American product liability law, where the 'test of reasonableness' of the consumers´ trust in a product is sometimes used to restrict liability of producers.

Regarding liability for defective certificates, the requirement of reasonable reliance could be of specific relevance within Article 6(1)(a), which constitutes liability for the completeness of information contained in a certificate. It might be questionable, if the recipient of a qualified electronic signature can be said to have reasonably relied on the respective certificate if the information specified in Annex I of the Directive is missing in that certificate. It might be possible that the technical expertise of the consumer will be taken into consideration to interpret the term reasonableness on an individual basis.

Another question of relevance for certification authorities is, to what extent a CA can exclude reasonable reliance by limiting its liability in his terms and conditions. Since the introduction of valid liability limitation clauses in relation to the relying party is legally doubtful due to the absence of a contractual relationship, the reasonableness requirement might open a door for CAs to limit their liability in a tort relationship. It will be up to the courts to decide whether a relying party can be said to have reasonably relied on a certificate if that certificate excludes liability of the issuer in a respect that is not covered by Article 6(3) and (4) and to what extent these kinds of liability limitations will be considered valid in a tortuous relationship. Possibly, the rules and provisions governing contractual liability limitations will be taken into consideration when answering that question.

Possibly, a disclaimer (which could e.g. appear to the relying party when he/she receives an electronically signed message) in which the CA states that its liability is limited could be used to prevent reasonable reliance. The advantage of that method would be that the relying party is confronted with the disclaimer 'up-front' – the disclaimer could e.g. state that by relying on the certificate the relying party agrees to the limitation of liability clause or to the terms and conditions of the CA in which a limitation of liability clause is inserted.

### 3.7.7 Absence of negligence

*Strict liability* – as it exists in product liability law[69] – is not demanded by the Directive. Instead, negligence of the provider is a precondition for a title to compensation for damages. This precondition is based on the typical situation of the relying party. The recipient of a signature that turns out to be invalid will often not be in a position to analyse the technical background of that failure, whereas the Certification Authority itself has much better insight into its own organisational and technical proceedings. Accordingly, the Directive imposes the burden of proof for negligence on the CSP, who has the necessary technical know-how to investigate the matter.

### 3.7.8 Limitation of liability

To reduce the financial risk associated with liability, Certification Service Providers will look for methods to limit their liability. A number of liability limitations are provided for in the Directive. These limitations have to be recognised by the Member States. To be considered valid, all liability limitation clauses generally have to be made available to the CA's contract partner or the relying party in clear and readable form.

Article 6(3) and (4) provide for certain liability limitations. E.g. a CSP can include a value limit for commercial transactions. If that limit is transgressed, the CSP 'shall not be liable for damage resulting from this maximum limit being exceeded.' If the wording of the Directive is taken literally, this does not offer a very extensive limitation option. If the CSP has to be at fault for liability to arise, the damage in a successful case will most likely be the result of a negligent act of the CSP rather than being caused by the excess of the maximum transaction limit. Thus, an interpretation of Article 6 that allows a CSP to limit his liability by referring to a maximum transaction value clause in the certificate should be followed.[70] The majority of legal literature that has been published on this topic so far interprets Article 6(4) to allow a relative liability limitation only, meaning that only the maximum value per transaction can be limited, but not the absolute liability for the certificate regardless of the number of transactions. This interpretation seems reasonable, since it is not possible for the relying party to see the number of previous transactions that have been conducted by the signatory or the extent to which the liability for the certificate has already been 'consumed' by these previous transactions.

---

[69] Council Directive 85/374/EEC on the approximation of the laws, regulations and administrative provisions of the Member States concerning liability for defective products, *OJ* L 141/20, 4.6.1999.

[70] The recognition of a per-incident and aggregate cap on a TTP's liability is also recommended by the ABA Science & Technology Information Security Committee, available at: <http://www.abanet.org/scitech/ec/isc/ukkeyr1.html>.

The provisions of the Directive also provide the possibility to indicate a limitation of use of a certificate. A Certification Practice Statement or a Certificate Policy[71] can, for example, mention that the certificate may only be used for a certain type of transaction or that it may only be used within one company, one country or within the EC. If the signatory then transgresses these limitations by using the certificate for purposes outside the limitation, the certification service provider will not be held liable for resulting damages.

Liability limitations can either be included in the Certificate Practice Statement that has to be brought to the attention of the relying party/signatory and that can for example be downloaded from the Website of the CSP or in a separate statement that the signatory or the relying party can easily access.

Outside the Electronic Signature directive, national laws govern the liability of certification authorities. The extent to which liability limitations will be allowed under these provisions, may depend on a number of factors, such as for example the class of the certificate. Some CAs offer three different classes of certificates depending on the level of confidence that can be placed in the certified signature. For example, a class I certificate will be issued on mere e-mail address verification, whereas a class III certificate will only be issued after identification of the signatory in person.

Thus, considering the liability limitations already included in the Directive, it is advisable for CSPs to establish a maximum cap for liability for qualified certificates. The maximum cap should include liability for all ancillary services that the certification authority may be held liable for. The maximum cap can for example vary depending on the quality of the certificate issued. CAs issuing cross-certificates to other CAs should clearly state the limitation of usage of these certificates to avoid liability to relying third parties other than CAs. In addition to that, a certificate may include a limitation that allows its use for a certain type of transaction only, e.g. a contract for the sale of movables.

While liability limitations that go beyond the ones foreseen in the Directive are only valid outside the scope of this Directive, a CSP might seek to prevent potential liability by explicitly stating that no liability will be assumed for any statements by the signatory that are not verified by the certificate. Moreover, to clearly avoid liability for potential conflicts regarding the legal validity of a digital signature in a certain context, the CSP may wish to make clear that he does not guarantee the legal effect of an electronic signature that bears its certificate. Since no case law regarding the interpretation of the liability provisions of the Directive exists yet, it is advisable to include liability limitations that are based on the narrowest possible interpretation of these provisions. For example, it is not clear at the moment to what extent courts will hold certification authorities liable for indirect damages arising from a defect

---

[71] A Certificate Policy (CP) is 'a named set of rules that indicates the applicability of a certificate to a particular community and/or class of application with common security requirements.' A model for drafters of a CP (RFC 2527) is available at <http://www.ietf.org/rfc/rfc2527.txt>.

certificate. Thus, exclusion of any form of liability for indirect damages incurred by either signatory or relying party may be useful.

Since national laws can go beyond the requirements of the liability provisions of the Directive, which does not foresee liability for this case, Certification Service Providers are advised to inform the relying party of the possibility of the loss of the private key by the signatory as not to appear to assume liability for damages incurring due to unauthorised use of a private key.

For certificates outside the scope of the Directive as well as for certificates that are relied on by parties located outside the European Union, limitation of liability may be possible to a wider extent.

To increase the probability that liability limitations in relation to relying third parties will be enforceable in court, it is advisable to require a relying party to agree on the terms and conditions for usage of the certificate list before enabling him to access the list. The statement that a relying party will be deemed to have agreed to the terms and conditions if he relies on the certificates issued by the certification service provider may be considered insufficient for that purpose if it cannot be established that the relying party had to take notice of the conditions prior to using the A' certificate for verification.

## 3.8    Articles 7-15 – Other provisions

The core of Directive is discussed above, in this section the remaining Articles are briefly addressed. Article 7 of the Directive is dedicated to international aspects. Also in recital 29 it is emphasised that the development of international electronic commerce requires cross-border arrangements involving third countries. Article 8 addresses the issue of data protection. Certification service providers and national bodies responsible for accreditation or supervision should comply with the requirements laid down in Directive 95/46/EC of the European Parliament and of the Council of 24 October 1995. Recital 25 specifies that 'provisions on the use of pseudonyms in certificates should not prevent Member States from requiring identification of persons pursuant to Community or national law.'

In the framework of the Directive, the Commission has received a number of implementing powers, e.g., in Article 3(4) (criteria for the designation of accreditation bodies) or Article 3(5) (publication of reference numbers of generally recognised standards). In the exercise of these implementing powers the Commission is assisted by an 'Electronic Signature Committee' with representatives of the Member States. Articles 4 and 7 of Decision 1999/468/EC[72] are applicable to this Committee. Article 4 describes the management procedure of the Committee:

---

[72] Council Decision of 28 June 1999 laying down the procedures for the exercise of implementing powers conferred on the Commission, *OJ* L 184 of 17.7.1999, p. 23 – 26.

1.　The Commission shall be assisted by a management committee composed of the representatives of the Member States and chaired by the representative of the Commission.
2.　The representative of the Commission shall submit to the committee a draft of the measures to be taken. The committee shall deliver its opinion on the draft within a time limit which the chairman may lay down according to the urgency of the matter. The opinion shall be delivered by the majority laid down in Article 205(2) of the Treaty, in the case of decisions which the Council is required to adopt on a proposal from the Commission. The votes of the representatives of the Member States within the committee shall be weighed in the manner set out in that Article. The chairman shall not vote.
3.　The Commission shall, without prejudice to Article 8, adopt measures which shall apply immediately. However, if these measures are not in accordance with the opinion of the committee, they shall forthwith be communicated by the Commission to the Council. In that event, the Commission may defer application of the measures which it has decided on for a period to be laid down in each basic instrument but which shall in no case exceed three months from the date of such communication.
4.　The Council, acting by qualified majority, may take a different decision within the period provided for by paragraph 3.

According to Article 7:
1.　Each committee shall adopt its own rules of procedure on the proposal of its chairman, on the basis of standard rules of procedure which shall be published in the　　　Official　　　Journal　　　of　　　the　　　European　　　Communities. Insofar as necessary, existing committees shall adapt their rules of procedure to the standard rules of procedure.
2.　The principles and conditions on public access to documents applicable to the Commission shall apply to the committees.
3.　The European Parliament shall be informed by the Commission of committee proceedings on a regular basis. To that end, it shall receive agendas for committee meetings, draft measures submitted to the committees for the implementation of instruments adopted by the procedure provided for by Article 251 of the Treaty, and the results of voting and summary records of the meetings and lists of the authorities and organisations to which the persons designated by the Member States to represent them belong. The European Parliament shall also be kept informed whenever the Commission transmits to the Council measures or proposals for measures to be taken.
4.　The Commission shall, within six months of the date on which this Decision takes effect, publish in the Official Journal of the European Communities, a list of all committees which assist the Commission in the exercise of implementing powers. This list shall specify, in relation to each committee, the basic instrument(s) under which the committee is established. From 2000 onwards, the Commission shall also publish an annual report on the working of committees.

5. The references of all documents sent to the European Parliament pursuant to paragraph 3 shall be made public in a register to be set up by the Commission in 2001.

The main tasks of the Committee are to clarify the requirements laid down in the Annexes of the Directive, the criteria referred to in Article 3(4) and the generally recognised standards for electronic signature products established and published pursuant to Article 3(5).

In Article 11(a) notification procedure is described. Two years after its implementation the Commission will carry out a review of the Directive so as, inter alia, to ensure that the advance of technology or changes in the legal environment have not created barriers to achieving the aims stated in the Directive (Article 12). The Member States have to transpose the Electronic Signature directive before 19 July 2001 and forthwith inform the Commission thereof (Article 13). Member States are required to communicate to the Commission the text of the main provisions of domestic law which they adopt in the field governed by this Directive.

# Chapter 4

# Directive 2000/31/EC on certain legal aspects of information society services, in particular electronic commerce, in the Internal Market

## Arno R. Lodder

Important dates regarding the Directive 2000/31/EC on certain legal aspects of information society services, in particular electronic commerce, in the Internal Market (Directive on electronic commerce) are in chronological order:

- **1998, November 18** – Proposal adopted by the Commission;[1]
- **1999, May 6** – Proposal approved by the European Parliament, subject to amendments;[2]
- **1999, August 17** – Amended proposal adopted by the Commission;[3]
- **2000, February 28** – Common position adopted by the Council;[4]
- **2000, May 4** – Approval by the European Parliament;[5]
- **2000, June 8** – Signed by the European Parliament and the Council;
- **2000, July 17** – Publication in the Official Journal;[6]
- **2002, January 17** – Directive should be implemented by the Member States.

## 4.1    Introduction

The Directive 2000/31/EC is usually called the e-commerce directive, or the Directive on e-commerce. Although several other Directives deal solely, or at least for the greater part, with e-commerce topics, Directive 2000/31/EC regulates central issues regarding electronic commerce, e.g. commercial communications, formation of online contracts, and liability of intermediaries. The Directive deals with key

---

[1]   COM (1998) 586 final, *OJ* C 30/4, 19.2.1999.
[2]   *OJ* C 279/403, 1.10.1999.
[3]   COM (1999) 427 final, *OJ* C 248 E/69, 29.8.2000.
[4]   *OJ* C 128/32, 8.5.2000.
[5]   *OJ* C 41/38, 7.2.2001.
[6]   *OJ* L 178, 17.7.2000.

*A.R. Lodder and H.W.K. Kaspersen (eds.),*
*eDirectives: Guide to European Union Law on E-Commerce, 67–93.*
© 2002 *Kluwer Law International. Printed in the Netherlands.*

issues of e-commerce, reason why the Directive is also known as the legal framework directive.[7]

The Directive consists of 24 Articles and 65 recitals. In the following sections are discussed the Articles and the recitals 17-52 that elucidate the meaning of the Articles, as well as the recitals 53-65 that contain some further considerations. The recitals 1-16 of the Directive elaborate upon what the Directive is (not) aimed at, and as such give a good impression of the scope of the directive. In the first place these opening recitals (1-16) express the high expectations the European Union has with respect to electronic commerce (recital 2). Therefore, free movement of information society services (cf. Article 14(2) EC Treaty) has to be realised by a high level of Community (legal) integration (recital 1, 3-6). The main objective of the Directive is to create a legal framework to cover certain legal aspects of electronic commerce in the internal market (recital 7-8). Criminal law as such is not harmonised, and the freedom of expression not affected (recital 8-9). The Directive in particular ensures the protection of minors and human dignity, consumer protection and the protection of public health, without prejudice to the level of protection in other Directives (recital 10-11). The Directive does not deal with fiscal aspects (recital 12-13), privacy (recital 14), confidentiality of communication (recital 15), and gambling activities, with the exception of promotional games to encourage sale of goods or services (recital 16).

The original proposal for a Directive considered five issues crucial:[8]
• Establishment of Information Society service providers;
• Commercial communications (advertising, direct marketing, etc.);
• Online conclusion of contracts;
• Liability of intermediaries;
• Implementation;
These issues are worked out in the following chapters and sections of the Directive:
• Chapter 1 – General provisions (Articles 1-3);
• Chapter 2 – Principles (Articles 4-15);
  ➢ Section 1: Establishment and information requirements (Articles 4-5);
  ➢ Section 2: Commercial communications ( s 6-8);
  ➢ Section 3: Contracts concluded by electronic means (Articles 9-11);
  ➢ Section 4: Liability of intermediary service providers (Articles 12-15);
• Chapter 3 – Implementation (Articles 16-20);
• Chapter 4 – Final provisions (Articles 21-24).

---

[7] See recital 7: ' (…) this Directive must lay down a clear and general framework to cover certain legal aspects of electronic commerce in the internal market.', and recital 8: 'the objective of this Directive is to create a legal framework (…).'

[8] COM (1998) 586 final, p. 4: 'The proposal therefore seeks to remove the obstacles that result from such conditions, for service providers established in Europe, by tackling five key issues that together form a coherent framework to bring about the free circulation of online services.'

The Article-by-article comments are grouped around the above topics.

At first glance the topics of the Directive seem randomly chosen, or seem not really to represent a coherent set. The logic behind that such divers topics are dealt with together, is that the Directive is intended to reflect the life cycle of electronic commerce activities. First, a service provider establishes, then the provider communicates commercially, and consecutively he concludes contracts online. While carrying out the contracts, liability of intermediaries may occur, and finally eventual disputes have to be resolved. In addition, the Commission stated 'the issues are all inter-related (...) and (...) none of these obstacles can be removed in isolation (for example, clarifying a service provider's liability is not possible without defining its place of establishment).'[9] Despite these explanations, the compilation of addressed topics remains somewhat unbalanced.

## 4.2 General provisions

### 4.2.1 Article 1 – Objective and scope

The main objective of the Directive is to <u>contribute to</u> ~~ensure~~ the proper functioning of the internal market <u>by ensuring</u> ~~, particularly~~ the free movement of information society services between the Member States (Article 1(1)). The underlined text is part of the final version of the Directive, the deleted words stem from the (amended) proposal. This slight change of wording is illustrative for the difficulty of regulating Internet related topics, like the Commission obviously found out. It is impossible to *ensure* the proper functioning of the internal market in such an open, global environment as the Internet. In the recitals the inherent global nature of information society services is recognised. Recitals 61-62 express that negotiation with third countries is necessary to make laws and procedures compatible, and that cooperation with third countries should be strengthened. Also, the Directive does not apply to services by a third country, and is without prejudice to results of discussions by international organisations (Uncitral, OECD) on legal issues (recital 58). However, the creation of an appropriate European regulatory framework may establish a strong negotiation position in international fora (recital 59).

Article 1(2) lists the topics necessary for realising the objective of Article 1(1). Articles 3-19 address these topics, e.g. the internal market in Article 3, commercial communications in Articles 6-8, electronic contracts in Articles 9-11,and code of conducts in Article 16.

The Directive complements existing Directives, but is without prejudice to the level of protection for, in particular, public health and consumer interest, as established by

---

[9]    COM (1998) 586 final, p. 3.

Community acts (Article 1(3)). Recital 11 gives an overview of the relevant acts, for instance, Directive 97/7/EC (see chapter 2) and Directive 84/450/EEC concerning misleading and comparative advertising. The Council added in the common position after Community acts: '(...) and national legislation implementing them, insofar as this does not restrict the freedom to provide information society services.'[10] To me, the last part of the sentence is a bit unlucky. Assume there is a conflict between the freedom to provide services and consumer interests or public health. Should then the freedom prevail over consumer interests or public health? This cannot be the case. What is probably meant is that for providing information society services prior permission is not needed. However, if a license is necessary to sell medicines (public health), this license is also needed for a website selling medicines, although this is a restriction of the freedom to provide information society services. This example is in line with Article 4(2), so Article 1(3) is better understandable if the phrase 'insofar ... services' is disregarded.

Already the proposal (recital 7)[11] indicated that the Directive does not aim to establish specific rules on private international law relating to conflicts of law or jurisdiction. Still, there has been quite some discussion on this point, in particular in relation to the country-of-origin principle (see section 4.2.2). In a late stage of the drafting of the Directive (common position), and probably in order to take away all remaining doubts, Article 1(4) now repeats the former recital 7 (the current recital 23).

In the (amended) proposal Article 22 and Annex I mentioned the exemptions that are now contained in Article 1(5). First, because other EU initiatives deal with taxation[12] and data protection[13] (under a-b), these areas are exempt. Second, cartel law (sub c) is not envisaged, probably because the topic is too complicated to be addressed in this Directive. Finally, under (d) activities are summed up that cannot be regulated, given the lack of mutual recognition by Member States or lack of sufficient harmonisation:[14] activities of notaries or equivalent professions, representation before the courts, and gambling activities. Note however that, according to recital 16, the Directive does apply to promotional games to encourage sale of goods or services.

Article 1(6) stresses that the harmonisation of information society services does not affect measures that promote cultural and linguistic diversity, and ensure the defence of pluralism. Recital 63 further explains this: 'the development of the information

---

[10]  SEC (2000) 386 final, p. 8.
[11]  The current recital 23.
[12]  See Communication on e-commerce and Indirect Taxation, COM (1998) 374 final, and the proposals regarding VAT for a regulation amending Regulation (EEC) No 218/92 and for a Directive amending Directive 77/388/EEC, COM (2000) 349 final. See also section 1.3.2.
[13]  Directive 95/46/EC (see section 6.2), and Directive 97/66/EC (see section 6.3).
[14]  COM (1998) 586 final, p. 32.

society is to ensure that Community citizens can have access to the cultural European heritage provided in the digital environment.'

## 4.2.2    Article 2 – Definitions

On their website, The European Commission claimed the proposal covers all sorts of Information Society services, both business to business and business to consumer, for example: online newspapers, online databases, online financial services, online professional services (such as lawyers, doctors, accountants, estate agents), online entertainment services such as video on demand, online direct marketing and advertising, and services providing access to the World Wide Web.

In the proposal *Information Society services* were defined in Article 2(a), from the amended proposal onwards Article 1(2) provides only a reference to the definition of Directive 98/34/EC.[15] However, the definition of information society services can be found in recital 17, and a number of examples are given in recital 18. The definition is:

– any service normally provided for remuneration;

It is not necessary that a service is paid for by the recipient. The costs of a service can also be covered by advertisement. For instance, free Internet providers fall under the scope of the Directive.

– at a distance;

The service should be provided without the parties being simultaneously present (see also Directive 97/7/EC). An interesting question from a theoretical perspective is whether a service ordered by mobile phone (WAP), while parties are simultaneously present, is an information society service. For example, a rental car could be ordered using a mobile, while one is standing at the desk of the garage where the car is parked. In my opinion the use of electronic means is the decisive criterion.

However, this does not mean that 'at a distance' should be deleted from the definition, because in almost all cases the criterion 'at a distance' is helpful. Moreover, deleting this criterion would for example mean that the Directive applies to Internet cafes where access to Internet is provided *not* at a distance. The rationale for the criterion is that parties at a distance cannot communicate face-to-face. So, the actual criterion should be whether face-to-face contact is possible. If parties are not at a distance and face-to-face contact is possible, the service is not of the information society; in all other cases, it is. For the example of the car rental this means the following. In case the rental car can be ordered at the desk, the service should not be considered one of the information society. In case the rental car cannot be ordered at the desk (e.g. easyrentacar.com), despite

---

[15]  Directive of 22 June 1998 laying down a procedure for the provision of information in the field of technical standards and regulations as amended by Directive 98/48/EC of 20 July 1998. For the sake of readability, the text of the definition better would have been included in the text, instead of a reference to the definition in another Directive.

the simultaneous presence of the representative of the rental company and the customer, the service should be considered one of the information society.
– by electronic means;
  The service should be sent and received using electronic equipment. Traditional distance selling methods, like mail-order firms, are not information society services. The services of a mail-order firm carried out using a website do fall under the scope of the Directive.[16]
– at the individual request of a recipient of services.
  The service should be delivered on demand. A visit to a website is always a service on demand, since the recipient 'requests' the website by typing the URL or by following a link. A standard example of a service that is not on demand is TV broadcasting, since the deliverance of the service does not depend on the request of the customer. One could well argue that this is also the case for WebTV, in particular for live reports, but the deliverance still is on demand because of the fact that one should visit a website before being able to watch WebTV.[17]

Traditionally, the term service providers refers to people or companies that provide services by telephone. In the Directive providers also include Internet service providers, and providers of online services, viz. a natural or legal person providing an information society service (Article 2(b)).

Article 2(c) defines in which country a service provider is established: 'a service provider who effectively pursues an economic activity using a fixed establishment for an indefinite period.[18] The presence and use of the technical means and technologies required to provide the service do not, in themselves, constitute an establishment of the provider.' The Commission claims that 'such a definition removes current legal uncertainty and ensures that operators could not evade supervision, as they would be subject to supervision in the Member State where they were established.' This country-of-origin principle has led to confusion, in particular in relation to consumer protection as regulated in the Rome convention. Would the consumer in case of e-commerce no longer have the possibility to apply its home-country law? This worry was especially fed by the fact that stimulation of e-commerce was given as a reason for this principle. Providers only had to take into account the law of their home country and not of all other Member States, as a result of which the starting of a website would become legally less complicated. On the issue of the country-of-origin principle a public hearing was held in Brussels on November 1999. The issue should be interpreted in the following way. As far as the

---

[16]  For example the Dutch site of the mail-order firm Wehkamp, <http://www.wehkamp.com>.
[17]  In some countries, like the Netherlands, at this moment Media Law does apply to TV but not to WebTV. Although applying the Directive to TV does not seem meaningful, for Media Law the border between these two basically identical services (WebTV and TV) will probably disappear.
[18]  This requirement is also fulfilled where a company is constituted for a given period, cf. recital 19.

requirements of the service provider are concerned, the country-of-origin principle applies. So, if a service provider is established in France, he has to fulfil the French requirements concerning for example issues belonging to the coordinated field (Article 2(f)). On the other hand, a consumer may apply the law of his home country to contracts that are concluded electronically, so the consumer protection still stands. This interpretation is also reflected in the current recital 22: '(…) Information Society services should *in principle* be subject to the law of the Member State in which the service provider is established (…)', while recital 8 of the (amended) proposal stated: '(…) should *only* be subject (…).'

The recipient of the service is defined in Article 2(d) as any natural or legal person who, for professional ends or otherwise, uses an Information Society service. According to recital 20 this covers all types of usage, both by persons who on the Internet provide and seek information. A provider of a service can at the same time as well be a recipient. For example, a person or company running a web store is both provider (online selling) and recipient (access to the Internet).

Following amendment 32 of the Parliament, Article 2(e) defines a consumer as a natural person who is acting for purposes which are outside his or her trade, business or profession. Although the Directive is not specifically targeted at consumers (like Directive 97/7/EC), in various Articles the consumer is given extra protection. In my opinion, 'outside his or her trade' should be given a wide interpretation. A webstore trading in books for example, should not be considered a consumer if office chairs are bought, although buying chairs is not part of their commercial activities.

Commercial communications are defined in Article 2(f) as any form of communication designed to promote. Both direct and indirect promotion is covered, in order to prevent circumvention of the ban on commercial communications for certain products (e.g., tobacco, alcohol).[19] Because the definition is wide, certain communications are explicitly excluded.[20] For example, mere ownership of a website or e-mail address, linking to a commercial site without getting paid for it, providing information not constituting promotion, consumer-testing services, and price or product comparisons (e.g., bargain finders). A communication is considered commercial if the goods, services or image are promoted of a company, organisation or person <u>pursuing a commercial, industrial or craft activity or exercising a regulated profession</u>. The Parliament proposed in amendment 31 to skip the underlined part in order not to exclude non-profit-making organisations or associations aimed at sales promotion or proselytism.[21] The amendment was not accepted, so on the basis of the

---

[19] COM (1998) 586 final, p. 20.
[20] COM (1998) 586 final, p. 21.
[21] See the Report from Committee on Legal Affairs and Citizens' Rights of 23 April 1999, A4-0248/99, p. 36.

Directive recipients are not protected against unsolicited e-mails (spam) from for example Scientology or Hara Krishna.

Regulated professions are defined in Article 2(g), under reference to Directive 89/48/EEC on a general system for the recognition of higher-education diplomas. The definition stems from recital 12 of the (amended) proposal (the current recital 32 from which the definition has been deleted). Examples of regulated professions are lawyers and physicians.

Because the definition of the coordinated field left some indistinctness, the common position contained a new recital 21 and an extended version of Article 2(h). The coordinated field concerns national requirements applicable to Information Society service providers and Information Society services. These requirements are either of a general nature, or specifically designed for the information society (Article 2(h), under (i)). In the first place requirements concerning the starting of an information society service, such as qualification, authorisation, and notification. Second, requirements concerning the pursuit of an information society service, such as the quality or content of the service (including regulation on advertisement and contracts), and liability. Obviously, beside existing legislation, the coordinated field includes issues that are regulated by the (implemented) Directive or other future legislation. Examples are the information requirements of Articles 5, 6, and 10, and the regulation regarding electronic contracting (Article 11). Excluded from the coordinated field are requirements applicable to goods as such, delivery of goods, and services not provided by electronic means (Article 2(h) under (ii)). Especially the last exception is rather peculiar. Hence, the coordinated field concerns requirements applicable to information society services or information society service providers. One of the elements of the definition of an information society service is 'by electronic means' (and a provider provides these services). So, the requirements apply to services provided by electronic means. Moreover, the requirements can be specifically designed for the information society or can be of a general nature. In the latter case such a requirement *is* in fact applicable to services not provided by electronic means.

### 4.2.3    Article 3 – Internal market

Service providers must comply with the provisions falling within the coordinated field of the Member States on which territory they are established (Article 3(1)).[22] The following example explains the scope of this paragraph. Assume that the Netherlands forbid promotion of firework. This means that a service provider established in the Netherlands is not allowed to promote firework. Service providers outside the Netherlands, let alone outside the European Union, may in principle promote firework, e.g. on their website. advertise

---

[22]   See the previous section for a discussion of the definitions of established service provider (Article 2(c)) and coordinated field (Article 2(h)).

A Member State may not restrict the freedom to provide Information Society services that are allowed by the Member State in which the service provider is established (Article 3(2)). This provision is similar to Article 2bis of the Television without frontiers Directive (89/552/EEC, and 97/36/EC). Because the freedom concerns only the coordinated field, restriction is allowed for reasons falling without the coordinated field. For example, a criminal information society service may be restricted, because criminal law is not part of the coordinated field.

Article 3(3) refers to the Annex of the Directive that sums up exceptions to the coordinated field regarding supervision (Article 3(1)) and the freedom to provide information society services (Article 3(2)). These field are, briefly described:
- intellectual property rights (dealt with in various other Directives, see also chapter 5);
- the emission of electronic money (dealt with in Directive 2000/46/EC);
- collective investments in transferable securities (dealt with in Directive 85/611/EEC);
- the freedom of the parties to choose the law applicable to their contract;
- contractual obligations concerning consumer contracts;
- formal validity of contracts concerning real estate;
- permissibility of unsolicited commercial communication by e-mail.

First, service providers do not have to comply with the rules of the Member State they are established in for any of these fields. At least, not as far as the Directive is concerned. This does not mean, however, that the service provider does not have to comply with other regulations in this area. Second, a Member State is allowed to restrict the freedom to provide information society services in any of those fields. Only if on the basis of other regulations the Member State is not allowed to restrict the service provider he cannot restrict, otherwise a restriction is allowed. For instance, if a website of a service provider established in the UK sells an Amsterdam house, it goes without saying that the transfer must be registered in the public registers of Amsterdam. The UK information society service cannot ignore this requirement. To give another example, there is no general ban on unsolicited commercial communication yet but instead each Member State may decide whether they allow it. Assume Denmark forbids unsolicited commercial communications, and Sweden does not. In that case it must be possible for Denmark to restrict the sending of unsolicited e-mail from Sweden, despite the existing permission from Sweden.

Article 3(4) contains another exception to paragraph Article 3(2). A Member State may restrict the freedom to provide information society services from another Member State under the following conditions. First, the measures must be necessary for public policy, public security, protection of public health, or protection of consumers. Second, the service must actually or potentially prejudice the objectives of the public policy, security, etc. Third, the measures must be proportionate to the objectives. Fourth, the other Member State must have been asked to take measures and they did it inadequately or did not it at all. Finally, both the other Member State and the Commission must be notified that the intention exists to take the measures. This is quite a detailed procedure (see further below), and I doubt whether the Member States are going to make much use of it.

According to Article 3(5), in case of urgency the just mentioned notification may be postponed, but only if the measures are almost immediately notified to, again, the other Member State and the Commission, and the reason for urgency is indicated.

As soon as possible the Commission has to examine whether the measures described in Article 3(4) are compatible with Community law (Article 3(6)). In case the measure is incompatible, the Member State is asked by the Commission to either not begin with, or end the measures.

The regulation regarding the coordinated field reveals that the Directive is apparently not as simple as was intended by the Commission (see recital 60). The definition of the coordinated field is quite difficult. The (nesting of) exceptions complicate the matter further. Article 2(h) mentions topics that do not belong to the coordinated field, the Annex contains a list of further exceptions, and yet other exceptions can be based on Article 3(4).

## 4.3    Establishment and information requirements

### 4.3.1    Article 4 – Principle excluding prior authorisation

The taking up or pursuit of the activity of an information society service is not subject to prior authorisation (Article 4(1)). So, Member States may not impose special authorisation schemes for Information Society services. This principle aims to prevent that potential providers restrain from offering information society services due to a demand of prior authorisation. Given the predicted economic impact of electronic commerce, it is important that no unnecessary barriers exist on this point. Especially, because Europe wants to catch up with the United States.

Authorisation may be required if this applies to the same services provided by other than electronic means (Article 4(2)). For example, a license to sell alcohol is also required in an electronic environment. Naturally also allowed and explicitly mentioned is prior authorisation based on Directive 97/13/EC on telecommunication services. One reason for prior authorisation in the field of telecommunication is the necessary supervision on the technical standards providers should meet.

## 4.3.2 Article 5 – General information to be provided

Notwithstanding information requirements established by Community law (such as Directive 97/7/EC), the information the service provider should at least provide is indicated in Article 5(a) to 5(g). Contractual relations are covered by the information requirements, but the requirements are also applicable if there is no contract between the provider and the recipient.

The information should be *easily*, *directly*, and *permanently* accessible. This means in the first place that it must be possible to obtain the information without much effort (easily) or additional acts (directly) being necessary. So, on a website the information must be stored in html-like language and the information must be found without the need to explore a number of the site's web pages. The information may not be (only) e-mailed or faxed. A good way to provide the information is by an icon or logo on each page with a link to a page containing the information.[23] The demand that information may not be altered, but remain permanently, must not be taken too literally. Several interpretations of this demand exist. First, that the information may not alter during a visit to a website. Second, that the recipient must have the opportunity to store the information. Finally, and related to the prior interpretation, that the information may not be presented in transitory way, e.g., a pop-up window. The term permanently is best explained if all interpretations are taken together.

Since all information society services are carried out at a distance, the information requirements of Directive 97/7/EC are also applicable in case the recipient is a consumer. There is some overlap on this point (see section 2.4). The information to be provided is in the first place the name of the service provider (Article 5(1)(a)). Second, the geographic address (Article 5(1)(b)), because the recipient must have the opportunity to complain outside the virtual world. In case of cross-border trade this will not be very helpful, the communication normally will remain at a distance. However, for the execution of a court order or for the return of goods, an address other than the URL is important. In the amended proposal *geographic* has been added to indicate that only a P.O. Box does not suffice. Article 5(1)(c) concerns the details of the service provider to contact him rapidly, like phone number and e-mail address. This completes the information necessary to communicate with the service provider quickly, and, if desired, not electronically. The remaining information requirements are not really interesting for the recipient of the service, but primarily for the other addressee of this Article, the competent authorities. Article 5(1)(d) concerns information of trade or similar public registers. In case the activity is subject to an authorisation scheme, information of the relevant supervisory authority has to be provided (Article 5(1)(e)). Concerning regulated professions, the professional bodies where the provider is registered, his professional title, and

---

[23] COM (1998) 586 final, p. 23.

reference to the applicable professional rules have to be provided (Article 5(1)(f)). If the activity of the provider is subject to Value Added Tax, the identification number has to be provided (Article 5(1)(g)).

Article 5(2) is about the mandatory price information. In the proposal the obligation was still 'prices of Information Society services are indicated accurately and unequivocally.' In the amended proposal the description was refined and especially the addition 'prices (...) must include all additional costs' helped getting a full picture of the costs and facilitated the comparison of offers by different service providers. In the Directive the price information has to be indicated clearly and unambiguously and '(...) must indicate whether they are inclusive of tax and delivery costs.' Neither all costs (e.g. not administrative costs) have to be indicated, nor should prices include all additional costs. The latter is difficult, since for example the costs for delivery may depend on the number of items ordered. To my opinion, a combination of the amended proposal and the Directive would have been better than the current text: 'must indicate all additional costs and in particular whether they are inclusive of tax and delivery costs.'

The phrase 'accurately and unequivocally' of the (amended) proposal has become 'clearly and unambiguously'. Is it possible that something is indicated clearly, but not unambiguously, or vice versa? Maybe if the price is indicated as 25/50 it is clear (the price is 25 or 50), but ambiguous (what is the price, 25 or 50?). All things considered, the information has to be transparent. For instance, a price in Euro meets the requirement 'clearly and unambiguously'.[24] At the time the Directive is implemented, the Euro will be the national currency in most Member States. Only websites established in the UK, Denmark, and Sweden have to present prices in at least two currencies. It would be a good service anyway if prices can be displayed in the currency that is preferred by the recipient (the Euro, the currencies of UK, Denmark, and Sweden, and, for example, US dollars). Because most exchange rates are online, this will not be too difficult to realise.

## 4.4    Commercial communications

### 4.4.1    Article 6 – Information to be provided

Commercial communications such as advertising and direct marketing are important for any company. Several forms of commercial communications can be distinguished on the Internet. The banner and interstitial are among the most used by websites. A banner is a small area on a website that is dedicated to commercial communications, an interstitial is a separate (small) browser window that pops up and can only be removed by closing it. Other forms of commercial communications are sites with (only) promotional information, postings to a newsgroup, or (bulk) e-mail.

---

[24] COM (1998) 586 final, p. 23.

The rather broad definition of commercial communications (Article 2(f)) already contained restrictions. Article 6 further restricts commercial communications to those which are part of, or constitute, an information society service. Article 2(f) would have been a more accurate place for this restriction.

According to recital 29 commercial communications are essential for financing and for developing new charge-free services. In the interest of fair trade and consumer protection, a number of transparency requirements are defined.

First, the communications must be clearly identifiable as such (Article 6(a)). For example, it must be clear that a website got paid for information that praises the quality of certain products, or that a banner contains an advertisement. Also, if e-mail is used the commercial purpose must appear from either the subject or the body of the mail.

Second, on whose behalf the commercial communication is made must be clearly identifiable (Article 6(b)). Does a Coca Cola banner on website already meet this requirement, or must it be made clear that the communication was made on behalf of Coca Cola Germany? If a banner links to information revealing the sponsor this suffices.[25] To my opinion, in case of an international trade mark information about the precise financier is not required. However, under certain circumstances information should be provided. If Spielberg sponsors spam for his latest movie, it must be clear that Spielberg did pay for it. This kind of information helps the recipient to distinguish (independent) information from commercial communications.

Third, Article 6(c) and 6(d) are about promotional offers and promotional competitions or games. Member States may forbid these promotional activities, but if they do not, these activities must be clearly identifiable as such (see Article 6(a)). Furthermore, the conditions for participation (competitions/games) or conditions which are to be met (offers) must be easily accessible, and presented clearly and unambiguously. For example, not allowed is small text at the bottom of the website containing all kinds of additional demands. The term 'easy access' was already discussed under Article 5(1), 'clearly and unambiguously' under Article 5(2).

### 4.4.2 Article 7 – Unsolicited commercial communications

Article 7 deals with unsolicited commercial communication (also known as spam) by electronic mail. Spam may disrupt the smooth functioning of interactive networks (recital 30), e.g. computer systems can go down if numerous e-mails are sent from or to the same server. The Directive focuses primarily on consumers protection. An argument often heard is that in case of downloaded spam consumers have to pay for services they never asked for. Some countries want to ban spam completely (if at all

---

[25] COM (1998) 586 final, p. 23.

possible). The Directive does not forbid the use of spam, but Member States can decide not to allow it. However, if spam is not prohibited by a Member State it should ensure that the spam is clearly and unambiguously identifiable as such. Without the need to open the mail, one must be able to identify email as spam.[26] Member States should also encourage appropriate filtering initiatives (recital 30). The fighting against spam (see section 2.8) is not in its final stage yet, for latest developments see chapter 6.

In the amended proposal Article 7(2) about opt-out registers was added. There are two types of registers, opt-out and opt-in. The latter requires that people who want to receive mail register, the former requires registration of people that do not want to receive mail. A problem with current off-line opt-out registers is that someone who registers because he does not want to receive unsolicited mail, still receives mails of companies which are not a member of the organisation that manages the register. According to Article 7(2), Member States that allow spam should ensure that service providers consult the opt-out registers regularly and that the registers are respected. Because the Member State has supervision over such a register, not only members of the organisation managing the register consult the register (as in the off-line world is the case), but all service providers have to. The Member States do not have an explicit duty to create an opt-out register, but since they should control the use of the register an indirect obligation exists.

Because of the State control and the obligation for all service providers to consult the register, opting out seems to sort more effect than it does now for ordinary direct mail. However, a national opt-out register is, given the global character of electronic commerce, probably not very effective, an international register would be more appropriate. A drawback of such an international register is its expected magnitude and as a consequence managing of the register will be hard (for example deleting no longer existing addresses) and consulting the register time-consuming. Maybe the already mentioned filters, making it possible to install a sort of commercial communications shield, will help. For that purpose, companies should be obliged to include in their commercial mailings an element by which the mailings can be identified as commercial and as a consequence be rejected automatically if desired. It is not sure whether all companies are willing to do this. Especially the type of companies that regularly spam (e.g., advertisement for travel arrangements and financial opportunities) might not be interested in cooperation on this point. Moreover, at this moment most spam comes from outside the EU, in particular from the USA. So for most spam the Directive will not sort any effect at all. This shows again the need for international cooperation.

---

[26]  COM (1998) 586 final, p. 24.

### 4.4.3 Article 8 – Regulated professions

Article 8 deals with commercial communications by members of regulated professions. Because for example lawyers and notaries are not allowed to communicate commercially in some countries, in the past it was not clear whether the sole use of an e-mail address or a website could be considered a commercial communication.[27] Note that in Article 2(f) mere using an e-mail address or having a website is excluded from being a commercial communication.

In general, Article 8(1) determines that commercial communications by a member of a regulated profession is permitted, but only if rules of professional ethics are regarded. So lawyers and physicians are allowed to have a website, as long as their professional norms are not violated. A website of an attorney claiming that he gets all criminals free, or a physician claiming that he can heal anyone, would not be allowed because of conflict with professional ethics.

Member States and the Commission should encourage the drawing up of codes of conduct by professional bodies and associations to determine what information may be provided in conformity with the rules of professional ethics (Article 8(2)). It is explicitly stated that this encouragement may not interfere with the autonomy of the professional bodies and associations.

In case the professional bodies do not sufficiently succeed in the drawing up of the codes of conduct, Community initiatives may become necessary to ensure a proper functioning of the Internal Market with regard to the information to be provided. Article 8(3) is in line with the general policy of the EU: self regulation is preferred, but in case self regulation does not work accurately the EU drafts regulation on the relevant topics. While drawing up these Community proposals, the Commission should consider the codes of conducts already drawn up by professional bodies and associations at a national level, and work in close cooperation with those bodies and associations.

A new paragraph 4 and recital 33 were added to the common position clarifying that the Directive only supplements existing Directives concerning access to, and exercise of, activities of regulated professions. I doubt whether anyone would have thought before the Directive could do more than that.

## 4.5 Online contracts

The provisions of Articles 9-11 on electronic contracts complements the Directive 1999/93/EC on electronic signatures (see chapter 3).

---

[27] COM (1998) 586 final, p. 4, p. 11.

### 4.5.1    Article 9 – Treatment of contracts

The formation of online contracts is an essential element of electronic commerce. Therefore, Article 9(1) determines that Member States have the duty to 'ensure that their legal system allows contracts to be concluded by electronic means.' Of particular importance is that legal requirements may not create obstacles for the use of electronic contracts, and that legal effectiveness and validity may not be not deprived on the account of contacts being electronic.[28] Formal requirements to be examined concern for example the medium used (paper, hand-written) or the presence of both parties.[29]

All necessary stages of the contractual process should be examined (recital 34). This means any requirement preventing the use of electronic means from negotiation and conclusion of the contract, to invoicing and filing of the contract. The implementation of the Directive into national law will not be an easy task for the Member States. All relevant legislation should be examined and amended in the above described way. The necessary amendments go beyond civil law, also procedural law concerning evidence has to be examined. For instance, allowing electronic invoices means that tax authorities may no longer require paper invoices.[30] The explanatory notes of the proposal mentioned the use of electronic agents.[31] Although neither in the recitals, nor in the Articles the electronic or intelligent agent returned, a systematic review of the legal system should in my opinion nonetheless lead to the acceptance of the conclusion of contracts by autonomous automated systems. All in all, as a consequence of appropriate amendments to the legal system of the Member States, the legal effect of paper and electronic contracts must become identical.

Member States have the freedom to not apply Article 9(1) to certain types of contracts, cf. Article 9(2):
(a) contracts that create and transfer of rights in real estate, except for rental rights;
(b) contracts requiring involvement of courts, public authorities, or professions exercising public authority;
(c) contracts of suretyship granted an on collateral securities furnished by consumers;[32]
(d) contracts governed by family law or law of succession.

---

[28] A similar definition can be found in article 5 and 5bis of the UNCITRAL Model Law on Electronic Commerce: 'Information shall not be denied legal effect, validity or enforceability solely on the ground that it is in the form of a data message.'

[29] COM (1998) 586 final, p. 26.

[30] R. Julia Barcelo (1999), 'Electronic Contracts', *Computer Law & Security Report* Vol. 15, no. 3, p. 150.

[31] COM (1998) 586 final, p. 25.

[32] For no obvious reasons Article 10(2) of the Directive does not use the term consumer, but the definition of consumer: 'persons acting for purposes outside their trade, business or profession'.

Mostly, the contracts under (a) need the intervention of a notary, and therefore would be covered by (b), viz. professions exercising public authority. Note, however, that the formal validity of contracts concerning real estate are excluded from the coordinated field (see 4.2.3). It would be too much to demand from the Member States to digitise their courts and public authorities in the short term (subparagraph (b)). The exceptions of subparagraph (c) and (d) are mainly given in by the fact that it is not clear how these contracts could hinder the Internal Market.

The Member States should indicate to the Commission to what type of contracts they do not apply Article 9(1). Furthermore, every five years Member States should submit a report on the application of Article 9(2). Also, in the report the reasons why Article 9(1) is not applied to the contracts of Article 9(2)(b) should be given.[33]

### 4.5.2    Article 10 – Information to be provided

Article 10 completes the triad on information requirements. The information concerns (a) the technical steps necessary to conclude the contract, (b) the filing and accessibility of the contract (c) the identification and correction of input errors and (d) the language of the contract. The requirements do not apply if parties who are not consumers have agreed otherwise.

The information should be given prior to the order being placed. If by clicking an OK button goods or services can be ordered from a website, all the above information should already been given. A general information page might suffice, given that the various information items can be found easily. However, unlike the general nature of the information of Article 5, the information required here is of interest only for those who want to enter into contracts. Therefore, the information could also be provided just before the placing of the order takes effect. So, if someone clicks on a specific product, the information can be provided at that point. Once the information has been provided, the handling of the order may begin.

The information should be given 'clearly, comprehensibly and unambiguously'. We have encountered these demands several times before, except for comprehensibly. Comprehensibly might have been added because the information concerns technical matters that can be explained clearly and unambiguously, but still in a way it cannot be understood by non-technical people.

The first information requirement (Article 10(1)(a)) needs to prevent that people are contractual bounded before knowing it. A simple click on an OK button may suffice to conclude the contract, but only if the recipient has been given information about this 'technical step' before he clicked. Otherwise, the contract is not binding.

---

[33]    SEC (2000) 386 final, p. 12.

Currently, most websites do not offer the possibility of contract filing, a stored contract can be used for the purpose of evidence.

A filed and accessible contract (Article 10(1)(b)) may give the recipient more confidence in the provider and influence his purchase.

Before goods or services are ordered, it must be possible to correct input errors. The recipient must be aware of this possibility (Article 10(1)(c)). If the website presents an overview of what has been ordered before the order is actually placed, the recipient should be informed how changes can be made in this overview.

Finally, it should be indicated in what language the contract is concluded. If the language of the site is Spanish, I assume the consumer does not have to be informed that the contract is concluded in Spanish (apart from the fact that the conclusion of the contract is actually electronically, so not in a particular language). Otherwise a strange of self-reference would occur, viz. 'do you realise that I am talking English?' Only in case other languages are offered than the language the website uses, the recipient should be informed about that. At this moment not so many sites offer more than one language to conclude a contract. Maybe this will change in the course of time. Especially if the translation into another language can be performed automatically, like Altavista's babelfish is doing already to some extent.

Article 10(2) is about code of conducts. The service provider should indicate any relevant code of conduct to which he subscribes, and how the code(s) can be consulted electronically. Usually so-called web seals refer to a code of conduct. For example, if a provider is connected to the Webtrader code, the Webtrader logo can be found on his site. If after a click on the logo or seal one is transferred to a page or site containing the text of the code, the requirement about the electronic consultation is met. Again, the requirement does not exist if parties who are not consumers have agreed otherwise.

Recall that the provider is not obligated to file the contract, but he has to indicate whether he does so or not (Article 10(1)(b)). The contract terms and general conditions, on the other hand, should be made available in a way they can be stored and reproduced. Note that this information requirement does not have to be met *before* the order is placed. Important is here that the recipient has the possibility to reproduce the information. Either for the purpose of making extra copies, or for simply viewing the contract. The reason not only storage is required but also reproduction is that otherwise the provider could store the information in such a way the recipient could not make use it.

The paragraphs 1 and 2 of Article 10 do not apply to contracts concluded exclusively by electronic mail or by equivalent individual communications (Article 10(4)). The latter addition is probably meant to make the regulation technically independent, not relying only on electronic mail (but allowing for example SMS). The rationale for this exception, that appeared in the common position for the first time, is probably that necessary information can be asked easily in case of individual communication.

If in an email a service or good is offered via a 'buy now' hyperlink, it depends on what happens after clicking the link whether paragraph 1 and 2 are applicable. If by clicking the link an order is sent to the provider, paragraph 1 and 2 are not applicable. If one is transferred to the website of the provider, paragraph 1 and 2 are still applicable. So, it seems that in case a service provider does not want to fulfil the requirements of Article 10 and 11, he should trade by e-mail only. However, according to recital 39 the exceptions of Article 10 and 11 should not enable the by-passing of those provisions by providers. So, two consumers contracting by e-mail do not have to meet all the requirements, but information society service providers have to provide this information in principle also in case only individual communication is used.

### 4.5.3    Article 11 – Placing of the order

Article 11 has gone through some changes during the drafting of the Directive. The original objective to determine the moment at which the contract is concluded has not been realised. One of the reasons Member States could not reach agreement was the limited time that was given. A major difficulty in determining the moment of conclusion has been that in some Member States a contract is concluded after delivery, while in most Member States agreement between the parties suffices.

In the original proposal the following acts were necessary:
1. The recipient of the service indicates to accept the service;
2. The service provider acknowledges the receipt of the acceptance;
3. The recipient of the service confirms the receipt of the acknowledgement of receipt.

In the amended proposal the third act was no longer necessary for conclusion of the contract. Although the third act may seem too much (the originally Article 11 was called the ping-pong-regulation), without the third act a contract can be concluded easily. Namely, if someone clicks on an OK button accidentally, and does not want to buy, the sole message of the service provider in which he confirms the acceptance is enough to conclude an, unwanted, contract. Although in case all steps are required the conclusion of the contract can take place rather quick, under the given circumstances a confirmation of the receipt would be helpful. Even if it is only a pop-up window displaying the acknowledgement. But, as already indicated, the steps necessary to conclude a contract are no longer part of Article 11, now called 'placing of the order'. Article 11(1) lays down some principles from which, again, professional parties can derogate. The Article is applicable to recipients placing an order by technological (electronic) means.

According to the first principle the service provider should acknowledge the receipt of the order without undue delay. The acknowledgement constitutes no longer the conclusion of the contract, but is merely a principle that if not complied with can lead to the contract being annulled. Recital 34 determines that acknowledgement of receipt may take the form of online provision of the service paid for.

The second principle is that the order and acknowledgement are deemed to be received at the moment parties are able to access them.[34] So, it is not necessary to take notice of a message. As soon as an e-mail has arrived at a mail server, it is deemed to be received.

Article 11(2) deals with technical means to identify and correct input errors. These means should be appropriate, effective and accessible. Prior to the placing of the order the means should be made available by the service provider. If by a simple click on an OK button an order is placed, it is hard to correct errors *before* the placing of the order. Under these circumstances it would be reasonable if within a short period input errors can be corrected in order to change or annul the contract. Some providers do sent recipients by e-mail an overview of the order and ask them whether they really wanted to order this. What I described in section 4.5.2 on information requirements, a website presenting an overview of what has been ordered before the order is actually placed, seems to be the most appropriate, effective and accessible way.

Similar to Article 10(4), paragraph 3 indicates that paragraph 1, first indent, and paragraph 2 do not apply to contracts concluded exclusively by individual communications. The moment messages are deemed to be received, the second indent of paragraph 1, is comprehensibly applicable to individual communications too.

## 4.6    Liability of intermediary service providers

Recital 40 states: 'Both existing and emerging disparities in Member States' legislation and case-law concerning liability of service providers acting as intermediaries prevent the smooth functioning of the internal market, in particular by impairing the development of cross-border services and producing distortions of competition (...) this Directive should constitute the appropriate basis for the development of rapid and reliable procedures for removing and disabling access to illegal information (...).' The appropriate basis referred to in this recital is defined in the Articles 12-15. In combination with the copyright directive (see chapter 5), these Articles should establish a clear framework of rules relevant to the issue of liability of intermediaries for copyright and relating rights infringements at Community level (recital 50).

---

[34] See also article 15 UNCITRAL Model Law on Electronic Commerce.

### 4.6.1 Article 12 – 'Mere conduit'

If the role of a service provider is only passive (information provided by the recipient is transmitted or access has been given to a communication network), he cannot be held liable for the content of the information that is forwarded by means of his system. Hence, the provider has neither knowledge of nor control over the information which is transmitted or stored (recital 42). A parallel can be drawn with postal services. For example, if a letter contains an illegally copied picture, the postal service cannot be held liable for the copyright infringement. The service provider is not liable for the transmitted information only if three conditions are fulfilled. First, the transmission may not be initiated by the provider. Second, the provider may not decide to whom the information is sent. Third, the provider may not select the information or modify it. Because in all three cases the provider takes the initiative, he cannot be considered to act as an intermediary. The initiative of the provider is the decisive criterion. As long as the initiative lies with the recipient, the intermediary is not liable. Note that this (lack of) liability concerns both civil and criminal law. However, according to recital 8 the objective of the Directive is not to harmonise the field of criminal law as such.

Article 12(2) further explains the scope of transmission and access. If information is transmitted in a network, the information goes from computer to computer. On any of these computers, information is temporally stored for a short period of time. This temporal storage is also seen as transmission, under the condition that the only purpose of the storage is facilitating the transmission, and the information is stored no longer than necessary for the transmission. The storage must be automatic (by machines, not humans), intermediate (in the course of the transmission) and transient (limited period of time).[35]

The possibility of prohibitory injunctions is addressed in paragraph 3. Despite the lack of liability of the service provider, a court or administrative authority may require to order the service provider to terminate or take measure to prevent a particular infringement.

### 4.6.2 Article 13 – 'Caching'[36]

The ratio of Article 13 differs from Article 12 and 14. The latter Articles protect the provider against liability for either transmission or storage of illegal information. Article 13 is not primarily aimed at illegal information, but rather aims to protect the recipient in different ways. Article 13 deals with liability regarding copies that are stored only temporary (caching). These are the same type of copies addressed in Article 12(2) (automatic, intermediate, and transient), except that the period they are

---

[35] COM (1998) 586 final, p. 28.

[36] I thank Cyril van der Net of the Dutch Ministry of Justice for providing useful information on the articles 12-15, in particular article 13.

stored is longer. Moreover, the purpose of the storage should be more efficient transmission of information delivered on demand of recipients. Although caching has a certain independent (economic) meaning, it is not considered a separate exploitation of the information transmitted.[37]

In case of caching, the provider is not liable if five conditions (a-e) of Article 13(1) are met. First, the provider may not alter the information (a), for then he cannot be considered an intermediary. Second, the provider has to comply with the conditions on access of information (b). For example, if a service has to be paid for, the cached page may not be free of charge. Another example is the use of banners. Normally, the computer hosting the banners gets paid for them. In case a website looses income because a provider receives the revenues for the banner on the cached page, the website may ask the provider compensation. Third, the provider has to update the information regularly (c). If he would not do this, it might occur that a recipient orders a book for, according to the cached page, 15 Euro, while the actual price is 17 Euro. Fourth, the provider is not allowed to interfere with applications (lawful use of technology) that measure the use of information (d). For instance, the statistical program that keeps track of the number of users visiting a web page may not get less hits solely as a result of the caching of the page. A solution could be to not have all elements of a page in cache. So, the banners and the statistical programs could be downloaded from the original source if the (remainder of the) page is in the cache of the provider. Fifth, the provider has to remove the information as soon as he knows that the initial source of the information is removed, access to it has been disabled, or court administrative authority have ordered such removal or disablement (e). The provider should take care that the information he provides is as accurate as possible. If he does not remove inaccurate information he will be held liable.

Article 13(2) deals, like Article 12(3), with the possibility of prohibitory injunctions.

### 4.6.3   Article 14 – Hosting

Hosting is the storage of information that is, unlike Article 12 and 13, not temporal. Service providers are not liable for the information that is stored by the recipient, under two conditions worked out in Article 14(1)(a) and 14(1)(b), respectively.

First, the provider must not have actual knowledge that the *information* or an *activity* is illegal. For example, if the provider knows that the recipient stores child porn or copyright infringing material, he is liable (information). He is also liable if he knows that in a newsgroup information is exchanged about where to obtain illegal material (activity). So, no exemption from both civil and criminal liability exists in case of actual knowledge. Moreover, the provider may not be aware of facts or

---

[37]   COM (1998) 586 final, p. 28.

circumstances from which the illegality is apparent, otherwise he is liable for claims and damages. Under these circumstances there is no criminal liability.

Second, the provider has to act promptly if he obtains knowledge or awareness of the illegality of information or an activity, either by removing the information or by disabling access. This second condition is somewhat problematic. It could lead to providers removing information after having been notified that the information is illegal, because they are afraid to be held liable. This fear of providers can be misused. One way out could be that the provider removes the material temporally and waits until he is acknowledged by his recipient that the information is not illegal. From that moment on he can make the information available again, and in case the information appears to be illegal after all, he can redirect claims to the recipient. However, this may lead to a catch-22 situation.[38] On the one hand the provider wants to remove the information because he is afraid to be held liable. On the other hand he does not want to remove the information because he is afraid of being held liable by the recipient for wrongfully removing the material.

In case a recipient is working under the authority or the control of the provider, there is no exemption possible from liability (Article 14(2)). For example, if a recipient is working for an Internet provider, the provider can be held liable due to its quality as employer or supervisor. Obviously, control concerns the control of the recipient's acts and not the control over the information as such.[39] Also, the liability does not extend to illegal information the recipient has stored off duty.

Article 14(3) deals, like Article 12(3) and 13(2), with the possibility of prohibitory injunctions. This paragraph also stresses that the other paragraphs do not affect the possibility for Member States to establish procedures governing the removal or disabling of access to information. This means that Member States are free to define rules that deal with the just described catch-22 situation.

### 4.6.4 Article 15 – No general obligation to monitor

Service providers do not have to turn into cyber patrols, at least they cannot be forced to. Article 15(1) indicates that no general obligation exists for service providers to monitor information they transmit or store. A general obligation to actively seek facts or situations indicating illegal activity does not exist either. Surely, with a general obligation the exemptions of the Articles 12, 13 and 14 would not be that meaningful. However, the fact that no general obligation exists, does not mean that a provider cannot have monitoring obligations in a specific case (recital 47).

In Article 15(2) two specific obligations for providers are specified. First, Member States may establish obligations on providers to inform the authorities of alleged

---

[38] Cf. the novel by Joseph Heller.
[39] COM (1998) 586 final, p. 30.

illegal activities or illegal information provided by recipients as soon as the provider becomes aware of it. Second, Member States may also establish obligations on providers to disclose the identity of recipients with whom they have storage agreements.

## 4.7     Codes of conduct and dispute settlement

### 4.7.1     Article 16 – Codes of conduct

For the development of a properly functioning digital economy, codes of conduct might turn out to be of equal importance as (or even more important than) the creation of a legislative framework. Contrary to legislation, codes of conduct can be altered in a flexible way. Changes in the market or technology can be dealt with in a code of conduct on a rather short notice. Since it takes considerable time to draft and implement EU directives, codes of conduct can also fill in a gap there. Years before the actual legislation enters into force, the topics can be dealt with in a code of conduct. An illustrative example is the Webtrader code, an initiative supported by the Commission, that includes several provisions of the Directives 97/7/EC and 2000/31/EC (before the Directives were implemented into national law).

According to Article 16(1), Member States and the Commission shall encourage the following 5 activities (a-e). In the first place the drawing up of codes that contribute to the proper implementation of Articles 5-15 (a). Secondly, the voluntary transmission to the Commission of draft codes at national or Community level (b). While in an earlier version of the Directive this was meant to check the compatibility of the codes with Community law, it no longer is. The purpose is now to keep an eye on the developments in this matter. Thirdly, the codes should be made available electronically in the Community languages (c). Assumedly, the demand concerning the language will not apply to national codes. The organisations (e.g., professional and consumer) that draw up the codes, should inform the Commission and the Member States about the application of the codes and their assumed impact (d). Finally, the drawing up of codes of conduct regarding the protection of minors and human dignity (e).

Article 16(2) stresses that consumer organisations should be involved in the drawing up of codes of conduct. This seems a relic of the original proposal, where consumer organisations were not mentioned in the first paragraph as organisations who should be encouraged to draw up codes. Now that they are, this part of the second paragraph is somewhat redundant. The other part of the second paragraph has been added to the common position and concerns the involvement of organisations representing the visually impaired and disabled, where appropriate. The European Parliament tried to add to this second paragraph the involvement of organisations representing copyright holders (amendment 58).[40] Apparently, the intellectual property rights lobby was not successful in the end.

### 4.7.2 Article 17 – Out-of-court dispute settlements

The legislation of the Member States may not hamper the use of alternative dispute resolution (ADR) in case of a dispute between the provider and the recipient. Moreover, legislation should also allow online ADR (ODR).[41] There do exist already quite some ODR-sites, as yet mainly American. The Directive should be an impulse for the development of European ODR-sites.

Because ADR is meant to save money and time, and resolve conflicts without too much technical legal discussion being necessary, consumers probably benefit most from ADR. The settlement of in particular consumer disputes is encouraged in Article 17(2). At this moment an Extra Judicial Network of the EU is under development (see also section 2.9.3), as well a particular Financial counterpart: FIN-NET.[42]

The Commission eagerly wants to follow the developments regarding ADR and ODR. Therefore, they encourage that bodies responsible for out-of-court dispute settlements inform the Commission about their services, and about their practices, usages or customs relating to electronic commerce.

### 4.7.3 Article 18 – Court actions

The effective exercise of the freedoms of the internal market makes it necessary to guarantee victims means to effectively settle disputes (recital 52). Therefore, the legal procedures of the Member States must be adapted to tackling illicit conduct or disputes on the Internet.[43] Member States should examine whether national law foresees in prompt court actions concerning the termination of any alleged infringement and to prevent any further impairment of the interests involved (Article 18(1)). For example, if illegal material is placed on a website in Spain, an Italian citizen must have access to effective Spanish court actions. If not, the mutual confidence between Member States could be damaged. Also the need for access by electronic means should be examined (recital 52). In case of information society

---

[40] See the Report from Committee on Legal Affairs and Citizens' Rights of 23 April 1999, A4-0248/99, p. 28.

[41] See the special issue on ODR, A.R. Lodder and R.W. van Kralingen (eds.), *Computerrecht* 2001-5 (in Dutch). See on this topic also the special ADR-site by the Joint Research Center of the EU, <http://dsa-isis.jrc.it/ADR/>.

[42] The site of the EEJ-network is at <http://europa.eu.int/comm/consumers/policy/developments/acce_just/acce_just04_nl.html>, FIN_NET is at <http://europa.eu.int/comm/internal_market/en/finances/consumer/intro.htm>.

[43] COM (1998) 586 final, p. 31.

conflicts, access to court actions can hardly be effective if for example the Italian does not have online access to the Spanish Courts.

Article 18(2) determines that the Injunctions directive[44] also applies to the Directive (see also section 2.9.2).

## 4.8    Cooperation and sanctions

### 4.8.1    Article 19 – Cooperation

Article 19 formulates several duties of the Member States concerning the implementation of the Directive. First, the Member States must have adequate means of supervision and investigation necessary to implement the Directive, and ensure providers supply them with requisite information (Article 19(1)). Second, Member States should also cooperate with one another by appointing one or more contact points (Article 19(2)). Third, Member States should provide assistance and information requested by other Member States (Article 19(3)). Contact points for providers and recipients, accessible by electronic means, should be established too. These contact points should provide information concerning contractual obligations and complaint and redress mechanisms (Article 19(4)(a)), and details of authorities and organisations for further information or practical assistance (Article 19(4)(b)). Finally, Member States should encourage that the Commission is informed of any significant administrative or judicial decision. The Commission on their turn communicates these decisions to the other Member States (Article 19(5)).

### 4.8.2    Article 20 – Sanctions

The provision that Member States shall determine effective, proportionate and dissuasive sanctions is standard for Internal Market directives. The Member States are within the given constraints free to determine sanctions for, e.g., a service provider that does not live up to the information requirements of Articles 5, 6, and 10.

## 4.9    Articles 21-24 – Final provisions

Before 17 July 2003, three years after the entry into force, the Commission reports on the application of the Directive to the European Parliament, the Council, and the Economic and Social Committee. After 2003 the Commission will report every two years. Where appropriate because of developments of the information society, the Commission will also include proposals for adaptations (Article 21).

---

[44] Directive 98/27/EC of the European Parliament and of the Council of 19 May 1998 on injunctions for the protection of consumers' interests; *OJ* L 166/51, 11.6.1998, at Article 1 and Annex.

Member States have until 17 January 2002 (18 months after the entry into force) to implement the Directive (Article 22(1)), and the measures necessary for complying with the Directive must refer to the Directive (Article 22(2)). On the day of its publication, 17 July 2000, the Directive has entered into force (Article 23). The last of the final provisions, Article 24, indicates as usual that the Member States are the addresses of the Directive.

## 4.10 Concluding remarks

The Directive is central to the regulation of e-commerce, and unprecedented in its extensiveness of regulating legal aspects of electronic commerce. By this Directive the EU obtains a strong position in negotiations with other countries concerning the regulation of electronic commerce. These negotiations will be necessary, since in cyberspace the borders of the EU are very easy to cross by both EU citizens and inhabitants of non-EU countries. A world-wide regulation of the topics addressed in this Directive in the future is needed, either by self regulatory mechanisms and/or governmental regulation. The former is probably easier to bring about. Anyway, the Directive is only a first, important step, further actions will be needed.

# Chapter 5

# Directive 2001/29/EC on the harmonisation of certain aspects of copyright and related rights in the information society

## Michel Vivant

Important dates regarding the Directive 2001/29/EC on the harmonisation of certain aspects of copyright and related rights in the Information Society of the European Parliament and of the Council of 22 May 2001 on the harmonisation of certain aspects of copyright and related rights in the Information Society are in chronological order:

- **1997, December 10** – Proposal adopted by the Commission;[1]
- **1999, February 10** – Proposal approved by the European Parliament, subject to amendments;[2]
- **1999, May 21** – Amended proposal adopted by the Commission;[3]
- **2000, September 28** – Common position adopted by the Council;[4]
- **2001, February 14** – Approval by the European Parliament;
- **2001, May 22** – Signed by the European Parliament and the Council;
- **2001, June 22** – Publication in the Official Journal;[5]
- **2002, December 22** – Directive should be implemented by the Member States.

## 5.1    Article 1 – Scope

The purpose of this Article is clearly indicated in its title: objective and scope.

### 5.1.1    Objective

This is a 'horizontal' directive, that is a Directive which concerns, if not the entire field of copyright and related rights, then at least a very wide part of it. This is not a Directive which relates to a discrete topic. The text purports to deal with copyright

---

[1]  *OJ* C 108/6, 7.4.1998.
[2]  *OJ* C 150/171, 28.5.1999.
[3]  *OJ* C 180/6, 25.6.1999.
[4]  *OJ* C 344/1, 1.12.2000.
[5]  *OJ* L 167/10, 22.6.2001.

*A.R. Lodder and H.W.K. Kaspersen (eds.),*
*eDirectives: Guide to European Union Law on E-Commerce,* 95–117.

and related rights, 'in the framework of the internal market', but, more, 'with particular emphasis on the information society.'

The text is directed at both copyright and related rights. It is less a concession to the *droit d'auteur* system than a necessity when in the European Union there coexist two systems – copyright and *droit d'auteur* – and when in the latter a distinction is precisely drawn between copyright *proprio sensu* on the one hand, and related rights (for instance, performers' rights or videogram producers' rights) on the other. The distinction is therefore necessarily in a text which is intended to apply to the two systems (anyway, these related rights are recognised under anglo-saxon regimes, even if they do not stand as an autonomous category of rights, but are incorporated into the bundle of rights generically known as copyright[6].

As with all Community texts, this Directive cuts across differences between member States' treatment of these various rights. We are in a transborder logic. And an European transborder logic. Actually, the visa of the Internal Market, in the language of Amsterdam Treaty, is both the justification and the measure of the intervention of the Community. Free circulation and free competition are important driving forces behind the Directive.

The Directive's first recital clearly suggests this:
'Whereas the Treaty provides for the establishment of an internal market and the institution of a system ensuring that competition in the internal market is not distorted. Harmonisation of the laws of the Member States on copyright and related rights contributes to the achievement of these objectives.'

There is also a strong economic perspective to the Directive. Certainly, the cultural aspect is not absent, and the recitals make reference to the question of 'creation' or 'creative content'. However, it is clear in these same recitals that the economic approach is fundamental. The European Community has not forgotten its past as the European Economic Community. The fourth recital is indisputably one of the most significant from this standpoint:
'A harmonised legal framework on copyright and related rights, through increased legal certainty and while providing for a high level of protection of intellectual property, will foster substantial investment in creativity and innovation, including network infrastructure, and lead in turn to growth and increased competitiveness of European industry, both in the area of content provision and information technology and more generally across a wide range of industrial and cultural sectors. This will safeguard employment and encourage new job creation.'

The emphasis placed on the information society suggests that inherited copyright, and related rights, systems must now be considered from a fresh perspective – the

---

[6]   See, for instance, G. Dworkin & R. Taylor, *Copyright, Designs and Patents Act 1988*, London, Blackstone, 1989.

'informational perspective' – and, if necessary, be reconsidered: 'The various social, societal and cultural implications of the information society require that account be taken of the specific features of the content of products and services.' We could add: that account be taken of the specific features of a new kind of work in the digital environment. Maybe that remark is more pertinent to the countries of the *droit d'auteur* system where the *droit d'auteur* (the author's right) is viewed, at least traditionally, as a strong personal right related to a totally original creation.[7] In the information society, copyright and related rights, are a part of industry (the cultural industries, but not exclusively) and the notion of 'work' changes in nature. The reference is no longer the literary work or the pictorial work but a new kind of work which a part of European doctrine has named 'informational goods': software, data bases, expert systems, and traditional works which have been converted into digitised format, to name but a few examples. 'Information' and 'work' have become related notions. Work and operating system are also closely linked.[8]

Copyright and related rights, accordingly, are a central component of the strategy of the 'actors' of the information society. As the Directive itself says, in one of its recitals, 'copyright and related rights play an important role in this context' (recital 2). This role is viewed as one of stimulating creation and innovation. These rights 'protect and stimulate the development and marketing of new products and services and the creation and exploitation of their creative content', says the text (*ibid.*).[9]

The cultural dimension is not absent from copyright in the information society. We can read in the recitals: 'Adequate legal protection of copyright works and subject matter of related rights is also of great importance from a cultural standpoint' (Recital 10).

But these rights are not only conceived as abstract rights but as having an active function of protection and, here, the recitals express the ambition of ensuring a high level of protection. For example, recital 8 states as follows: 'Any harmonisation of copyright and related rights must take as a basis a high level of protection.' And, in this approach, these rights are economic rights, with an economic purpose and an economic effect. The emphasis is placed on the necessity of offering to authors and others contributors an appropriate reward and a satisfactory return on their investment (see recital 9). The aim is legitimate and, *de facto*, is present in all the national systems of copyright or *droit d'auteur*. This approach is reminiscent of that adopted in TRIPS (Agreement on Trade-Related Aspects of Intellectual Property Rights of 1994). We are in a similar logic where copyright and related rights are

---

[7] On the opposition between the two systems, see – in French – A. Strowel, *Droit d'auteur et copyright, Divergences et convergences*, LGDJ, 1993.

[8] On the idea of « operating works », see – in French – M. Vivant, *Une épreuve de vérité pour les droits de propriété intellectuelle : le développement de l'informatique, in L'avenir de la propriété intellectuelle*, Litec, 1993, p. 43.

[9] By way of comparison, in the French language version of the text, the 'development' becomes '*conception*' – conception, creation – that, perhaps, is not only a semantic variation.

apprehended as economic instruments, and as implements of (economic) development.

### 5.1.2   Scope

The Directive's scope follows naturally from its objective. The Directive purports to 'seize' the entire field of copyright and its various related rights (see, for instance, Article 2). We have already said this is a 'horizontal' directive, one which operates in the context of the information society (see above).

However, despite the Directive's wide-ranging ambitions, not all the aspects of copyright *sensu largo* are present in the Directive. Moral rights are one notable absence. Moreover, the text itself, in Article 1(2), takes care to mark out the limit between this Directive and past Directives which have had something to say on the subject of copyright. Matters which have already been treated by other Directives are expressed to be 'reserved': 'This Directive shall leave intact and shall in no way affect specific existing Community provisions' (Article 1(2)). This would conceivably apply in equal measure to both 'vertical' directives – such as the Directives dealing with computer programs and databases – and other 'horizontal' directives – such as the Directives on rental and lending rights, satellite broadcasting, cable retransmission and on the duration of copyright.

Also reserved are the provisions of previous Directives, the object of which is not specifically copyright or related rights, but which indirectly relate to this topic as, for instance, of the question of liability for online activities under the Directive on electronic commerce (see section 4.6). It is simply a matter of preservation of the '*acquis communautaire*'.
Lastly, the new text also amends old Directives, in particular in order to comply with international law as WIPO Performers and Phonograms Treaty.

This is clearly an ambitious text with a broad scope.

## 5.2    Article 2 – Reproduction right

At the head of chapter 2 on 'rights and exceptions', Article 2 specifically concerns the 'reproduction right'. This right can be presented as the basic right, as regards both copyright and related rights, from which flow all the other prerogatives of the owner. Irrespective of the different legal systems, reproduction can be defined broadly as the 'fixation' of the work in a medium. The right of reproduction gives the owner a monopoly with respect to authorising any such fixation and thereby control over the exploitation of the work.

By way of example, in the French Intellectual Property Code (Article L. 122-3), reproduction consists in the material fixation of the work by any process which allows the communication of the work by indirect means to the public (*'La reproduction consiste dans la fixation matérielle de l'œuvre par tous procédés qui permettent de la communiquer au public d'une manière indirecte'*). The reference to 'indirect' communication may seem a little confusing, however, this is explained by the fundamental distinction that must be drawn between a work and the medium through which it is communicated, a principle which is established both under the *droit d'auteur* and copyright systems.

Under the English Copyright Designs and Patents Act 1988 (CDPA), 'reproduction' finds its equivalent in the exclusive right of the owner to copy or authorise the copying of his or her work. For literary, musical or artistic works, 'copying (...) means reproducing the work in any material form' (section 17(2) CDPA).

So far as the Directive is concerned, the recitals have little to say in relation to the right of reproduction. Recital 21 is little more than a declaration of general policy in that it proclaims that the Directive 'should define the scope of the acts covered by the reproduction right with regard to the different beneficiaries', and that in the light of the *'acquis communautaire'*. This concern is commendable as, even if the approaches of the different systems of law are more or less the same, they do not exactly coincide. However, the text of the Directive does not advance our understanding of how the right of reproduction is to be viewed in the context of the information society.

More interesting is the Directive's call for a broad definition of the reproduction right: 'A broad definition of these acts [of reproduction] is needed to ensure legal certainty within the Internal Market' (same recital). To ensure legal certainty... but, also, at the same time to ensure the high level of protection which is one of the aims of the Directive (see above) given that such a broad definition of the right would confer a large degree of protection to the its holder.

So far as Article 2 itself is concerned, it envisages this right for each of the following holders respectively: authors, performers, producers, etc. However, the precise scope of the right for each holder is determined by the specific nature of the exploitation which the Community legislator has considered worthy of monopoly protection. For instance, the right of producers of cinematographical works is not expressed in abstract and general terms (as one would expect, for example with respect to authors or literary works), but in precise language. Hence, the right is conferred upon producers 'of the first fixation of films' (because the right of these exists in respect only of the *first* fixation) and with the precision 'in the respect of the original and copies of their films.' We will find again that in the others Articles related to rights.

Having said this, the definition of the content of the right is broad. It is a right 'to authorise or prohibit' (which are really, two facets of the same reality) 'direct or

indirect, temporary or permanent reproduction, by any means and in any form, in whole or in part.'
Each expression used is significant and warrants a (brief) comment.

'Direct or indirect': the reproduction need not be a direct one; if the object of the copyright is a form, the only question is to know if this can be recognised in the allegedly infringing work, the precise manner of the reproduction does not matter.

'Temporary or permanent': in the digital world, this is a very important issue because many fixations are fleeting and the question has been asked if such fixations are really reproductions. It is a question to which various answers have been advanced. So far as the Directive is concerned, a reproduction need not be permanent. The act or the fact of fixation is sufficient. But this implies that certain restrictions are needed to limit and give a degree of certainty to the right of reproduction. Accordingly, the Directive provide for an exception in Article 5(1): temporary acts forming part of a technological process are not considered to constitute a reproduction (see below).

'By any means and in any form': it is well established, both under *droit d'auteur* and copyright systems, that the means employed in carrying out a reproduction or a copying matter little. Hence, a photograph of an architectural work and the storage of a literary work in digital format on the hard disk drive of a computer are treated in exactly the same way as the pirated copy of a literary work. It is irrelevant that the infringing act is carried out in a medium of fixation different from that in which the original work was fixed. As for the form of reproduction is concerned ('any form'), the position is analogous: the work can be 'repeated' in this original form (or a form which closely approximates it) but may also be rather substantially changed, as in the reproduction of the architectural work in photographical format. What is essential is that the protected work can be recognised in the infringing reproduction. The English Copyright Designs and Patents Act 1988 specifically recognises this when it provides that 'copying includes the making of a copy in three dimensions of a two-dimensional work and the making of a copy in two dimensions of a three-dimensional work' (Section 17(3)).

Finally, reproduction 'in whole or in part': this needs little comment. The reproduction is not a question of volume but one which has regard to the quality of that which has been taken. Hence, the rightsholder can prohibit a partial reproduction, as well as a reproduction of the entire work, subject to any applicable exceptions provided for in national laws (on these exceptions see Article 5(2)).

In summary all possible kinds of fixations are likely to constitute reproduction and therefore be subject to the exclusive prerogatives of the relevant rightsholder.
The Directive clearly makes a 'maximalist' – and in our view desirable – choice as far as the scope of the reproduction is concerned.

## 5.3 Article 3 – Communication to the public

Article 3 tackles the second fundamental aspect of the exclusive rights which constitute copyright: the right of performing, showing, playing, broadcasting the work... If one adopts a synthetic view of intellectual property rights (IPRs) (which seems to me the desirable one), one can speak of a general 'right of communication to the public'. However, not all legal systems share such a view of IPRs. Although it may be present, for instance, in the Dutch and French systems, it is absent in their English and Irish counterparts. So the Directive has made a significant choice in speaking precisely about a 'right of communication to the public', with this addition: 'And right of making available to the public other subject-matter.'[10]

The first point to note is that the Directive establishes, in EU law, the notion of an autonomous right to communicate the work to the public. The manner in which the work is communicated is not, however, relevant to the existence of the right.

In a revisited approach to copyright (or *droit d'auteur*) (that is one liberated from the constraints of inherited juridical chauvinism and dogmas!) it is perhaps 'communication' which is the core notion, the author's entire creative activity being turned towards the public. Indeed, it is this very notion of 'public' which gives sense to the creative act, and the link between creator (author) and public lies in the act which allows the work to reach this public: the communication.[11]

But if the notion of 'public' has occasionally been problematic (for example, does the entire guest body of a hotel form a distinct public, or are these people merely a collection of separate, discrete, individuals?), the emphasis placed by the Directive on the information society, and, more specifically, the rise of information networks and the Internet has forced a reconsideration of what constitutes the public in this context. The recitals rightly proclaim that there exists 'legal uncertainty regarding the nature and the level of protection of acts of on-demand transmission of copyright works and subject matter protected by related rights over networks' (recital 25).

Actually, the mechanism of 'on-demand transmission' leads to wonder whether it is still possible to speak of 'public' where it seems that this notion has been to a certain degree 'dismembered' from three conceptual points of view: space, time and object. Each person to whom the work is communicated may be in a different place (as in the example of the hotel guests). Each demand may be made at a different time. And even the object of the demand may not be the same since the possibilities offered by interactivity allow each Internet user to structure his progress through for example a

---

[10] See B. Hugenholtz, *Copyright problems of electronic document delivery*, European Commission DG XIII, 1995.

[11] See – in French – D. Masson, *Les droits patrimoniaux de l'auteur à l'épreuve de la communication au public*, Thesis, Montpellier, 1997, who describes the communication as a new 'crystallisation' of the rights which make the copyright as the *droit d'auteur*, in more usual words a kind of 'summarisation' of these rights.

website (and hence the works) which he consults. Having said this, the perception of the public as a virtuality oblige to give a positive answer. The question is not to know if the persons are here or there and visit a website at a specific hour ... but if the message is able to reach anybody. And thus the act, more or less active, of 'making available' works or other subjects is a form of this communication.

It is in an effort to deal with these questions that the WIPO Copyright Treaty of 20 December 1996 expressly states in Article 8 dealing with the same right of communication (the same words have been chosen): 'Authors of literary and artistic works shall enjoy the exclusive right of authorising any communication to the public of their works in such a way that members of the public may access these works from a place and at a time individually chosen by them.' The terms are almost the same in the two texts and exactly the same for the 'hard core' of the formula: right of communication to public includes 'making available to the public of their works in such a way that members of the public may access them from a place and at a time individually chosen by them.'

The same right is recognised to the holders of related rights in the second WIPO Treaty dealing with the related rights: for performers on fixations of their performances, for phonograms producers on their phonograms, and so on... And for the broadcasting organisations, it is specified that these organisations have such a right 'whether these broadcasts are transmitted by wire or over the air, including by cable or satellite.'
So the understanding of this right – both in European and international law – is the broadest possible. The rightholder is able to control the 'dissemination' of his work or his particular subject matter through all possible media and specifically information networks and digital media.

This control over the dissemination of a work is all the stronger because point 3 provides, with reason, that this right shall not be exhausted by any act of communication to the public of a work or other subject matter. Exhaustion of rights is an important doctrine of European law which has radically modified intellectual property rights in the European Union. But everyone who is familiar with this field of IPRs, knows also that, the overwhelming opinion of both practitioners and academics is that this exhaustion does not affect the right of representation (right of communication). In the well known 'Coditel' case, the Court of Justice of the European Communities decided, in a matter concerning a TV cable retransmission of a film, that the rightsholder was entitled to prohibit the retransmission of the film in the territory in respect of which he enjoyed the exclusive right of communication of the work (Country 1), notwithstanding the fact that the retransmission came from a country (Country 2) where the broadcaster was entitled to retransmit the work. The Court held that the right was still effective and had not been exhausted (Court of Justice 18th march 1980, *Recueil* p. 881). The Directive leaves this reasoning undisturbed and it specifies that the exclusive right will applies in the case of a on-demand transmission.

The recitals of the Directive clearly indicate that its author wanted to provide a high level of protection of intellectual property rights (see above). This legislative intention is clearly translated in the operative provisions of the Directive.

Concretely, that signifies that the rightholders, at least in theory, have a perfect control of their work or subject matters. Every act of use of these works or other subject matters must be authorised, subject obviously to the possible legal exceptions (see after). But, considering the highly publicised Napster or MP3 cases, the text brings a powerful reinforcement to those who have made themselves the defenders of intellectual property. It is not possible lawfully to download a music or a photograph without an authorisation from the relevant rightsholder. Hence, even if global networks have given birth to new social relations, new ways of interacting with works and a new economic model, the legal model relating to intellectual property remains the same: a model centred on the power of prohibit.

## 5.4    Article 4 – Distribution right

The object of Article 4 is very specific and related to a sophisticated notion which is not understood in the same way in all countries and, in some cases, may not be understood at all.

It deals with a 'distribution right' which is already present in the WIPO Treaty of December 1996, but is the subject of some controversy. The recitals give interesting indications: it is intended, they state, to confer an 'exclusive right to control distribution of the work incorporated in a tangible article' (recital 28). We are no longer in the field of a 'dissemination' through networks as in Article 3. It is a new way of control for an other form of diffusion.

But, before attempting to define the exact substance of this right, it is necessary to observe that it is conferred only upon authors, and not to the owners of related rights: it is a specific prerogative to the copyright *stricto sensu*. Is it then a prerogative arguably linked to the act of creation? (It should be noted that this position is to be contrasted with that adopted in the WIPO Treaties since the Performances and Phonograms Treaty gives a similar right to the holders of related rights.)

Whether it relates exclusively to copyright stricto sensu or to related rights as well, the question which arises is what is the precise scope and nature of this right within the European legal order.

In Continental doctrine, the idea, full of interest, began to circulate some years ago, that the right of reproduction includes a 'right of destination'. One of the first systematic, and very valuable, studies was carried out in Belgium by Gotzen.[12] According to Gotzen, this right entitles an author to forbid contracting parties as well as the ulterior purchasers one or several uses of the copy of the work. It is a manner of controlling not only the commercialisation of the copies but also of the possible uses made by the buyers of these. It is easy to understand that such a right is not one which is susceptible to be exhausted. The two notions of wide control by this right of destination and of exhaustion are even directly conflicting.

Right of destination, right of distribution: does the semantic proximity suggest an intellectual proximity? Certainly a superficial, and cursory, analysis could lead to such a conclusion. But the observation according to which the right of destination cannot be exhausted is not compatible with the affirmation of a (delimited) exhaustion of the right of distribution in the Directive (Article 4(2)).

The right of distribution is altogether different and is less ambitious in scope. It made a discreet, although significant appearances in the Software directive of 1991 and Data Bases directive of 1996. In the WIPO Treaty on Copyright, the word 'distribution' itself is used. Article 6 is expressly entitled 'Right of distribution'. The text, it is true, is very elliptical: 'Authors of literary and artistic works shall enjoy the exclusive right of authorising the making available to the public of the original and copies of their works through sale or other transfer of ownership' (Article 6(1)). To authorise the making available... (WIPO Treaty). Exclusive right to any form of distribution... (European directive). What do these expressions mean and consequently what is the power of the rightholders? These expressions, taken together and read in contemplation with Article 4(2) which provide an exhaustion 'with the first sale or other transfer of ownership in the Community of (the work)' – the physical expression of the work ('*support*' in French or '*soporte*' in Spanish) –.

Thus the first and easy answer is that this right concerns only the physical object (what is perfectly consistent with the non-exhaustion in an immaterial environment we have seen in the precedent Article).
As for the substance of the right one's first reaction would be to consider that its holder can control both placement on the market and subsequent marketing of the item (tangible Article). The common meaning of the word 'distribution' leads to this interpretation. In relation to the first of these powers: to decide setting or not the work on the market, it indubitably belongs to the holder of this right of distribution. The Court of Justice of European Communities does not say otherwise in its jurisprudence, beginning with the emblematic cases 'Centrafarm' (Court of Justice 31st Oct. 1974, Centrafarm Vs Sterling Drug Recueil p. 1147, Centrafarm Vs Winthrop: Recueil p. 1183). But it could not be true for the second point: to control the marketing of the Article after it has been placed on the market, and this precisely

---

[12]  F. Gotzen, *Het Bestemmingsrecht van de Auteur*, Brussels, Larcier, 1975, in Flemish, with a summary in French.

because the text of the Directive provides exhaustion of the right. The control cannot be maintained after the placement of the Article upon the market, cabbot persist. In fact, the following distinction needs to be drawn.

Either the first act making the work available realises a transfer of property in the article in which it is embodied (whether this be by means of a sale or a contract of an equivalent nature). Provided this has been carried out by or with the consent of the owner (a well known expression drawn from the ECJ's jurisprudence), then there will be an exhaustion of the right to control any subsequent resale (as mentioned in recital 28) but also exhaustion more widely of the right to control the distribution of the item in any way (*ubi lex non distinguit...*). Alternatively, if the first «act» done in relation to the item has not had the effect of transferring property in it (for example, the owner decides to rent rather than sell copies of an item), then the right will not be exhausted.

That said, in most cases there will be exhaustion, since the model of the sale is the more widespread of the two. Therefore, the statement that «the right of distribution shall not be exhausted...» may be misleading. Exhaustion will generally, but not exclusively, be the rule.

All that nevertheless with the reserve that the present Directive does not affect the specific provisions provided by specific Directives as the Directive on computer programs. That signifies that, when this last text provides for exhaustion except for the rental right, this peculiar provision conserves effect when the work is a computer program.

We shall conclude by returning to the question we posed earlier: the compatibility of the rights of distribution and destination. We have said that it was not really possible to conceive a right of destination subject to exhaustion. But André and Henri-Jacques Lucas ask this interesting question: would it be possible to provide for exhaustion limited to the 'distribution aspect' considered by the Directive, leaving unaffected the faculty for the author to limit the material use of the copies? Their cautious conclusion is that it is not certain that this solution would find favour with the Court of Justice.[13] In my opinion, this solution effectively cannot be sustained since the recognition of a right of distribution means the death of any right of destination.

In fact, the rightholder, according to the analysis of the European Court, may, when it is matter of a tangible Article, decide upon the conditions for its placement on the market. That is the extent of his rights. No more.

## 5.5 Article 5 – Exceptions and limitations

This Article deals with the 'exceptions and limitations' to the restricted acts set out in Articles 2, 3 and 4. It is indisputably the weak point of the text. It is the longest

---

[13] A. and H-J. Lucas, *Traité de la Propriété littéraire et artistique*, Paris, Litec, 2001, n° 252.

article of the Directive, but does not establish any real harmonisation since the Member States are not obliged to adopt the same exceptions! 'Member States may provide...'

### 5.5.1   General observations

A preliminary comment: the Directive has finally chosen to speak of exceptions *and limitations*, and not only about exceptions as it had at one time been intended. This is more than a question of nuance. The specialists of the matter know that the second expression suggests a particular limit beyond which a right granted or recognised cannot extend. By contrast, an exception is more an anomaly (some speak about a 'paralysis' of the right for particular reasons) and it seems that it is always possible to return to an irregular provision. Whether the choice taken by the drafters of the Directive to provide for both exceptions and limitations has any practical ramifications remains to be seen.

If Member States are free to elect one exception and not another one, recital 32 says, in a very clear way, that the Directive 'provides for an exhaustive enumeration of exceptions.' Exhaustive enumeration: the possible exceptions (or limitations) are only those expressly provided for by the Directive so there is no risk of any additions to the list through the intervention of national legislators. The text of the Directive is the only pertinent reference.

However, if Member States cannot create new exceptions (or limitations) and so new distortions, the possibility offered to them by the Directive to elect between the exceptions they want is a potential source of 'disharmonisation' (if I can allow myself this expression). Recital 31 correctly observes that 'existing differences in the exceptions and limitations to certain restricted acts have direct negative effects on the functioning of the Internal Market of copyright and related rights; (that) such differences could well become more pronounced in view of the further development of transborder exploitation of works and cross-border activities; (that) in order to ensure the proper functioning of the Internal Market, such exceptions and limitations should be defined more harmoniously.' And maybe it is right too when it adds that 'the degree of their harmonisation should be based on their impact on the smooth functioning of the internal market.' But the question is to determine concretely what will be the relevant degree of harmonisation.

The recitals again provide some guidance in that with two just finalities: consideration of the information society and search for a balance of interests. 'The existing exceptions and limitations to the rights as set out by the Member States have to be reassessed in the light of the new electronic environment' (recital 31). 'A fair balance of rights and interests between the different categories of rightholders, as well as between the different categories of rightholders and users of protected subject matter must be safeguarded' (same recital). These two ideas provide fertile ground for reflection; the second one is present in many doctrinal reflections, particularly in German literature on copyright.[14] It is also present in German jurisprudence and notably the interesting 'school book case' decision of the German Federal Constitutional Court in which the court considered that 'the legislature is not only obliged to secure the interests of the individual but it is also charged with setting limits on the individual rights and powers that are necessary to preserve the interest of the general public; it must bring about a just balance between the sphere of the individual and the interests of the public' (BverfGE 31, 229, Kirchen- und Schulgebrauch).

But, to appreciate concretely the tenor of the possible exceptions, so far as the Directive is concerned, a close analysis of the text is required.

### 5.5.2 Specific commentaries

There are two categories of exceptions, considering their object. Some that only apply to the reproduction right, and others that apply to both reproduction and other rights. With a common provision (point 5) on the necessity to have due consideration to the international obligations of the Member States.

#### 5.5.2.1 Exceptions to reproduction right

The first category of exceptions applies to the reproduction right, and includes a specific provision dealing with temporary acts of reproduction. For these acts, the right of reproduction *is* extensive and the Member States have no freedom. For the others, they *may* provide an exception.

It is necessary to refer to the text: it is not only the temporary acts of reproduction which are exempted from the right of reproduction but acts 'which are an integral and essential part of a technological process' etc. These acts, as says the text itself, 'have no independent economic significance' (Article 5(1)) and, accordingly, there is no reason to prohibit them. A similar idea is present in the WIPO Copyright Treaty (Article 10). More fundamentally, one can question if a fixation without human purpose but with only a technical function is still a reproduction.[15] In any case, the solution adopted by the Directive is the desirable one.

Regarding the other exceptions to the reproduction right, Members States have a freedom of choice. The number of possible exceptions has grown since the initial proposal for the Directive in 1997. In the final version there are five such possible exceptions. If each one has its own proper logic, two remarks on the spirit and intent of the text can be made. The first is that, if at one time a separate treatment had been

---

[14] For instance, E. Ulmer, *Urheber- und Verlagsrecht*, Berlin, Heidelberg,... Springer Verlag, third ed., 1980, p. 6.

[15] This question was raised some years ago by André Lucas and the present author, in a report made for the French Ministry of Culture : *Les nouvelles technologies de l'information, Recension technique et première analyse de leur impact sur la propriété littéraire et artistique*, Montpellier, IDATE, 1993.

intended for the 'analogue' and for the 'digital' copy, this distinction has finally been repealed. Secondly it is possible to identify a concern, common to three exceptions : the need to ensure to the rightsholders a 'fair compensation', which is a the manifestation of the need to strike a balance between competing interests, to which we have already alluded.

Article 5(2)(a) is globally aimed at 'reprography'. It does not speak about private copy (that is the object of the following paragraph) but concerns all kinds of reproductions on paper or any similar medium, effected by the use of any kind of photographic technique or other process having similar effects. (It excepts musical scores – which would appear to demonstrate the effect of efficient lobbying.) In fact, this exception (except in so far as it exempts music scores) is in accordance with the solutions adopted in all Members States' systems.

The requirement of fair compensation is certainly the most interesting rule, although the concept is already present in many legal systems. Of course, it could be possible to argue that compensation is owing only in cases of a real and quantifiable loss... with the consequence that, if the copy is judged as not having any real economic impact, compensation would not be owing! Recital 35 considers this situation, saying that 'in certain situations where the prejudice to the rightholder would be minimal, no obligation for payment may arise.' But, following the explicit provision of the text, in my opinion this situation would only be a marginal case. And it is sure that compensation can be obtained through a general system. In this context it is notable that, in recital 37, the Community Authorities assert that any eventual national schemes on reprography 'do not create major barriers to the internal market'). It is positively a way for a flexible mechanism.

In contrast to an earlier draft which distinguished between analogue and digital reproductions, Article 5(2)(b) now deals with reproductions 'on any medium'. The private character of the reproduction determines the scope of the provision. The final text refers to all reproductions 'made by a natural person for private use and for ends that are neither directly or indirectly commercial' (the European Parliament having added the idea of a directly or indirectly commercial end). That constitutes an important limit to the potential exception (or limitation because it can be noted here that the private sphere is usually considered as out of the 'natural' field of the copyright). And we find again the fair compensation 'which takes account of the application or non-application of technological measures referred to in Article 6 to the work or subject-matter concerned', about which we can note that the recital 38 says that 'this may include the introduction or continuation of remuneration schemes to compensate for the prejudice to rightholders' (remuneration schemes meaning reasonably general system of compensation). It is to be noted that the Directive does not specifically opt for either of the two systems of fair dealing or formal and strictly delimited right of private copy.

The exception of Article 5(2)(c) has changed notably with the evolution of the text. In its earlier version, it could be classed in the category of exceptions, partially justified by their non-economic impact, but which were also intended to realise the balance of interests which is one of the guiding principles of the Directive. In the final version, the institutions targeted by the exceptions remain libraries, cultural establishments, museums, and the purpose is no more determined ('specific acts of reproduction'). However the emphasis is set on the non-commercial or economic finality of the activity of the author of the reproduction (activity and not act of reproduction), which 'opens' widely the scope of the exception.

Article 5(2)(d): this exception to the single reproduction right is totally new for a number of Member States. At first blush, it appears to confer a specific right of 'ephemeral fixation', but for the limited purposes of broadcasting entities, and, in contrast to paragraph 1, without any compulsory effect. However, given the possibility of archiving of documents, this temporary or transient fixation is susceptible to become permanent! The question will be to find the correct interpretation of the expression: 'On the ground of their exceptional documentary character.'

Article 5(2)(e), an example of social purpose and again with the requirement of fair compensation.

### 5.5.2.2      Exceptions to different rights
The following exceptions (Article 5(3)) potentially concern both the reproduction right and the right of communication to the public. As they are numerous (fifteen!) – it is the great litany of the exceptions – we are not examine each of them. They are well known exceptions in several systems of law whilst in others they either do not currently exist or are the subject of considerable controversy. Accordingly, it is understandable that Member States are not required by the Directive to provide for these exceptions.

On the whole, these exceptions are justified by a concern for the defence of some fundamental or important liberties, and represent different manifestations of the same end sought to be achieved.
The quality of the beneficiary of the exception can be the determinant cause of the exception: this is the case of the exception for the benefit of people with a disability (the exceptionally authorised use having to be 'directly related to the disability') (subparagraph (3)(b)) or for the cultural establishments referred to in Subparagraph (2)(c) (see subparagraph (3)(n)).

The specific aim of the exception can be an other justification: teaching or scientific research (subparagraph (3)(a) and also, in a particular perspective, subparagraph (3)(n)); reporting of current events (subparagraph (3)(c)); 'use for the purposes of public security or to ensure the proper performance or reporting of administrative, parliamentary or judicial proceedings' (subparagraph (3)(e)) which is really new for some systems of law but is also certainly pertinent (in France, a litigant has been sentenced for counterfeiting for have reading a text under copyright during the plea) or further use during religious or official ceremonies (subparagraph (3)(g)).

But the reporting of events is also a manifestation of the freedom of speech, which of itself constitutes an important and proper justification for an exception. This same consideration of freedom of speech, freedom of expression is also present in the traditional exception relating to quotations, for example for purposes of criticism (subparagraph (3)(d)), and more obviously in the exception of quotation for direct purpose of information (subparagraph (3)(f): use of political speeches, public lectures,...), also, in filigree, in the exception for the purpose of caricature, parody or pastiche (subparagraph (3)(k)) which was absent from the initial proposition (proof that the 'right to humour' is alive and well in Europe!), and further in more 'technical' exceptions (see subparagraph (3)(j): 'advertising').

Other exceptions are considerably more specific in nature. Some have material aims: repairing (subparagraph (3)(l)) or reconstructing (subparagraph (3)(m)). And even, works located in public places can be 'withdrawn' from copyright's hold (subparagraph (3)(h): 'use of works, such as works of architecture or sculpture, made to be located permanently in public places').

Lastly, one cannot ignore the rather odd catch-all provision : 'Use in certain other cases of minor importance where exceptions or limitations are already exist under national law, provided that they only concern analogue uses and do not affect the free circulation of goods and services within the Community, without prejudice to the other exceptions and limitations contained in this Article', Subparagraph (3)(p).
Of course the exceptions do not exist abstractly and specific conditions are required for the application of each one. That said, two or three elements are often, if not in all cases, present, which are worthy of closer attention.

The first point to note is that the reference often made to the objective serves in that case to be the measure of the scope of the exception (for instance subparagraph (3)(a, b, j): in b, exception for the benefit of people with a disability is possible 'to the extent required by the specific disability'). This is probably a general – if unstated – principle underlying most exceptions (for example, the exceptions relating to parody).
The second observation is that in many cases the exception requires indication of the source (see subparagraph (3)(a, c, d, f)).
The third one, linked to the second, can be read as a rule of reason. In these cases, the requirement having been posed, the text adds : 'unless this proves impossible' (see subparagraph (3)(a, c, d), and, using similar words, (3)(f). The requirement is a condition for the application of the exception but the requirement must not render the exception impracticable.

For the rest, it is of course necessary to refer to each provision... Usual problem of reading...

### 5.5.2.3     Right of distribution

All the possible exceptions can be extended to right of distribution (Paragraph (4)). Reproduction, communication, distribution: the text specifies that each of these shall only apply in cases 'which do not conflict with a normal exploitation of the work or other subject matter and do not unreasonably prejudice the legitimate interests of the rightholder' (Paragraph (5)). Recital 44 provides an explanation for this provision, reminding the reader that European Law must be conceived in accordance with international obligations of Member States and the EU. One cannot but recognise in the formulation of the Directive a requirement of the Berne Convention (Article 9).

### 5.5.3    Valuation

The wording of the Directive is lengthy and, paradoxically, at the same time often vague, this may be viewed as a good thing because it means freedom for the legislators. But, precisely, is it a good thing? And when these legislators may decide to adopt one exception and not another, is it possible to speak about harmonisation? Maybe the relatively rapid success of the proposed directive can be explained by the feeling, in each Member State, that the projected directive does not carry out the harmonisation which is the natural object of this kind of texts! I am not sure that the 'legal landscape' is going to change with the adoption of this text.

This Article, in my opinion, constitute a real fault line in the Community's copyright regime. To give an example in the cyberspace which is emblematic of the information society, it is possible in the Dutch legal system lawfully to make excerpts of visual works and to place these excerpts onto computerised networks. This sort of 'quotation' remains legal in the Netherlands but may be held to be illegal in France. Thus, a single act of fixation and communication receives two different analyses in the territory of the European Union : the appearance of the same picture on the screen of a computer is going to be judged licit in a country and possibly infringing in an other... One could legitimately ask: where is the Single Market? Much ado about nothing, it would seem.

And this in light of the 'motherhood' statement contained in recital 32 which says that it is desirable 'that Member States should arrive at a coherent application of these exceptions and limitations, which will be assessed when reviewing implementing legislation in the future.' Let us wait... and hope.

## 5.6    Article 6 – Technological measures

With this Article, we leave the domain of copyright and related rights, strictly speaking, to address the issue of technical measures designed to protect and support such rights.

The recitals underline that new technological development will increasingly allow rightsholders to make use of technological measures to protect copyright and related rights (see recital 47). The concept is not a novel one: similar provisions exist in the WIPO Copyright Treaty (Article 11), in the WIPO Performers and Phonograms Treaty (Article 18) and also in the Directive on Computer Programs of 1991 (Article 7).

For the purposes of the Directive, these measures are defined as 'any technology, device or component that (...) is designed to prevent or restrict acts, in respect of works or other subject-matter, which are not authorised by the rightholder of any copyright or any right related to copyright as provided by law or the *sui generis* right provided for in Chapter III of Directive 96/9/EC' (Article 6(3)). Only the 'effective' measures are required to be protected according to the text and, rather than leaving the interpretation of this expression – «effective measures» – to judicial wisdom, the text makes a rather awkward attempt at defining it, what is a little strange (See Article 6(3)). That observation having been made, it should be noted that the scope of the provision is particularly broad since it extends to the *sui generis* database right.

As for the protection afforded, it is double. First, it is a direct protection against 'the circumvention of any effective technological measures' (Article 6(1)), circumvention 'which the person concerned carries out in the knowledge, or with reasonable grounds to know that he or she is pursuing that objective' (*ibid.*). But secondly, it is also a protection against manufacture, importation, distribution, sale,... of this type of devices which permit such a circumvention, carried out in furtherance or assistance of to the principal prohibited act (Article 6(2)). However, there is no question of forbidding all sorts of acts of commercialisation. As recital 48 well specifies: 'Such legal protection should respect proportionality and should not prohibit those devices or activities which have a commercially significant purpose or use other than to circumvent the technical protection.' It is for this reason that that the Directive requires that the relevant legal protection must be provided against devices which are 'primarily designed, produced, adapted or performed for the purpose of enabling or facilitating the circumvention' (Article 6(2)(c)).

The precise manner and form of the legal protection does not matter (only an 'adequate' protection is required). And so Member States are not required to provide penal protection (in the project of the European Council against cybercrime, the question has been sharply debated but finally no provision has been adopted).

In fact the Community Authorities even encourage a voluntarist policy (in the form of agreements between rightholders and other parties concerned). But, if at the end of the day, member States must adopt a legal policy, it is advisable to ensure an equitable balance between different interests. Technological measures must not prevent the normal play of the exceptions and limitations. These measures have a specific aim but they must not lead to a result which exceeds this aim and, since they claim to ensure the defence of rights, must not be transformed into an unreasonable restriction upon freedom. This concern appears in the recitals but it is even clearer in the Statement of Council's Reasons at the time of the adoption of the Common Position on where it can be read: 'Technological measures designed to prevent or inhibit acts allowed by law (e.g. by virtue of an exception) were not protectable under Article 6. In other words (...), the exceptions provided for in Article 5 prevailed over the legal protection of technological measures provided for in Article 6' (Sept. 2000, n° 43). That explains the provisions of paragraph 4: a general one and a specific one about right of reproduction. In this last case, the States can adopt measures to maintain the desired balance of interests 'unless reproduction for private use has already been made possible by rightholders'; in other words, if it is possible to obtain the same result by other than coercive means (a parallel can be drawn with the text of the Software directive of 1991 where decompilation is forbidden if the information sought therefrom has already been voluntarily provided by the rightsholder or is otherwise readily available: Article 5). This is a good example of the principle of economy in the art of law-making.

It remains the last but one provision of the Article, a particularly opaque provision: 'The provisions of the first and second subparagraphs shall not apply to works or other subject-matter made available to the public on agreed contractual terms in such a way that members of the public may access them from a place and a time individually chosen by them.' If this means that freely accessible works (for example, those appearing on a website or the website itself) are exempt from the provisions of the Article, then we could well ask ourselves whether there is any genuine point to the Article. And if this is not its meaning, then what interpretation is to be given to the provision? One would have hoped for a clearer expression of legislative intention!

## 5.7   Article 7 – Rights-management information

The provisions of Article 7 ('Obligations concerning rights-management information') are even more novel than those of the previous Article. It is directed to the ease of diffusion of works which networks such as the Internet offer. As recital 54 states: 'Technological development will facilitate the distribution of works, notably on networks, and this will entail the need for the rightholders to identify better the work or other subject-matter, the author or any other rightholder, and to provide information about the terms and conditions of use of the work or subject-matter in order to render easier the management of rights attached to them.' And the recital continues: 'Rightholders should be encouraged to use markings indicating, in addition to the information referred to above, inter alia, their authorisation when putting works or other subject-matter on networks.'

In a way, in this 'information society' of which one of the characteristic features resides in these new 'informational goods' that we have encountered (see above), the information – the information provided by the rightsholders in association with their works – becomes an element of strategy for the management of rights.

Given the strategic nature acquired by such information, the Directive attempts to fight against illegal activities intend 'to remove or alter the electronic copyright-management information' (recital 55). Anyway, the same idea and almost the same provisions are present in the WIPO Copyright Treaty of 1996 (Article 12).

The intervention of a Community text is further justified by the risk that fragmented national legal approaches 'could potentially hinder the functioning of the internal market' (as says the same recital 55).

Given the foregoing, the text is easy to understand and does not require very extensive comment.

Point 2 of the Article provides a definition, for the purposes of the text, of 'rights-management information', a definition which repeats the presentation made by the recitals: 'Any information provided by rightholders which identifies the work or other subject-matter....' The definition is broad: broad in reference to the relevant information ('any information'), broad in reference to the rights concerned (it concerns not only copyright and related rights but also the *sui generis* right provided in Data Base directive). The concern of protection is clearly significant insofar as the last paragraph specifies that the obligation for the states to adopt adequate protections of this rights-management information is also imperative when only a partial information is linked to the works or other subject-matters (for instance information on the rightholder or information about the conditions of use of these items).

Member States' obligations: the first one is the prohibition of 'removal or alteration of any electronic rights-management information.'

Secondly, there is the obligation to provide for adequate legal protection against any person performing one of these indirect acts of 'aggression': distribution, importation for distribution, broadcasting,... of items from 'which electronic right-management information has been removed or altered without authority.' The processes are similar to those adopted for the protection of the technological measures that we have considered above in Article 6.

From a legal point of view, it must be noted that an intentional element is required. The author of an alteration must have acted 'knowingly' and of course 'without authorisation'. In the second case (legal protection against indirect acts), it is even necessary that the person 'knows, or has reasonable grounds to know, that by so doing he is inducing, enabling, facilitating or concealing an infringement of any copyright or any rights related to copyright as provided by law, or of the *sui generis* right provided for in Chapter III of Directive 96/9/EC.'

If it were legitimate to adopt the vocabulary of penal law, it could be possible to speak of a sort of *dolus specialis.* But it is important to note that the Directive does not impose any kind of measures, penal or otherwise. The only requirement is that an 'adequate legal protection' be provided. That is, one may observe in passing, not a very satisfactory form of harmonisation!

In this respect, it appears that the European text takes a step back from the WIPO provisions that we have mentioned. If this treaty leaves the same liberty to the states in the choice of the 'adequate' remedies, it restricts indirectly the field of the (potential) penal law since it says that the Contracting Parties shall provide adequate remedies against persons performing some acts 'knowing, or *with respect to civil remedies* having reasonable grounds to know, that will induce, enable, facilitate or conceal an infringement of any right covered by this Treaty or the Bern Convention' (the Directive, in saying nothing about application of penal provisions potentially leaves their application open, whereas the WIPO treaty normally excludes their application).

We shall add, finally, that the recitals say (although not the text itself) that 'any such rights-management information (...) may, depending on their design, at the same time process personal data about the consumption of patterns of protected subject-matter by individuals and allow for tracing of on-line behaviour' and that therefore 'these technical means, in their technical functions, should incorporate privacy safeguards in accordance with Directive 95/46/EC of the European Parliament and of the Council of 24 October 1995 on the protection of individuals with regards to the processing of personal data and the free movement of such data' (recital 56). This question of protection of personal data is an other important facet of the information society and the point which the recital emphasises is particularly important, the risk especially grave. So it could be considered regrettable not to have a provision dealing with the important issue of data protection in the operative provisions of the Directive. However, in any event the Directive on the protection of personal data will continue to apply. Therefore, the recital simply serves as a timely reminder of the importance of the protection of personal data in the European Union.

That is perhaps the last lesson to be drawn from the Directive: the information society is a whole.

## 5.8    Articles 8–15 – Common provisions

A brief comment will be made on this Article, the first of the 'Common provisions' and the only one which really justifies any comment.

The text is clear: the Member States are required to adopt sanctions to give concrete effect to the provisions of the Directive. But the language is very diplomatic: 'Appropriate sanctions and remedies'. That could potentially mean any number of things. In fact, the Directive leaves the decision to the States. What is not open to criticism. A Directive only provides for harmonisation. If the result can be obtained by different ways, it does not matter if one solution is preferred to another.

The text presents only a kind of 'guidance' and states a specific requirement.
The guidance provided: that the sanctions shall be 'effective, proportionate and dissuasive.' It is the translation of a double concern of efficiency and measure. It is possible to recognise a general principle that the European Court of Human Rights of Strasbourg calls a general principle of democratic societies. In this respect, maybe it is interesting to note that the TRIPS Agreement (Agreement on Trade-Related Aspects of Intellectual Property Rights of 1994) also requires remedies, which are efficient ('effective action...' says Article 41) but with an additional requirement of procedural fairness (procedures shall 'be fair and equitable').
Specific technical requirement: the paragraph 2 specifies different kinds of measures such as injunctions or seizure of infringing material.

Finally, regarding the last paragraph, the recitals explain the rationale of the provision. Recital 58 says: 'In the digital environment, in particular, the services of intermediaries may increasingly be used by third parties for infringing activities. In many cases such intermediaries are best placed to bring such infringing activities to an end. Therefore, without prejudice to any other sanctions and remedies available, rightholders should have the possibility of applying for an injunction against an intermediary who carries a third party's infringement of a protected work or other subject-matter in a network.'

'In the digital environment', e.g. in the information society: we have thus come full circle...

## 5.9    Concluding observations

How to conclude? Opinion on the Directive must remain qualified and even reserved.

The first merit of this text is that it exists. After various Directives of limited scope, this one offers a global and 'transverse' view of the matter of copyright and related rights. But a global view does not signify a general one. Many subjects are absent from the text. Some omissions are natural and understandable: for instance, it does not seem possible for the European authorities to intervene, at least directly, on the problem of moral rights ; at the same time, this does not really fall within the European Community's competence and it is politically a sensitive, even thorny issue. For other subjects, it would had been possible to offer, if not answers, at least some indications, a beginning of harmonisation, on the important problem of employees' creation, for example, which was the case in the Directive on software. This is also too sensitive an issue perhaps!

It was easier to adopt provisions on questions where consensus exists, and not only in the European Union. The provisions on technological measures (Article 6) or the obligations concerning rights-management information (Article 7) are perfect examples of the case in point. They are the direct echo of similar provisions which have been adopted at the international level in the WIPO Copyright Treaty and offer an answer to a concrete interrogation (how to manage rights effectively in a digitised environment?), a question which is no more French than German or European than American. Thus, in these cases, if European harmonisation can indeed be observed, it is in fact closer to being the birth of a new international rule. The same can be said about the new definition of the right of communication to the public or the definition of the new right of communication to the public (Article 3) with its specific emphasis on the 'on demand' system. The WIPO Treaty gives a similar definition and, here also, tries to answer a question which is not specific to one country or regional area. Having said that, the interest of the text is real ; does it matter if a problem is not specifically European? The effect of harmonisation in Europe is genuine. And from the European angle, that is important. What is more, on these questions, Europe is in the forefront of a modern law, adapted to the context of the new technologies of information.

All of this, thus, is positive.

However, not everything in the Directive is so. Most peculiar aspect is not, to my mind, the effect of harmonisation but the fact that it singularly avoids any harmonisation! The differences between the national laws on the content of the rightsholders' prerogatives are not very important but they are of consequence when they involve exceptions. We have seen that the Member States are completely free to adopt any exceptions from the list given by the Directive (with a sole exception of a compulsory case) (Article 5). Thus, the state of the law(s) can be exactly the same before and after the supposed harmonisation. As I have said, this perhaps explains why the Directive was so easily adopted (see above observations on Article 5) but the fact is it does not result in harmonisation. An example of this? In the world of networks, it is still possible to put a text or graphics on line legally in one country, where in another country such a reproduction could be considered illegal. For instance, reproducing material for (electronic) teaching purposes could be legal in Denmark but illegal in France.

How then can this be a 'single market' of Treaties when the rules are radically different? How can we play the same game when the teams do not use the same rules? 'Much ado about... little'? Let us hope not!

# Chapter 6

# Data protection and e-commerce

## Henrik W.K. Kaspersen

## 6.1 Data protection and data protection instruments

E-commerce-practises may interfere directly or indirectly with private life of e-commerce parties in many ways. Protection of private life is subject of different international arrangements like in Article 8 of the European Convention for the Protection of Human Rights and Fundamental Freedoms, Article 12 Universal Declaration of Human Rights, Article 17 International Convention on Civil and Political Rights, and, of course, subject of constitutional and other fundamental national regulations. Under the EC-Treaty a high level of consumer protection goes hand in hand with respect for human rights, as an interest to be guarded by the institutions of the Community when enacting or enforcing regulation. In particular, data protection has become an integrating element of European legislative policies.

The respect for private life is a human right as established in the long row of decisions of the Court of Human Rights in Strasbourg. The possibilities of automatic data processing in order to gather, store, retrieve and combine data about persons, raised concern in Europe about the impact on the private life of the persons involved. In 1981 the Council of Europe drafted a Convention[1] on the protection of personal data based upon the privacy principles as developed by the OECD.[2] Herewith, the concept 'data protection' was introduced in many European legislation. The Convention 108 is the most important source of data protection legislation – at least in Europe – and came into force on October 1, 1985. Although at present not all members of the Council of Europe have ratified this Convention, as a data protection instrument the Convention has great value. Surprisingly, at present the Convention is ratified by the smallest possible majority.[3] The continuing development of information technology caused some erosion to Convention 108, being an instrument from the early eighties and mainly based upon the concept of traditional databanks as an alternative for the paper filing cabinet. For this reason, the Council of Europe is

---

[1] Convention 108, full name: Convention for the Protection of Individuals with regard to Automatic Processing of Personal Data, ETS NR. 108.
[2] Guidelines on the Protection of Privacy and Transferred Flow of Personal Data, Paris 1981.
[3] Signed by 30 out of the 42 Council of Europe Member States and ratified by 21. (<http://www.conventions.coe.int> status per July 2, 2001).

*A.R. Lodder and H.W.K. Kaspersen (eds.),*
*eDirectives: Guide to European Union Law on E-Commerce,* 119–145.
© 2002 *Kluwer Law International. Printed in the Netherlands.*

currently working on a modern additional protocol to the Convention. The European Union, however, decided to create an alternative data protection instrument for its Member States, maintaining most of the definitions and principles of Convention 108 but embedded in more detailed and specific data protection rules. The result was the Directive 95/46/EC on Data Protection.[4]

The reasons for EU action was threefold. EU-members did not rush to ratify Convention 108. Therefore, the Commission made an urgent invitation to do so, and announced an own EU-initiative in case the situation would not change.[5] Further, the Commission felt that Article 16 of Convention 108 concerning transborder data flows was too weak and would allow Member States to create legal barriers, which indeed happened in a number of cases.[6] Further, the object of protection under the Convention 108 is the static personal data file, where the EU directive concentrates on the dynamic concept of the processing of personal data. The Directive provides more rights and stipulates more precise criteria to be met, such as the data protection concept of necessity. A detailed discussion of the differences between the Convention and the directive would go too far within the frame of this Article.

The intent of the European legislator, by enacting the Directive 95/46/EC, was to create a general data protection framework, possibly followed by a number of specific or sectorial data protection instruments. Although it is not sure that there will be many more data protection directives, since the concept of self-regulation is being enhanced, Directive 95/46/EC hereafter will also be refereed to as the mother directive. Directive 97/66/EC is the only sectorial directive so far, addressed to providers of telecommunication services, in earlier days baptised as the ISDN-directive. A draft of this sectorial directive circulated long before the mother directive was adopted, but it was finalised and put into force formally in 1998 (see hereafter). Nevertheless, the structure and content of the ISDN-directive were developed before 1995, the year in which the importance of communication networks like Internet became clear. A revision of the Directive in the light of the market and technology changes was therefore inevitable. In this chapter the proposed amendments are discussed, but only while this book is being printed a final text is decided upon.

Some aspects of the protection of private life have been dealt with in EU-directives referred to in other chapters of this book. Where useful a cross reference will be made. This chapter first recalls the main issues of the mother directive, with some limitation since in e-commerce not all the situations or relations as described in the

---

[4]  Directive of the European Parliament and the Council of 24 October 1995 on the protection of individuals with regard to the processing of personal data and on the free movement of such data, *OJ* L 281, 23.11.1995.

[5]  Recommendation of the Commission, July 29, 1981, *OJ* L 246/13, 29.8.1981.

[6]  Irene Vassilaki, 'Transborder Data Flow of Personal Data, an Empirical Survey of Cases Concerning Transborder Data Flow of Personal Data', *Computer Law & Security Report*, 1993, 9, p. 34f.

directive will occur (section 6.2). Next, the outline of the specific directive 97/66/EC is given. Section 6.4 discusses the content and the background of the proposed amendments to the latter directive. A selected number of privacy-related aspects of e-commerce are discussed in section 6.5, and to what extent data protection rules and other related rules apply is demonstrated. The chapter concludes with some general observations on privacy protection in the field of e-commerce.

## 6.2 Directive 95/46/EC

### 6.2.1 History and Implementation

The first draft proposal was from the year 1990,[7] which was two years later replaced by a fully revised second version.[8] The common position was reached in February 1995, and the final text adopted in June 1995. The directive was formally adopted on October 24, 1995. The Member States are obliged to implement the Directive within three years after adoption, *in casu* before 24 October 1998.[9] Not all Member States appeared to be willing to meet this requirement,[10] and some of them still fail to do so now,[11] which lead to proceedings of the Commission. Hereafter, I will deal with the most important aspects of the Directive. Reference to definitions and main principles will be made.

### 6.2.2 Scope

Article 2(a) provides for a definition of personal data. The concept is very much the same as already defined in Convention 108, be it that directive 95/46/EC does not relate to 'personal' data of legal persons. The text reads: 'any information relating to an identified or identifiable natural person.' Information is personal data if 'it enables the direct or indirect identification of the person concerned.' Further 'identification is possible if the personal data contains or consists of identifiers such as an identification number.' It may also be possible to identify someone 'by means of factors which are specific to the physical, physiological, mental, economic, cultural or social identity.' The definition of personal data is very broad and may include any piece of information. The question therefore is by whom a person needs to be identified or to whom a person need to be identifiable and to what extent before the relating information can be qualified as personal data?

---

[7] COM (90) 314 def.-SYN 287.

[8] *OJ* C 311, 27.11.1992.

[9] See Article 32(1).

[10] In July 1999 the Commission send reasoned opinions for failing to comply with the obligation under Article 32(4) of the Directive to nine EU Member States (Fourth Annual Report, Article 29 Working Party, 5019/01/EN WP 46, p. 13).

[11] The Commission started proceedings on the basis of Article 226 EC against France, Luxembourg, Germany, the Netherlands and Ireland. In the mean time, Germany and the Netherlands have implemented the directive in the year 2001.

Recital 26 points at the controller and 'any other person'. Article 2(c) defines the controller as the party that determines the purpose and means of the processing of personal data, and Article 2(b) defines the processing of personal data as any handling with personal data. The latter two definitions will be discussed further hereafter, but should be mentioned here to clarify the concept of personal data. The 'other person' of recital 26 must be seen in relation with the controller – who may seek assistance from a third person – and the purpose of the processing, including the intended dissemination of the data or the result of the processing to 'other persons'. Recital 26 adds to this 'by all means likely reasonable'. Data is personal data if the controller himself or with the help of a third person can identify the person concerned. The efforts to identify must be 'reasonable' and need not consist of lengthy and extensive technical or even forensic investigations. Under circumstances such investigations would even make it possible to trace anonymised data back to the person to whom it related before.

Personal data concerns data contained in any data carrier, from traditional paper to other electronic formats. In addition, the definition of processing, in Article 2(b) reads '(processed) whether or not by automated means'. The limitation, however, to particular personal data, is found in Article 3(1). Under the scope of the directive come only personal data wholly or partly processed by automatic means. Data not suitable for automatic processing fall under the scope of the directive only if they are a part or are intended to form a part of a so-called filing system. Article 2(c) defines a personal data filing system as a facility which enables to access the data according to specific predefined criteria. In order to prevent circumvention or evasion of the rules, recital 27 encompasses the principle that the protection of personal data should not be different depending on the technical means used for its processing. However, unstructured files are excluded from the scope of the Directive. To my opinion, in a computer environment unstructured files *per definitionem* do not exist. It is left to the Member States to define unstructured files. Only fully unstructured files should not fall under the Directive. In addition, it should be said that the distinction between automated processed personal data and manually or otherwise processed data becomes blurred anyway. Scanning techniques enable any paper data to be put in an electronic format for further processing. For this reason, very few personal data will not come under the scope of the Directive.

The definition of processing in Article 2(b) refers to any handling of personal data from the collection, the storage, organisation, retrieval, elaboration, dissemination to others and even deletion. Although not mentioned explicitly in the recitals, the mere transmission of data is not included in the definition of processing (dissemination by transmission, on the contrary, is) because the mere transmission is not directed to the meaning and content of the personal data involved.

The definition of the controller in Article 2(d) is also very broad. It includes natural persons as well as legal persons, and also private and public bodies. A controller determines the purpose and the means for the processing of personal data. This is a clever set of criteria, clearly referring to the responsible person or body. It is left to the Member States to determine on the basis of the criteria in Article 4 to which controllers national law applies. These criteria are:

a) the data processing is actually carried out in the frame of activities of an establishment in the territory of the Member State;

b) the controller is established in any other place under the jurisdiction of the Member State;

c) the controller is outside the territory of the European Community, but uses equipment for personal data processing on the territory of the Member State, except if the equipment is used for transit only.

The Directive thus is applicable to controllers who even process personal data somewhere abroad. Both the law of the state of settlement and the other state may apply. If a European controller moves the processing of personal data outside the Union's territory (or European Economic Area, EEA), the law of the place of settlement applies. Article 25 prohibits the transfer to countries outside the EEA if they do not provide an adequate level of personal data protection (see hereafter).

The other definitions in Article 2 such as (e) the processor, (f) the third party, (g) the recipient, and (h) data subject's consent are rather obvious and need not be discussed here.

Article 3 exempts some forms of processing of personal data from the scope of the Directive, i.e. processing within the frame of the Union, as defined in Titles V and VI of the treaty on the European Union, and processing related to public security, national security and criminal matters. In both areas, however, separate initiatives are undertaken to apply the principles of the Directive also to those fields.[12] Article 9 further allows to wholly or partly exempt processing of personal data solely for the purpose of journalistic or artistic or literary expression in the light of freedom of expression.

### 6.2.3    Elaboration of the data protection principles

In the Articles 5-13 the data protection principles as incorporated in Convention 108 are further elaborated. Recital 11 states the Directive should give substance to and amplify those principles.

Article 6 embodies the *data quality principle* stating that personal data must be processed by or on behalf of the controller, fairly and lawfully (which seems rather self-evident to me, but apparently not that simple to implement in national law) and

---

[12] In particular is referred to the application of data protection rules to personal data processed by the institutions of the EC. In the frame of negotiations the EU third pillar there is some agreement to apply common data protection rules to the police domain.

further proscribing criteria for keeping the personal data correct, up to date, and not redundant for the purposes for which they were collected or further processed.

Article 7 provides for the criteria which make data processing legitimate. Six cases are distinguished in the Article.
The consent of the data subject (a) should be read in conjunction with Article 2(h), i.e. the consent must be given unambiguously. A controller may not take for granted that a data subject is aware of the intended data processing and does not oppose it. In addition, Article 7(b) says: if necessary to perform a contract with the data subject, separate consent need not to be asked.
The further conditions under (c)-(e) are rather obvious: if the controller is under a legal obligation; if by processing vital interests of the data subject are protected; and if the controller performs a task of public interest. The last criterion (f) is the most frequently occurring situation: the interests of the controller related to the processing of personal data should be balanced against the right of the data subject not to be involved in the processing of data relating to him. At least, such processing must be necessary for the legitimate purposes of the controller. In particular the criterion under (f) sees to the dissemination of data to other persons. Therefore, the right of the data subject to object to a specific processing (Article 14), including the dissemination to others, is particularly related to Article 7 (e) and (f). Article 14 also provides the data subject with a right to object against the first dissemination of his personal data for direct marketing purposes, which involves a corresponding obligation to the controller to inform the data subject. Recital 30 regrettably does not provide much clarification about the criteria in Article 7. Moreover, it is left to the implementing Member States to come up with more specific conditions how to deal with personal data in legitimate business practises and direct marketing activities. One can imagine that legitimate business interests will draw the balance in the direction of business, in particular where the privacy sensitiveness of the data involved is considered to be rather low as is for example the case with only names and addresses. In these cases, however, the data subject must have an unconditional right to opt-out.

Article 8 defines and provides for very precise conditions of processing of sensitive personal data. The sensitiveness is related to the content or meaning of such data (data revealing racial or ethnic origin, political opinions, religious or philosophical beliefs, trade-union membership, health and sex-life). A national identification number is also considered as a special category of such personal data. The processing of personal data which does not fall within one of the specified categories, even if it is of a sensitive nature in certain circumstances, has to follow the general set of rules.

Article 10 regulates the amount of information to be given to the data subject, if the personal data are obtained from the data subject himself and Article 11 does the same for the situation where the data are obtained from other persons. These provisions reflect the *openness principle*, the right to know what is being processed by whom, and facilitate the *individual participation* by the user as further regulated in Articles 12-15. The data subject has a right to know if and what information about him is processed by the controller, including a right of correction.

Article 13 allows the Member States to restrict the scope of the rights and obligations as specified in Articles 6, 10, 11, 12 and 21 in case of national security, public order, criminal law enforcement and some additional overriding interests such as the rights of other data subjects.

### 6.2.4    Other safeguards

The *safeguard principle* is embodied in Article 16 and Articles 17-21 regulate the obligations of the controller to notify the supervising authority, the criteria and procedures. Article 25 formulates the principles in case of transfer of personal data to non-EU states. Transfer of personal data to non-EU Member States is only allowed if the state in question provides for an adequate level of data protection. In this field two type of measures haven been taken in order to prevent impediments of international data transfers and relating trade. Agreements have been concluded with individual countries, of which the USA is the most important. With the USA the so-called *safe harbour arrangement* has been negotiated, necessary because the USA do base privacy protection upon the concept of personal data protection. The *safe harbour arrangement* refers to equivalent privacy protection mechanisms enabling international transfer without violating Article 25 of the Directive. It should, however, be noted that these arrangements will only have a limited effect since it does not apply to banking and insurance companies and, moreover, there will always be situations where it appears simply impossible to reconcile US and EU legal requirements.[13]

In addition the Commission approved standard contractual clauses to be applied by European controllers in their relationship with non-European Union parties in order to ensure what is considered to be an adequate level of protection, in particular concerning the rights of the data subject. Member States should legally recognise that if the clauses are applied in individual private agreements the processing of personal data is adequately protected and cannot be forbidden by the Member State involved on the basis of Article 25 of the Directive.[14] The flaw in such contract clauses, of course, is how to ensure the rights of the data subject if a party further down in the chain ignores the spirit and meaning of the original agreement.

Article 27 allows to draw up Codes of Conduct. Specific reference should be made to Article 29 on the basis of which the so-called Article 29 Working Party was

---

[13]    Gillian Bull, 'Data Protection –Safe Harbour, Transferring personal data to the USA', *Computer Law & Security Report* Vol. 17 no. 4, 2001, 239-243 (241).

[14]    Decision of the European Commission of June 18, 2001, see
<http://www.europa.eu.int/comm/internal_market/en/dataprot/news/clauses2.htm>.

established, composed of representatives of the national data registrars. The Working Party publishes recommendations, reports and other documents on privacy related issues which to their opinion should be brought to the attention of the European Commission, European Parliament, national governments or the public at large. The Working Party publishes a yearly report on its activities, which due to the proceedings is regrettably only published more than a year after the concerning period of activity.

In the mean time, self-regulatory initiatives may have a favourable impact on the enforcement of privacy rules. Here is referred only to an initiative to have a pan-European logo and relating certification procedure for e-commerce enterprises. One of the criteria to meet is adherence to the existing data protection legislation (which at least will be formed by the implementation of Directives 95/46/EC and 97/66/EC) and the participants will in particular inform the persons concerned about the intended processing of their personal data. If consent from the data subject is necessary, this will be asked by means of a separate mouse click.[15]

## 6.3    The Telecommunications directive 97/66/EC

### 6.3.1    History and implementation

The drafting of Directive 97/66/EC[16] started simultaneously with the mother directive of 1995. Nevertheless, Directive 97/66/EC is adopted much later, because technological and market development caused a need for revising the draft text. The Council Resolution of June 30, 1988 already called for a specific data protection instrument and the Directive was adopted by the European Parliament and the Council on December 15, 1997. It was due to be implemented by the Member States by October 24, 1998 at the latest.[17] The Member States were even more indolent in transposing this Directive than with regard to the Directive of 1995. The European Commission, therefore, started proceedings against a considerable number of Member States, some of which could be dropped during the year 1999 and 2000. At present, Ireland, France, Greece and Luxembourg have still failed to notify (full) implementation and will have to face proceedings before the Court of Justice in Luxembourg.[18]

The aim of Directive 97/66/EC is the harmonisation of data protections rights for the telecommunication sector in light of Article 94 (old: 100a) and the relating procedure

---

[15]  <http://www.shopinfo.net/pruefkriterien.shtml>.

[16]  Directive 97/66/EC of European Parliament and the Council of December 15, 1997 concerning the processing of personal data and the protection of private life in the telecommunication sector *OJ* L 24/1, 30.1.1998.

[17]  397L0066, *OJ* L 24/1, 30.1.1998.

[18]  Fourth Annual Report Article 29-Data Protection Working Party, 5019/01/EN WP 46, p. 13-14

under Article 95 of the EC Treaty, in other words, the Directive is a harmonisation instrument. It is meant to enable a free international flow of information within the European Union or the EEA. The directive was known under the informal name ISDN-directive, but now is usually referred to as the Telecommunications directive. Recital 4 stresses in particular the need for harmonised protection of privacy because the occurrence of digital networks with integrated services, since consumers would not have confidence in such services when their privacy would not adequately be protected all over the Union. In particular, video on demand and interactive television are considered as privacy sensitive services (recital 3 and 10). In the light of what was to come – the full emergence of the Internet – the definition of the relevant services seems rather outdated but, generally speaking, the concern for adequate privacy protection in those or similar areas was not unjustified.

### 6.3.2 Scope

Article 1(1) restricts application of the Directive to what is called the telecommunications sector. Article 2 further clarifies what is meant by this, and recital 12 clarifies what should not fall under the scope of the directive. The protection of fundamental rights and fundamental freedoms as such are not addressed. The Member States are allowed to take the (legislative) measures they think necessary for the protection of state security, public order, enforcement of criminal law, etc., the regular exemption under EC law. The Directive does not affect the ability of Member States to intercept telecommunications. The rules of both Directives have no direct interference with the authority for the state to intercept telecommunications, provided if it executes this competence within the limits and under the circumstances as set by Article 8 ECHR and its relating case law.

Article 1(2) clarifies the relation to the general data protection directive 95/46/EG. Directive 97/66/EC can be considered as a *specialis* of the latter directive but also as a supplement. For instance, the mother directive does not apply to the mere transmission of signals or data, where directive 97/66/EC does to the extent that it requires only some technical facilities closely related to the process of transmission. Article 1(2) includes legal persons in the circle of persons whose 'privacy' has to be protected, whereas the mother directive does not deal with such legal persons (recital 13). It could be a lengthy but not fruitful debate whether or not legal persons should enjoy the protection of their 'privacy' or that another legal justification should be found. The inclusion of legal persons in the telecommunications directive is restricted to certain subscribers. The provisions of directive 97/66/EC have to be interpreted in the light of the mother directive 95/46/EC.

Article 2 delineates the scope of the Directive by giving some definitions. Subject of the regulation is the subscriber, both natural and legal persons (a). A subscriber is a person who has concluded a contract with a telecommunications service provider who offers a publicly available telecommunications service. In my opinion, free use of telecommunications services on the basis of registration should also be considered as a contract. Article 2(b) mentions the user, any person who makes use of telecommunications services. This notion includes both the subscriber and other users. The latter will use telecommunication services on the basis of a contract on his behalf too, but that is only relevant where it concerns the obligations of his service provider. The Directive puts obligations on the service provider, in particular in its relation with the subscriber, and other obligations which concern any user of such services, irrespective the legal title for such use. Users are, e.g. the employees of a subscriber as well as any person with whom a communication is sought.

A public telecommunications network is in essence a communication system consisting of technical components, for the provision of telecommunication services (Article 2(c)). The key element of such services is the transmission and routing of signals, except radio and television broadcasting, cf. Article 2(d).

Article 3(a) further restricts the types of services to ISDN and digital mobile networks. Since the transmission may be enabled by means of wire, radio waves or other electromagnetic means, a telecommunication network includes a wide range of systems, like fixed cable networks, digital mobile systems and satellite communication systems. The key subject of this Directive is the telecommunication service, which mainly consists of the transmission and the routing of signals over a telecommunication network. According to this criterion the transmission of signals over a fixed cable between two points will not constitute a telecommunication service, whereas Internet communication in most cases is considered to be a telecommunication service. The providers of such communication services make use of the TCP/IP protocol. An Internet user or the provider of a website is not a provider of such telecommunication services, because the traffic from and to the users of his site is not controlled by him (routed) but by the whole of service providers by means of the Internet protocol.

A part of the provisions of the Directive also extend to analogue systems if such features can be implemented technically and at reasonable costs (Article 3(2) and 3(3)). Since analogue systems will be hard to find nowadays, I do not discuss these paragraphs. From the Directive and its recitals is clear that mainly traditional telecommunication services were envisaged. The intended amendment proposal to the Directive therefore is more important than the Directive itself, but for a good understanding a brief overview of the provisions should be given.

### 6.3.3    Relation to Directive 95/46/EC

The interrelation with the mother directive 95/46/EC is worked out further in Article 14. Article 14(2) states, similar to Article 13 (1) of the mother convention, that Member States may, by law, restrict the scope of obligations and rights of the Directive if necessary for national security, national defence, public order, the fighting of crimes, etc. A very important addition has been made: in case of unauthorised use of the telecommunication system. Under Article 6 (see below) I will come back to that addition. Article 14(2) is applicable only to those Articles that may have an impact on the (public) interests specified, viz. Article 6 and 8. Article 14(2) includes Chapter III of Directive 95/46/EC on remedies, liability and sanctions, Article 14(3) gives the Article 29 Working Party the authority to give advice, and the updating of the Annex (see hereafter under Article 6) is attributed to the European Commission and the committee under Article 30 of the mother directive.

### 6.3.4 The obligations under Directive 97/66/EC

Article 4(1) requires appropriate security measures for the communications services to be applied by the provider of such services. Security is used here in the sense that not only the operation of the service is ensured but also that measures must be taken to protect the confidentiality of the communications. A similar rule can be found since long in the ITU-Convention and Article 17 of Directive 95/46/EC, with the state of the art, appropriate level of security risks and costs of the measures may be taken into account. Recital 15 adds that the security measures taken under directive 97/66/EC should be evaluated on the basis of the same criteria as applied in Article 17 of directive 95/46/EC. Moreover, the measures are obviously not intended to be only technical and organisational. According to recital 16, the implementing Member State apparently is expected – not obliged – to take other measure as well, like the criminalisation of unauthorised access to (non-public) communications. In relation thereto recital 16 notes that some Member States have only criminalised the intentional unauthorised access. In this respect the coming Cyber Crime Convention will assist the European Commission.[19]

Article 4(2) obliges the service provider, if a particular risk for the security of the telecommunications network occurs, to inform subscribers about such risks and about possible remedies, including the relating costs. In the recitals nothing specific can be found about this obligation. Article 4(2) only has meaning if particular security risks occur which the service provider has not foreseen and against which, within the limits of Article 4(1) he was not obliged to take effective measures. One could question whether the provider in practice will be in the circumstances to give the information as required by the Article. With regard to Internet providers the question can be raised what their obligation towards their subscribers would be, in case malicious viruses or worms have been launched[20] or in case of denial of service attacks against certain websites? Or, in case of systematic hacker activities against the systems of such providers? In my opinion, there is a difference between the content of a communication and the communication itself. Internet service providers

---

[19] The Treaty will oblige parties to criminalise unauthorised access to computer systems and networks, and unauthorised interception of electronic communications (Article 3). See Final activity report <http://conventions.coe.int>.

[20] Such as in July 2001 the 'red worm' that was feared to slow down Internet traffic considerably or even block it.

are in principle not liable for the content of the transmissions they carry out – provided the conditions as stipulated in Articles 12-15 of the e-commerce directive are met[21] – but there is a difference when such content jeopardises the security of the underlying communication services. Under Article 4 Internet service providers would have no obligation in case of massive attacks by means of viruses like 'I love you' but would be obliged to inform their subscribers in case of the red worm virus and also in case of specific hacker activities. This discrepancy is hard to understand. Apart from the content of Article 4, would it not be a matter of due care that service providers inform their subscribers about certain concrete security risks and incidents?

Article 5 deals with the confidentiality of what is called 'calls' by means of telecommunication services over public communication networks. In Article 5 the right of Article 8 ECHM – 'freedom of correspondence' – has been worked out for telecommunications. Most Member States will make no difference between traditional telephony and communication over electronic network and offer the same protection. For those states who do not, Article 5 is a welcome supplementation.

Traffic data relating to both subscribers and users must immediately after the termination of the communication be erased. A part of this traffic data may be needed for billing purposes. Article 6(2) authorises the use of such data, which is specified in an Annex. Would this be necessary due to technical developments, Annexes can be amended in a more flexible way than the text of the Directive itself (recital 27). The maximum period of preservation is not specified, but should not exceed the maximum term during which subscribers may challenge the bill. This term is not specified in the Directive, but will be specified in service provider's general terms and conditions. Article 6(3) entitles a service provider to process the data referred to in paragraph 2 for marketing purposes, but only if the subscriber has given his consent. This is in line with Article 10 of the mother directive. Consent should be explained here in the sense of Article 2(d) of the mother directive, i.e. freely given and informed. The marketing is restricted to the telecommunication services of the provider in question. If he would like to sell a copy of the (elaborated) traffic data to another party. Article 14 of the mother directive applies, including the right of the subscriber to object.

Article 6(4) says that traffic data may be processed only by employees with specific tasks: billing or traffic management, customer inquiries, fraud detection and (internal) marketing, as far as necessary for the purposes of their tasks. This is a very specific partly translation of Article 17 about security of processing in the mother directive. Moreover, the service provider should apply Article 17 to the very processing of traffic and billing data as well.

Costumer enquiries and fraud detection are mentioned in Article 6(4) where they are not in the preceding paragraphs of the Article. Obviously, that processing of traffic and billing data is considered to fall within the scope of the purpose for which it was

---

[21] See section 4.6.

collected. Traffic data may, however, not be kept for those purposes longer than the final term defined by Article 6(2). In relation thereto, I could imagine that service providers have a need to collect traffic data in particular cases such as misuse of the telecommunications system in order to protect their own interests and those of their subscribers, which is broader than fraud alone. Investigations to e.g. electronic stalking and frequent anonymous calls would fall outside the scope of Article 6. To that purpose Article 13(1) enables Member States to allow by law the processing of traffic data for such investigations. Article 13 uses the term 'unauthorised use' which may be narrower than misuse as presented above. Anyway, it is left to the Member State to determine what constitutes unauthorised use of the telecommunications system, which is to regret from a point of harmonisation.

In case of court or other proceedings traffic data or billing data may be used as evidence. Article 6(5) allows to preserve and hand data over to the competent authorities, also if the period of time following from paragraph 2 has expired. Of course, the relevant data must have been kept, otherwise there is nothing left to hand over.

Article 7 refers to itemised billing and thereby to traditional telecom operators only. Behind the Article is the debate how specified a bill must be, given the legitimate privacy interests of users. The general drift here is that a bill should not reveal more information of the user than necessary for the purpose of the bill. In some cases, where there is a special relationship between the subscriber and the user, even less information should be given. The Article shows that it is hardly possible to provide a common and adequate solution at a detailed level. Therefore, it is left to the Member States to prescribe by law the system or alternative systems they prefer. Article 7 has little significance for those service providers that apply a flat rate of subscription, e.g. cable operators and Internet providers.

Article 8 and Article 9 concern the feature of calling line identification or CLI. This facility refers also rather to traditional telecommunications. Part of a communication are data about its source. Article 8 regulates to what extend and under which circumstances the data should be made available to the receiver of a call and to what extend a sender must have the possibility to suppress such data. This Article is only applicable for those service providers who offer CLI to their subscribers. On the Internet the TCP/IP protocol passes e-mail addresses and URL's to the recipient of a communication. If one would like to conceal those data, one should make use of anonymous remailers or encryption services. CLI in e-commerce applications seems to have little use, so I will leave the Articles, and Article 10 on automatic call forwarding systems for what they are.

Article 11 regulates the content of subscriber directories, in paper as well as in electronic format. The Article takes as a starting point that no more information about a subscriber should be given than necessary to identify him, i.e. necessary for a communication. Other information can only be given with consent of the subscriber (unambiguous!). A subscriber can demand to be not included in a directory. In principle there should be no costs involved.

Article 11(2), nevertheless, allows to charge the subscriber. If a subscriber so wishes his personal data may not be used for direct marketing purposes. The latter reflects the general rule in the mother directive under Article 14. Since directive 97/66/EC includes also legal persons in the circle of subscribers, the question should also taken into account how far the rule of Article 11 applies to information about legal persons as well.

Opposite to the detailed rule of the previous paragraph, Article 11(3) does not get any further than imposing a very open obligation to the Member States to sufficiently protect the legitimate interests of legal persons in this respect. Other service providers than traditional telecom operators will generally not publish directories of their subscribers, or directories of e-mail addresses. Many of such directories came into place with voluntary cooperation of the persons concerned. In other cases, search engines collect e-mail addresses on the Web. Since Article 11 is only applicable to service providers in relation with their subscribers, the lawfulness of building e-mail directories without express consent of the person concerned should be judged on the basis of the mother directive. The justification for the building and making available of such a directory by others than the accountable service providers may be found in Article 7(e): a task carried out in the public interest, regardless possible legal impediments which would come from intellectual property rights, including rights on databanks. If the controller of a subscriber file or his equipment are located outside the territory of the Union, the privacy interests of the data subject may not be protected in a similar way.

Article 12 deals with unsolicited *calls*. A call is not defined in the Directive, but Article 12(1) indicates that a call should be interpreted as a communication over a (traditional) telecommunications network. The means by which the calls in question are undertaken are also related to such telecommunication systems, as automatic calling machines or fax machines. Subscribers must have given prior consent. See also the parallel provision on such technical tools in Article 9-10 of the Distance selling directive (see section 2.8).

Article 12(2) allows other calls for direct marketing purposes only if subscribers gave their prior consent thereto (opt-in) or if subscribers were given the opportunity to express their wish not to receive such calls (opt-out). The Article embodies the principle that the unsolicited calls affect the privacy of a subscriber. It is obvious that an opt-in system would be more privacy-friendly than an opt-out system. An opt-in system has serious disadvantages from a point of costs and organisation for direct marketeers. Article 12(3) refers to subscribers that are legal persons in the same way as in Article 11.

Article 13 deals with technical features and standards of equipment, and Article 15 sets the term of implementation on October 24, 1998 and gives some rules of transition.

## 6.4 Proposal for amendment of Directive 97/66/EC

### 6.4.1 History and background of the proposal

Under the title 'Electronic communications: processing of personal data, protection of privacy' the European Commission launched a proposal to amend directive 97/66/EC on July 12, 2000.[22] The Telecommunication Council reached agreement on the text in its meeting of June 2001,[23] except on the point of unsolicited (e)mail. The decision of the Council was to study the proposals of the European Parliament on this issue first.[24] The remaining text therefore seems rather final.

The purpose of the proposal is to replace directive 97/66//EC by the amended text. The intended changes are not major. The original structure of 97/66/EC is maintained. Technological developments, not foreseen at the time of the enactment of 97/66/EC, are addressed. The proposal is a consequence of the 1999 Review of the regulatory framework for electronic communications, which aims at technology neutral regulation for any communication service. This implies that also consumers and users should profit from the same protection, regardless the technology of the communication service. The draft proposal thereto comes up with a number of new definitions showing the convergence between traditional telecommunication networks and Internet, including the communication services rendered by means of it.

### 6.4.2 New definitions

The present definitions under Article 2(c) and (d) of telecommunications services and networks, will be replaced by the broader terms electronic communications services and networks. The definitions are no longer part of Article 2 but are included by a dynamic reference to the new Framework directive.[25] By this the circle of service providers is expanded to Internet providers as well, as long as they in their service supply meet the routing criterion in the definition of the service provider. Recital 5 explicitly refers to the Internet. In this way, the Directive applies to all communication service providers irrespective the technological means by which they offer such services. It should, however, be borne in mind that technological differences may cause that not all Articles apply to all service providers, or not in the same way. This is not a problem as long this does not cause loopholes in the system of privacy protection.

Some new definitions were added. Article 2 now consists of the following definitions: a) user (text unchanged); b) traffic data: data processed in the course of

---

[22] *OJ* C 365, 19.12.2000.

[23] Results of the Telecommunications Council of 27 June 2001, Memo/01/247.

[24] The tabled proposal was sent back in the session of September 6, 2001. Discussions continue.

[25] COM (1999) 539.

or for the purpose of the transmission of a communication; d) communication: the exchange or transmission of information by means of a publicly available electronic communication service between a finite number of parties (this is supposed to exclude broadcasting, if finite indeed may be interpreted as restricted); e) call: establishing a connection by means of a publicly available telephone service allowing two-way communication in real-time. The latter definition excludes e-mail communications as not being two way in real time, but on the other hand includes chat and chat box activities. In addition, c) defines location data as data indicating the geographic position of the terminal equipment of a user of a publicly available communication service. Location data occur in mobile terrestrial and satellite telecommunication systems.

### 6.4.3    New important elements in the Directive

Article 4 and 5 (security and confidentiality of communications) had only minor editorial changes. The relating recital 13 is more balanced now and suggest that service providers should inform subscribers about risks which are beyond the control of the service provider. In addition, service providers are now obliged to inform subscribers about particular software and encryption technology in order to protect their communications. The Directive does require that certain technical measures are applied by the service provider or put by him at the disposal of the subscriber. For instance, Internet providers must do more in preventing the propagation of computer viruses than informing the victims of what they could do or – usually – could have done.

Article 6 was subject to some editorial changes and the wording 'calls' was replaced by 'communication' and 'transmission' without changing the meaning of the Article. Article 6(2) is redrafted and the reference to the Annex is deleted; since there is a new functional definition of traffic data, a specification can be missed. Article 6(3) is extended in the sense that the processing of traffic data for the provision of value added services is allowed too, as long as necessary for such services and if the subscriber has given his consent. A new paragraph is inserted under number 4 (and the remaining paragraphs are renumbered) imposing a duty on service providers to inform subscribers what type of traffic data are processed for the purposes under the previous paragraphs, i.e. for billing, interconnection, direct marketing, and value added services.

A wholly new Article 9 (the remaining Articles are renumbered) is dedicated to location data. Location data are given here as 'location data other than traffic data'. This rather strange expression should make a difference between location data during a communication – which are usually part of the communication and as such are traffic data– and location data which are registered in the telecommunication central in order to be able to forward a call to standby equipment in the indicated geographical zone (see also recital 17). Location data may not be processed (I would say: further processed) unless rendered anonymous or if necessary for the offering of a value added service; only with consent of the subscriber or user and for the period of the service only. The duty upon the service provider to inform subscriber and user is similar to the new Article 6(4). In addition, the user or subscriber must be offered the opportunity to withdraw his consent.

Location data have no meaning in the traditional Internet-environment but may become more significant if mobile equipment is used with WAP-technology or with the future UTMS. Notwithstanding, traffic data, including location data, are under control of the intermediate communication service provider and cannot be disseminated to communicating parties without consent of the party concerned.

Article 12 (the former Article 11) on directories of subscribers received some editorial changes. Recital 20 points out that the general data protection principles should also be applied in the sense that subscribers have a right of correction and should be informed of the purpose of the file, also regarding unsuspected possibilities offered by search functions which may reveal more information about the subscriber than he had reasons to assume.

The unsolicited calls of Article 12 become unsolicited communications in Article 13. Electronic mail is added as a specific means for unsolicited communications. For the rest the text is unchanged awaiting the debate in the European Parliament about a possible preference for a opt-in or opt-out regime. The relating recital 22 states that the rate of privacy protection should not depend on the technological environment. This may lead to the establishment of technical standards for terminal equipment. Such equipment may pass certain personal data to other communicating parties, of which the sender is not aware or has no control over.[26]

The changes in the remaining Articles are minor. Some transitional arrangements have been added in Article 16 and 17.

### 6.4.4 Conclusion

The text of the directive and its recitals has been improved and made more precise. The inclusion of Internet as a communication network and related communication services was inevitable, although not all the provisions apply to Internet service providers. The broadening to communication networks and communication services reflects the need to think in technology neutral terms. A number of the Articles in the Directive still refer to typical technical features and services in the traditional telecommunication domain. The obligations towards legal persons as subscriber remains vague. Important questions related to directive 97/66/EC have not been

---

[26] A legal basis for such standards will be provided by Directive 99/5/EC of March 9, 1999 on Radio Equipment and Telecommunications Terminal Equipment and the Mutual Recognition of their Conformity.

solved yet, such as with regard to unsolicited communications. The principle that traffic data must be deleted after the communication took place may incite Member States to introduce by law an opposite system of mandatory retention for the purposes of criminal law and other public interests.

## 6.5    Some specific aspects of data protection in e-commerce

### 6.5.1    Particular Privacy risks in e-commerce

E-commerce may involve the intended and not intended exchange of information which falls in the terms of personal data as defined by Directive 95/46/EC or within the scope of Directive 97/66/EC. For an extensive analysis of all the possible privacy-related risks for online communications, the Working Document of the Article 29 Data Protection Working Party[27] provides a good insight in the technical context of the Internet for the layman and a complete overview of all privacy related issues.

Marketing e-commerce parties are interested to know as much about their customers as they can. Apart from gathering such information by means of other sources, the online contact technically allows to compose what is called online customer profiles. These profiles are a product of any information e-commerce parties obtain, i.e. from direct input by customers, from agreed transactions, and by means of technical facilities such as *cookies*.[28] On the basis of such profiles and by means of invisible *hyper links* commercial *banners* that may be of interest of the user are accessed.[29]

Of course, there is a realistic possibility that those data are not collected and further processed in accordance with data protection rules. Moreover, because of the global nature of modern communication networks, it may even happen that in the country where such data are being processed no data protection rules exist at all. This can be the case in the online world as well as in the offline world, be it that the electronic environment makes it very easy to collect and process personal data and also makes a connection between worlds ruled by different legal systems. It is therefore imperative that at least at the European level a single legal system of privacy protection is established and a broader application than Europe alone is striven for.

In this section a number of specific privacy sensitive issues are discussed related to the fact that third parties are involved in providing communication services which enable to do e-commerce. I have chosen to discuss the topics traffic data (6.5.2), cookies (6.5.3), e-mail directories (6.5.4), unsolicited e-mail (6.5.5) and e-mail

---

[27]   Privacy on the Internet- An integrated EU Approach to On-line Data Protection, November 21, 2000, 5063/00/EN/FINAL WP 37, hereafter referred to as WP 37.

[28]   See about how to obtain user profiles e.g. Peter Scholar, 'Persönlichkeitsprofile im Internet', *Datenschutz und Datensicherheit*, 25 (2001) 7, 383-388 (384-385).

[29]   WP 37, 18.

systems (6.5.6). Section 6.5.7. concludes with some observations about the legal impact of technical measures to protect one privacy: anonymity and pseudonymity.

## 6.5.2    Traffic data

E-commerce transactions may leave a number of electronic traces, by which information can be obtained about the consumer/user. The communication phase is a vulnerable one, in particular because the communications have to be trusted to third parties, such as telecom network and telecom service providers. Their systems systematically collect data about the communications that passed through such systems. In addition to constitutional rights that protect the confidentiality of written correspondence and telecommunications, like Article 8 ECHR does, Directive 97/66/EC restricts the purposes for which and the period of time during which such traffic data legally can be preserved. Since traffic data may be important material for law enforcement and secret services there is a counter movement in the direction of mandatory retention of traffic data. In the draft Cyber Crime Convention[30] mandatory retention of traffic data has been considered but not adopted. Article 20 allows law enforcement authorities to order telecom operators and Internet service providers to collect traffic data relating to specific communications for a certain period in the future. Article 18 provides for the legal power to submit certain traffic data that were registered in the past. If an order based upon Article 18 would be issued shortly after the communication took place, the relating traffic data in most cases will still be available. In the sense of the convention are only considered those data registered by the computer system that were part of the chain of communication, by which the origin, destination and route can be determined, and which provide information about time, data, size, duration of the communication service. Other data that may be stored are not included in the definition.

By opting for a system of traffic data 'as is' criminal investigations may sometimes have to apply other means to gather evidence – if possible – , in particular when there is a considerable lapse of time between the moment of the crime and the relating investigation. Mandatory retention of traffic data for a certain period may help in this respect, but involves serious disadvantages. The first one, of course, concerns the protection of private life of the communicating parties, e.g. Article 6 and 14 of Directive 97/66/EC. If a system of mandatory retention was to be applied, say for a period of 6 month or one year, telecom operators and Internet service providers would have to collect, store, retrieve and up-date high numbers of gigabytes. This huge collection of privacy sensitive data should be secured against illegal access or other abuse. If such a file existed it could also be object of individual requests for information. For providers the maintenance of such data collections would involve substantial costs, for which they probably will not receive (full) compensation. The second argument against mandatory retention, of course, is the high privacy risk for

---

[30]   Draft included in final activity report of June 29, 2001, see
<http://conventions.coe.int/Treaty/EN/projects/FinalCybercrime.htm>.

the persons concerned, such as becoming involved in a criminal investigation – whether justified or not – and the risk that others may obtain information about of communications between individuals.

The Cyber Crime Convention reflects a minimum basis. As in any international treaty Parties may go beyond what is agreed. *In concreto*, this means that a Party to the Cyber Crime Convention may apply a system of mandatory retention, but cannot demand that other Parties apply the same system. A Party cannot refuse international cooperation solely on the ground that other Parties are not able to execute a request for dissemination of traffic data.

In individual cases telecom operators and Internet service providers may have a need to collect and store traffic data in order to protect the well-functioning of their system and in order to prevent misuse. This covers a broad range of conduct, e.g. where subscribers harass other subscribers by means of frequent anonymous calls or where subscribers try to hack into the telephone switches or Internet provider systems. Directive 97/66/EC actually does not provide the legal basis for the collection of such traffic data, but Article 9(f) Directive 95/46/EC does, provided that the necessity requirement is fulfilled, and that the interest of the provider is indeed overriding. This means that the measure under all circumstances has to pass the proportionality test. Systematic collection and preservation of any traffic data would not meet the criteria of Article 9 and would, therefore, be unlawful. In the frame of the draft revision of directive 97/66/EC the discussion about mandatory retention has not lead to a different system.

### 6.5.3    Cookies

E-commerce parties may use cookies to collect personal data from the data subject himself or from other persons. Cookies are small pieces of information, automatically stored in the computer of a user (or sometimes remote) to smoothen further access to a particular web-site. When a user sends out a request for information to be obtained from a particular website, the web server where the website is hosted is addressed. In sending back the requested information to the user, a cookie may be included and stored in the user's computer system. Cookies may contain personalised information in relation to the web-site that was visited, such as login codes, pass words, credit card numbers or a list of shopping items. Web servers may look for the presence of relevant cookies in the user's system and use the information to personalise the next access. Web servers may also look for cookies which were not generated by this particular Web server but by other Web servers. They may use this information, e.g. by including banners with advertisements within the preference of the individual user.

The storage of cookies happens unnoticed and cannot be prevented by the user unless by making some efforts. With some browsers cookie-files can be defined as read only and reduced to zero bytes, but this may be only a temporal solution until the cookie-makers find out how to circumvent this.[31] Some Web browsers allow to refuse the instalment of any cookie, but this will cause that some Web-sites cannot be accessed anymore. A possible option is to give separate permission for the instalment thereof each time again. Not accepting cookies will reduce the facilities of user's system and the possibilities to communicate. The cookie file can be opened for inspection, and cookies can be deleted from this file. However, if the concerning website is visited once more a new cookie will be stored in the user's computer system.[32]

The use of cookies may infringe upon the right of privacy. A cookie collects and passes information about a user to the website owner. Whether this information has to be considered as personal data depends on the circumstances. For instance, a single IP-address will not enable the website owner to identify the individual person behind it without the help of a third person (the ISP), but additional data may enable identification and therefore have to be considered as personal data and have to be processed in a fair and lawful manner. In particular where the user is not aware of the use of cookies has to be considered as problematic in the light of data protection rules. Personal data may be collected lawfully from the user under the conditions as described in Article 7 of Directive 95/46/EC. The user must have given his consent unambiguously. Some persons would argue that a user should be aware of the options and features of the browser he applies, and therefore should be aware of the fact that cookies are installed as part of the communication process. Others would construct consent from the fact that the user has the possibility to remove installed cookies from his system and refrains from doing so. Anyway, the burden of proof that the user consented in the installation and use of a cookie is on the website owner. In my opinion, the examples do not represent an unambiguous consent as required by Article 7(a) of Directive 95/46/EC since most users are not aware of technical details of the software they apply. From a privacy point of view the transparency – or better the lack of transparency – of the cookies mechanism is problematic. Cookies may be part of accepted business practices, but this does not necessarily lead to the conclusion that the average user is or should be aware of it and has accepted it. Therefore, in my opinion, more information should be given about the meaning and use of cookies in general and *in concreto* when they are applied in practise. It seems just a matter of due care that the user is asked for permission to store a cookie in his system before it is stored or inform the user how to delete it afterwards. This is not a very complicated feature to realise in the communication protocols or browser programs.[33]

---

[31] The dark side of cookies, <http://www.cookiecentral.com/content.phtml?area=2&id=2>.

[32] The cookie concept, <http://www.cookiecentral.com>.

[33] The Article 29 Working Party proposes such measures because of 'invisible' processing of personal data (Recommendation 1/99 on Invisible and Automatic Processing of Personal Data on the Internet Performed by Software and Hardware, WP 17 (5093/98), see also Fourth Annual Report, 5019/01/EN WP 46, adopted May 17, 2001, p. 22).

Application of criminal law will not lead to a different conclusion. The storage of the cookie in the system of the user can be seen as illegal access and as a consecutive illegal alteration of data.[34] The modalities of the cookie-technique allow to subsume these acts under the mentioned criminal provisions. There is intent of the website-owner, since he applies the technique for further use. If the acts have been committed illegally depends on whether the user gave permission, directly or indirectly, and how this circumstance is appreciated under domestic law. The mere fact that a computer can be accessed and that data therein can be altered will not be considered as authorised access or alteration. It is, therefore, not unlikely that the presence of such authorisation will be judged differently under criminal law and the Data protection directive.

### 6.5.4    E-mail directories

E-mail addresses are personal data in the sense of the privacy Directives. Internet Service Providers (ISPs) will keep records of their subscribers and provide the user with an e-mail address. Other than with telephone directories, e-mail addresses are not published. The publishing of telephone directories often is an obligation under the national Telecommunications Act, and a remainder of public interest policies in the field of telecommunication. The collection and further processing of such an e-mail directory may not be necessary for a certain purpose (Article 6(1)(b) of the mother directive), or there is a right to opt-out according to Article 11 of Directive 97/66/EC. In particular the latter provision could prevent the publishing of such a list, because the regular e-mail-user seems to prefer not to have his name and address included in such directories. Nevertheless, some organisations manage to collect e-mail addresses by technical surreptitious means, by search activities on the net or even by completely illegal means.[35] The lawfulness of such activities should be judged on the basis of the mother directive. For instance, the application of illegal or surreptitious means for the collection of such personal data is a direct violation of Article 3(1)(a) that states that the processing (that means also the collection) must be fair and lawful. The current discussions on opt-in or opt-out concerning commercial communications in Article 13 of the proposal for amendment of 97/66/EC may lead to the adoption of a similar system for e-mail directories, e.g. also an *opt-out* system.[36]

### 6.5.5    Spam (unsolicited communications)

Under the rather colloquial terms *spam* – which literally means canned pork – and *spamming* has to be understood unsolicited commercial messages or e-mails (UCE), respectively the practice of sending such communications. UCE or *junk-mail* can be

---

[34]  See e.g. Draft Cyber Crime Convention, Article 2 and 4. Both Articles are already implemented in most domestic criminal codes.

[35]  See for a number of examples: WP 37, 32.

[36]  WP 37, 40.

sent to individual Internet users or to news groups. If done in large quantities it is not only a nuisance for the recipients, but it may lead to serious blocking of communication facilities. The latter aspects are not envisaged here. The sending of unsolicited e-mail is in the literature considered as a violation of the recipients right of privacy, in this respect literally the right to be let alone. The respect for privacy is a fundamental right. Others stress the need of consumers to be informed about available products and sales offers. The right to gather information is also a fundamental right. Businesses and direct marketing organisations have a strong interest in sending commercial communications to the broadest possible circle of potential buyers. These conflicting interests cannot be easily reconciled. Some recipients would like not to receive UCE, where others would regret if they did not receive such information.

In the frame of the proposal to amend Directive 97/66/EC there are two options, known as *opt-in* and *opt-out*. Opt-in means that recipients will not receive UCE, unless they have given their express consent. Opt-out stands for the systems where recipients must be given the opportunity to indicate that they have no preference for further UCE from the same sender. Such systems will require the maintenance of central registers which will have to be consulted before UCE is sent out. Both systems have their advantages and disadvantages as well. Direct marketeers prefer opt-out systems, because the broadest possible number of persons can be reached and registering only persons who opt-out is not too costly. Those costs can be further kept under control by allowing a registration for only a limited period of time, e.g. one year. In both systems the weak point is the enforcement of the rules and possible sanctions for violations, in particular because of the international component. Further, consumers as well as direct marketeers may have more flexible needs which cannot be completely served by either a fully regulated opt-in or opt-out system. Any regulation, therefore, should be supplemented by self-regulation of enterprises and consumer parties involved.

The debate has not yet been finished. The Telecommunication Council, in its meeting in Luxembourg in June 2001, did not take a decision, but left it to the European Parliament to come up with a concrete proposal. The Parliament itself looked at a proposal for regulation of *opt-in* but sent it back to the drafters as inadequate. Given the argumentation above, my feeling is that the European Parliament eventually will choose for an *opt-out* system. However, the modalities of such regulation will determine its value for all parties concerned.

Rules on specific unsolicited commercial communications can be found in the Distance selling directive (see section 2.8) and in the e-commerce directive (see section 4.4.2). It is recommendable to come up with a general system for such communications, independent from the technology used and from the parties involved. Therefore, the proposal for amendment of directive 97/66/EC in my opinion should also amend the other Directives with regard to unsolicited commercial communications and should regulate not only electronic communications but also paper distribution.

### 6.5.6    E-mail systems

E-mail is a hybrid form of communication. Like the traditional mail it has two different aspects: the communication process and the object of the message which has an independent meaning. Protection of e-mail communication may be subsumed under Article 8 ECHR but nevertheless a number of questions are not solved yet. As far as the communication process is concerned most European Member States will grant protection under their constitution. However, the legal status of e-mail messages not engaged in such a process, e.g. stored in a mailbox, is uncertain and may depend on relating case law. The legal status of e-mail systems within an organisation is even more unclear.

The Directive 95/46/EC does in principle not apply to the mere transmission of personal data. Recital 47 states that the sender of the message is the controller of the personal data contained in the message. The service provider as such is not. He is the controller of additional personal data, such as traffic data, for which the rules of Directive 97/66/EC apply. Of course, the recipient of an e-mail message has to be considered as a controller for the personal data contained in it.

A different situation is at stake within an organisation. The employer determines the equipment and the purpose of the e-mail system and therefore has to be considered as the controller of the e-mail system, including the personal data that is being handled by it. Most obligations under the Directives will apply to the employer/controller. However, no criteria are given to delineate the private sphere of an employee and his right of confidentiality in relation to the employer/controller.

### 6.5.7    Remedies: Anonymity/pseudonymity?

Concerning the Internet, the debate in legal and other circles today is about a right of anonymity, i.e. the right to communicate or the right to engage oneself to legal agreements without revealing one's identity towards other parties. Closely related to anonymity is pseudonymity, the right to act under a self-chosen identity. From the position of the Internet user, the advantages of anonymity or pseudonymity are clear. Electronic traces of the activities of this user will loose interest for other persons if the real identity of the user involved cannot be found. This will directly serve the privacy needs of the users who will not be exposed to the (professional) curiosity of those parties that collect personal information for commercial or for other reasons. Anonymity/pseudonymity leaves it to the user to decide if he wants to reveal his identity or other personal data, if such would be necessary for the communication or for the execution of the agreement. A delivery order would make little sense without a delivery address. The wordings 'necessary' are very much in place here, since this term occurs frequently in Directive 95/46/EC in order to express that any processing of personal data must be necessary for the purposes of the controller in the first place. In the context of anonymity/pseudonymity it should be established whether it is really necessary to know the identity of a user in order to have a communication, to enter into a contract or to handle its relating transactions. Under the term 'Privacy Enhancing Technologies' (PET) all kind of technical instruments have been developed, which can be applied by Internet users to participate in communications anonymously and to carry out electronic payments anonymously, without the possibility to establish the real identity of the user involved. Further, in Article 17 of Directive 95/46/EC the incentive could be found for the making available of such technologies by controllers of personal data, in particular to prevent that others are able to collect the personal data that necessarily have to be exchanged in the relation between the data subject and the controller.[37]

The other side of the coin is that users may misuse their anonymity in order to evade the consequences of their conduct, e.g. by breaching a contract or by committing a crime, or that circumstances demand that the real identity of a user is known, e.g. in cases of state security or other overriding societal interests. If a right to anonymity/pseudonymity would be recognised, it would be necessary to recognise, at the same time, the interests and situations for which this right wholly or partly may be set aside. In the USA, where the first amendment guarantees free speech, the use of anonymity/pseudonymity may be an important condition for the freedom of speech and should therefore be restricted as little as possible. According to Reno v. ACLU constitutional standards for printed media should at least as an initial matter be applied to the electronic environment as well.[38] This does not necessarily lead to completely identical standards given the occurrence of different circumstances.[39] In a recent decision, a US court nevertheless formulated a number of conditions under which an Internet service provider by means of a subpoena could be forced to reveal the identity of persons who had posted messages in a newsgroup.[40] Those conditions come down to that the information sought is needed to serve a legitimate interest of some importance and that the information cannot be obtained otherwise. Courts in other countries may raise similar conditions, but the US thresholds are probably higher because of the overriding right of freedom of speech. For other jurisdictions, such conditions may also follow from principles of fair trial or procedure.

Therefore, a general and generic right to anonymity does not yet exist. In the off-line world, most countries oblige their citizens to carry means of identification.[41] The law recognises certain rights in particular circumstances which could be indicated as examples of such a right. For example, the right of a defendant to remain silent, the

---

[37] H. van Rossem, *et al. Privacy Enhancing Technologies; the path to Ano*, The Hague 1995, second edition R. Hes *et al.*, Idem, The Hague 1998.

[38] Reno v ACLU, 117 S.Ct 2329 (1997).

[39] See e.g. A. Michael Froomkin, 'Legal Issues in Anonymity and Pseudonymity', *The Information Society*, 15: 113-127.

[40] Doe v 2THEMART.Com Inc., No. C01 453Z (W.D. Wash., 27 april 2001), see comment *Computer Law & Security report* Vol. 17 no. 4 2001,279-280.

[41] My country does not know a general duty of identification. Only in specific circumstances a citizen is under the obligation to identify himself.

right of journalists to conceal their source, a new right for persons who act as whistleblowers to remain anonymous when they reveal scandals within an organisation[42] and many more examples can be given. These examples have too little in common to form the basis for a general right of anonymity. The establishment of such a general right would lead to a very broad scala of exemptions and relating conditions. Regulating anonymity for the electronic environment only would be against the legislative trend not to exempt the electronic environment from any applicable rule as embodied in present law.

In the mean time it would be useful to know how anonymity/pseudonymity would work in practise between parties. A German pilot project on on-line shopping, started in 1998, demonstrated that anonymity/pseudonymity does not intervene with legal security concerning deliveries and payments if appropriate measures are taken. The final evaluation, in particular whether such a system should be recommended, is still to come.[43]

## 6.6    Concluding observations

The regular data protection rules, as laid down in Directive 95/46/EC, apply to e-commerce activities to the same extend as they apply to such activities in off-line situations. The Directive formulates obligations for the controllers of the processing of personal data and provides the data subjects with certain rights of control. The processing of personal data is only lawful if necessary for a pre-defined purpose and should be balanced against the right of respect for privacy of the data subject, except in particular circumstances. The controller is obliged to keep the personal data up to date and relevant for the purpose of the processing. The data subject has a right to know what data are kept about him and should be informed actively in a number of cases. The data subject further has a right to request correction of the personal data relating to him and to object against the processing of personal data for purposes of direct marketing. There may be some coincidence of privacy rules of the mother directive and other Directives in the field of e-commerce. The privacy rules in other directives, like the e-commerce directive, do not derogate to the rules of the mother directive unless it concerns specific rules further elaborating the mother directive.

Directive 97/66/EC concerns – or better: will concern soon – the service providers of public communications services. For e-commerce its meaning is in specific provisions on traffic data, e-mail-directories and unsolicited e-mail. The precise regulation of unsolicited mail will be decided on in the last month of 2001. Anyway, the outcome will have to match with the mother directive on the processing of personal data for direct marketing, with the distance selling directive concerning the

---

[42]   Raising concerns about serious wrongdoings, European Commission, SEC 2000
[43]   Datenschutzberater 9/2001, 6 (<http://www.dasit.myshop.de>).

means for commercial communication, and with the e-commerce directive on unsolicited mail.

E-commerce may involve particular risks for the privacy of consumers. Firstly, legal protection or remedies against the intrusion of privacy have to be found in the given Directives and their consecutive implementations in national law. It seems that the discussed Directives provide adequate standards for the protection of the privacy of consumers and other parties in e-commerce. However, it should be borne in mind that the enforcement of data protection rules is left to the data subject and not to a public authority. Data subjects may not always be aware of what is happening with their personal data. Therefore, it is understandable that in new data protection instruments the emphasis is more on mechanism to enhance the transparency of data processing which may lead to a better enforcement of data protection rules. In addition, self-regulation in the form of Codes of Conduct, enacted by the parties involved, can and will lead to a higher level of protection.

A second flaw is the international component. Data protection rules may differ or not exist in the other countries where an e-commerce party is settled and the EU data protection system may be circumvented. Some enterprises may even deliberately choose for an (electronic) settlement outside the EU to circumvent certain rules. From a point of privacy protection it is therefore important to take international initiatives to arrive at a global system for data protection or equivalent level of protection. The safe harbour arrangement with the USA shows that there is still a lot of work to do.

The consumer or user can restrict the risks for his privacy by applying certain technical measures. PET (privacy enhancing technologies) is a valuable contribution to the protection of personal data in e-commerce. In the mean time it raises questions about a possible right to be not identified in electronic communications.

# Appendix 1

**Directive 97/7/EC of the European Parliament and of the Council
of 20 May 1997
on the protection of consumers in respect of distance contracts**

THE EUROPEAN PARLIAMENT AND THE COUNCIL OF THE EUROPEAN UNION,

Having regard to the Treaty establishing the European Community, and in particular Article 100a thereof,

Having regard to the proposal from the Commission[1],

Having regard to the opinion of the Economic and Social Committee[2],

Acting in accordance with the procedure laid down in Article 189b of the Treaty[3] , in the light of the joint text approved by the Conciliation Committee on 27 November 1996,

(1) Whereas, in connection with the attainment of the aims of the internal market, measures must be taken for the gradual consolidation of that market;

(2) Whereas the free movement of goods and services affects not only the business sector but also private individuals; whereas it means that consumers should be able to have access to the goods and services of another Member State on the same terms as the population of that State;

(3) Whereas, for consumers, cross-border distance selling could be one of the main tangible results of the completion of the internal market, as noted, inter alia, in the communication from the Commission to the Council entitled 'Towards a single market in distribution`;

whereas it is essential to the smooth operation of the internal market for consumers to be able to have dealings with a business outside their country, even if it has a subsidiary in the consumer's country of residence;

(4) Whereas the introduction of new technologies is increasing the number of ways for consumers to obtain information about offers anywhere in the Community and to place orders; whereas some Member States have already taken different or diverging measures to protect consumers in respect of distance selling, which has had a detrimental effect on competition between businesses in the internal market; whereas it is therefore necessary to introduce at Community level a minimum set of common rules in this area;

(5) Whereas paragraphs 18 and 19 of the Annex to the Council resolution of 14 April 1975 on a preliminary programme of the European Economic Community for a consumer protection and information policy[4] point to the need to protect the purchasers of goods or services from demands for payment for unsolicited goods and from high-pressure selling methods;

(6) Whereas paragraph 33 of the communication from the Commission to the Council entitled 'A new impetus for consumer protection policy`, which was approved by the Council resolution of 23 June 1986[5], states that the Commission will submit proposals regarding the use of new information technologies enabling consumers to place orders with suppliers from their homes;

(7) Whereas the Council resolution of 9 November 1989 on future priorities for relaunching consumer protection policy[6] calls upon the

[1] OJ No C 156, 23.6.1992, p. 14 and OJ No C 308, 15.11.1993, p. 18.
[2] OJ No C 19, 25.1.1993, p. 111.
[3] Opinion of the European Parliament of 26 May 1993 (OJ No C 176, 28.6.1993, p. 95), Council common position of 29 June 1995 (OJ No C 288, 30.10.1995, p. 1) and Decision of the European Parliament of 13 December 1995 (OJ No C 17, 22.1.1996, p. 51). Decision of the European Parliament of 16 January 1997 and Council Decision of 20 January 1997.

[4] OJ No C 92, 25.4. 1975, p. 1.
[5] OJ No C 167, 5.7.1986, p. 1.
[6] OJ No C 294, 22.11.1989, p. 1.

A.R. Lodder and H.W.K. Kaspersen (eds.),
eDirectives: Guide to European Union Law on E-Commerce, 147–154.
© 2002 Kluwer Law International. Printed in the Netherlands.

Commission to give priority to the areas referred to in the Annex to that resolution; whereas that Annex refers to new technologies involving teleshopping; whereas the Commission has responded to that resolution by adopting a three-year action plan for consumer protection policy in the European Economic Community (1990-1992); whereas that plan provides for the adoption of a Directive;

(8) Whereas the languages used for distance contracts are a matter for the Member States;

(9) Whereas contracts negotiated at a distance involve the use of one or more means of distance communication; whereas the various means of communication are used as part of an organised distance sales or service-provision scheme not involving the simultaneous presence of the supplier and the consumer; whereas the constant development of those means of communication does not allow an exhaustive list to be compiled but does require principles to be defined which are valid even for those which are not as yet in widespread use;

(10) Whereas the same transaction comprising successive operations or a series of separate operations over a period of time may give rise to different legal descriptions depending on the law of the Member States; whereas the provisions of this Directive cannot be applied differently according to the law of the Member States, subject to their recourse to Article 14; whereas, to that end, there is therefore reason to consider that there must at least be compliance with the provisions of this Directive at the time of the first of a series of successive operations or the first of a series of separate operations over a period of time which may be considered as forming a whole, whether that operation or series of operations are the subject of a single contract or successive, separate contracts;

(11) Whereas the use of means of distance communication must not lead to a reduction in the information provided to the consumer; whereas the information that is required to be sent to the consumer should therefore be determined, whatever the means of communication used; whereas the information supplied must also comply with the other relevant Community rules, in particular those in Council Directive 84/450/EEC of 10 September 1984 relating to the approximation of the laws,

regulations and administrative provisions of the Member States concerning misleading advertising[7]; whereas, if exceptions are made to the obligation to provide information, it is up to the consumer, on a discretionary basis, to request certain basic information such as the identity of the supplier, the main characteristics of the goods or services and their price;

(12) Whereas in the case of communication by telephone it is appropriate that the consumer receive enough information at the beginning of the conversation to decide whether or not to continue;

(13) Whereas information disseminated by certain electronic technologies is often ephemeral in nature insofar as it is not received on a permanent medium; whereas the consumer must therefore receive written notice in good time of the information necessary for proper performance of the contract;

(14) Whereas the consumer is not able actually to see the product or ascertain the nature of the service provided before concluding the contract; whereas provision should be made, unless otherwise specified in this Directive, for a right of withdrawal from the contract; whereas, if this right is to be more than formal, the costs, if any, borne by the consumer when exercising the right of withdrawal must be limited to the direct costs for returning the goods; whereas this right of withdrawal shall be without prejudice to the consumer's rights under national laws, with particular regard to the receipt of damaged products and services or of products and services not corresponding to the description given in the offer of such products or services; whereas it is for the Member States to determine the other conditions and arrangements following exercise of the right of withdrawal;

(15) Whereas it is also necessary to prescribe a time limit for performance of the contract if this is not specified at the time of ordering;

(16) Whereas the promotional technique involving the dispatch of a product or the provision of a service to the consumer in return for payment without a prior request from, or the explicit agreement of, the consumer cannot be permitted, unless a substitute product or service

---

[7] OJ No L 250, 19.9.1984, p. 17.

is involved;

(17) Whereas the principles set out in Articles 8 and 10 of the European Convention for the Protection of Human Rights and Fundamental Freedoms of 4 November 1950 apply; whereas the consumer's right to privacy, particularly as regards freedom from certain particularly intrusive means of communication, should be recognised; whereas specific limits on the use of such means should therefore be stipulated; whereas Member States should take appropriate measures to protect effectively those consumers, who do not wish to be contacted through certain means of communication, against such contacts, without prejudice to the particular safeguards available to the consumer under Community legislation concerning the protection of personal data and privacy;

(18) Whereas it is important for the minimum binding rules contained in this Directive to be supplemented where appropriate by voluntary arrangements among the traders concerned, in line with Commission recommendation 92/295/EEC of 7 April 1992 on codes of practice for the protection of consumers in respect of contracts negotiated at a distance[8];

(19) Whereas in the interest of optimum consumer protection it is important for consumers to be satisfactorily informed of the provisions of this Directive and of codes of practice that may exist in this field;

(20) Whereas non-compliance with this Directive may harm not only consumers but also competitors; whereas provisions may therefore be laid down enabling public bodies or their representatives, or consumer organisations which, under national legislation, have a legitimate interest in consumer protection, or professional organisations which have a legitimate interest in taking action, to monitor the application thereof;

(21) Whereas it is important, with a view to consumer protection, to address the question of cross-border complaints as soon as this is feasible; whereas the Commission published on 14 February 1996 a plan of action on consumer access to justice and the settlement of consumer disputes in the internal market; whereas that plan of action includes specific initiatives to promote out-of-court procedures; whereas objective criteria (Annex II) are suggested to ensure the reliability of those procedures and provision is made for the use of standardised claims forms (Annex III);

(22) Whereas in the use of new technologies the consumer is not in control of the means of communication used; whereas it is therefore necessary to provide that the burden of proof may be on the supplier;

(23) Whereas there is a risk that, in certain cases, the consumer may be deprived of protection under this Directive through the designation of the law of a non-member country as the law applicable to the contract; whereas provisions should therefore be included in this Directive to avert that risk;

(24) Whereas a Member State may ban, in the general interest, the marketing on its territory of certain goods and services through distance contracts; whereas that ban must comply with Community rules; whereas there is already provision for such bans, notably with regard to medicinal products, under Council Directive 89/552/EEC of 3 October 1989 on the coordination of certain provisions laid down by law, regulation or administrative action in Member States concerning the pursuit of television broadcasting activities[9] and Council Directive 92/28/EEC of 31 March 1992 on the advertising of medicinal products for human use[10],

HAVE ADOPTED THIS DIRECTIVE:

## Article 1
### Object

The object of this Directive is to approximate the laws, regulations and administrative provisions of the Member States concerning distance contracts between consumers and suppliers.

## Article 2
### Definitions

For the purposes of this Directive:

(1) 'distance contract' means any contract concerning goods or services concluded between a supplier and a consumer under an

---

[8] OJ No L 156, 10.6.1992, p. 21.

[9] OJ No L 298, 17.10.1989, p. 23.

[10] OJ No L 113, 30.4.1992, p. 13.

organised distance sales or service-provision scheme run by the supplier, who, for the purpose of the contract, makes exclusive use of one or more means of distance communication up to and including the moment at which the contract is concluded;

(2) 'consumer' means any natural person who, in contracts covered by this Directive, is acting for purposes which are outside his trade, business or profession;

(3) 'supplier' means any natural or legal person who, in contracts covered by this Directive, is acting in his commercial or professional capacity;

(4) 'means of distance communication' means any means which, without the simultaneous physical presence of the supplier and the consumer, may be used for the conclusion of a contract between those parties. An indicative list of the means covered by this Directive is contained in Annex I;

(5) 'operator of a means of communication' means any public or private natural or legal person whose trade, business or profession involves making one or more means of distance communication available to suppliers.

## Article 3
### Exemptions

1. This Directive shall not apply to contracts:
- relating to financial services, a non-exhaustive list of which is given in Annex II,
- concluded by means of automatic vending machines or automated commercial premises,
- concluded with telecommunications operators through the use of public payphones,
- concluded for the construction and sale of immovable property or relating to other immovable property rights, except for rental,
- concluded at an auction.

2. Articles 4, 5, 6 and 7 (1) shall not apply:
- to contracts for the supply of foodstuffs, beverages or other goods intended for everyday consumption supplied to the home of the consumer, to his residence or to his workplace by regular roundsmen,
- to contracts for the provision of accommodation, transport, catering or leisure services, where the supplier undertakes, when the contract is concluded, to provide these services on a specific date or within a specific period;

exceptionally, in the case of outdoor leisure events, the supplier can reserve the right not to apply Article 7 (2) in specific circumstances.

## Article 4
### Prior information

1. In good time prior to the conclusion of any distance contract, the consumer shall be provided with the following information:
(a) the identity of the supplier and, in the case of contracts requiring payment in advance, his address;
(b) the main characteristics of the goods or services;
(c) the price of the goods or services including all taxes;
(d) delivery costs, where appropriate;
(e) the arrangements for payment, delivery or performance;
(f) the existence of a right of withdrawal, except in the cases referred to in Article 6 (3);
(g) the cost of using the means of distance communication, where it is calculated other than at the basic rate;
(h) the period for which the offer or the price remains valid;
(i) where appropriate, the minimum duration of the contract in the case of contracts for the supply of products or services to be performed permanently or recurrently.

2. The information referred to in paragraph 1, the commercial purpose of which must be made clear, shall be provided in a clear and comprehensible manner in any way appropriate to the means of distance communication used, with due regard, in particular, to the principles of good faith in commercial transactions, and the principles governing the protection of those who are unable, pursuant to the legislation of the Member States, to give their consent, such as minors.

3. Moreover, in the case of telephone communications, the identity of the supplier and the commercial purpose of the call shall be made explicitly clear at the beginning of any conversation with the consumer.

## Article 5
### Written confirmation of information

1. The consumer must receive written confirmation or confirmation in another durable

medium available and accessible to him of the information referred to in Article 4 (1) (a) to (f), in good time during the performance of the contract, and at the latest at the time of delivery where goods not for delivery to third parties are concerned, unless the information has already been given to the consumer prior to conclusion of the contract in writing or on another durable medium available and accessible to him.

In any event the following must be provided:

- written information on the conditions and procedures for exercising the right of withdrawal, within the meaning of Article 6, including the cases referred to in the first indent of Article 6 (3),
- the geographical address of the place of business of the supplier to which the consumer may address any complaints,
- information on after-sales services and guarantees which exist,
- the conclusion for cancelling the contract, where it is of unspecified duration or a duration exceeding one year.

2. Paragraph 1 shall not apply to services which are performed through the use of a means of distance communication, where they are supplied on only one occasion and are invoiced by the operator of the means of distance communication. Nevertheless, the consumer must in all cases be able to obtain the geographical address of the place of business of the supplier to which he may address any complaints.

## Article 6
### Right of withdrawal

1. For any distance contract the consumer shall have a period of at least seven working days in which to withdraw from the contract without penalty and without giving any reason. The only charge that may be made to the consumer because of the exercise of his right of withdrawal is the direct cost of returning the goods. The period for exercise of this right shall begin:
- in the case of goods, from the day of receipt by the consumer where the obligations laid down in Article 5 have been fulfilled,
- in the case of services, from the day of conclusion of the contract or from the day on which the obligations laid down in Article 5 were fulfilled if they are fulfilled after conclusion of the contract, provided that this period

does not exceed the three-month period referred to in the following subparagraph.

If the supplier has failed to fulfil the obligations laid down in Article 5, the period shall be three months. The period shall begin:
- in the case of goods, from the day of receipt by the consumer,
- in the case of services, from the day of conclusion of the contract.

If the information referred to in Article 5 is supplied within this three-month period, the seven working day period referred to in the first subparagraph shall begin as from that moment.

2. Where the right of withdrawal has been exercised by the consumer pursuant to this Article, the supplier shall be obliged to reimburse the sums paid by the consumer free of charge. The only charge that may be made to the consumer because of the exercise of his right of withdrawal is the direct cost of returning the goods. Such reimbursement must be carried out as soon as possible and in any case within 30 days.

3. Unless the parties have agreed otherwise, the consumer may not exercise the right of withdrawal provided for in paragraph 1 in respect of contracts:
- for the provision of services if performance has begun, with the consumer's agreement, before the end of the seven working day period referred to in paragraph 1,
- for the supply of goods or services the price of which is dependent on fluctuations in the financial market which cannot be controlled by the supplier,
- for the supply of goods made to the consumer's specifications or clearly personalised or which, by reason of their nature, cannot be returned or are liable to deteriorate or expire rapidly,
- for the supply of audio or video recordings or computer software which were unsealed by the consumer,
- for the supply of newspapers, periodicals and magazines,
- for gaming and lottery services.

4. The Member States shall make provision in their legislation to ensure that:
- if the price of goods or services is fully or partly covered by credit granted by the supplier, or

- if that price is fully or partly covered by credit granted to the consumer by a third party on the basis of an agreement between the third party and the supplier,

the credit agreement shall be cancelled, without any penalty, if the consumer exercises his right to withdraw from the contract in accordance with paragraph 1.

Member States shall determine the detailed rules for cancellation of the credit agreement.

## Article 7
### Performance

1. Unless the parties have agreed otherwise, the supplier must execute the order within a maximum of 30 days from the day following that on which the consumer forwarded his order to the supplier.

2. Where a supplier fails to perform his side of the contract on the grounds that the goods or services ordered are unavailable, the consumer must be informed of this situation and must be able to obtain a refund of any sums he has paid as soon as possible and in any case within 30 days.

3. Nevertheless, Member States may lay down that the supplier may provide the consumer with goods or services of equivalent quality and price provided that this possibility was provided for prior to the conclusion of the contract or in the contract. The consumer shall be informed of this possibility in a clear and comprehensible manner. The cost of returning the goods following exercise of the right of withdrawal shall, in this case, be borne by the supplier, and the consumer must be informed of this. In such cases the supply of goods or services may not be deemed to constitute inertia selling within the meaning of Article 9.

## Article 8
### Payment by card

Member States shall ensure that appropriate measures exist to allow a consumer:

- to request cancellation of a payment where fraudulent use has been made of his payment card in connection with distance contracts covered by this Directive,
- in the event of fraudulent use, to be recredited with the sums paid or have them returned.

## Article 9
### Inertia selling

Member States shall take the measures necessary to:

- prohibit the supply of goods or services to a consumer without their being ordered by the consumer beforehand, where such supply involves a demand for payment,
- exempt the consumer from the provision of any consideration in cases of unsolicited supply, the absence of a response not constituting consent.

## Article 10
### Restrictions on the use of certain means of distance communication

1. Use by a supplier of the following means requires the prior consent of the consumer:

- automated calling system without human intervention (automatic calling machine),
- facsimile machine (fax).

2. Member States shall ensure that means of distance communication, other than those referred to in paragraph 1, which allow individual communications may be used only where there is no clear objection from the consumer.

## Article 11
### Judicial or administrative redress

1. Member States shall ensure that adequate and effective means exist to ensure compliance with this Directive in the interests of consumers.

2. The means referred to in paragraph 1 shall include provisions whereby one or more of the following bodies, as determined by national law, may take action under national law before the courts or before the competent administrative bodies to ensure that the national provisions for the implementation of this Directive are applied:

(a) public bodies or their representatives;

(b) consumer organisations having a legitimate interest in protecting consumers;

(c) professional organisations having a legitimate interest in acting.

3. (a) Member States may stipulate that the burden of proof concerning the existence of prior information, written confirmation, compliance with time-limits or consumer consent

can be placed on the supplier.

(b) Member States shall take the measures needed to ensure that suppliers and operators of means of communication, where they are able to do so, cease practices which do not comply with measures adopted pursuant to this Directive.

4. Member States may provide for voluntary supervision by self-regulatory bodies of compliance with the provisions of this Directive and recourse to such bodies for the settlement of disputes to be added to the means which Member States must provided to ensure compliance with the provisions of this Directive.

## Article 12
### Binding nature

1. The consumer may not waive the rights conferred on him by the transposition of this Directive into national law.

2. Member States shall take the measures needed to ensure that the consumer does not lose the protection granted by this Directive by virtue of the choice of the law of a non-member country as the law applicable to the contract if the latter has close connection with the territory of one or more Member States.

## Article 13
### Community rules

1. The provisions of this Directive shall apply insofar as there are no particular provisions in rules of Community law governing certain types of distance contracts in their entirety.

2. Where specific Community rules contain provisions governing only certain aspects of the supply of goods or provision of services, those provisions, rather than the provisions of this Directive, shall apply to these specific aspects of the distance contracts.

## Article 14
### Minimal clause

Member States may introduce or maintain, in the area covered by this Directive, more stringent provisions compatible with the Treaty, to ensure a higher level of consumer protection. Such provisions shall, where appropriate, include a ban, in the general interest, on the marketing of certain goods or services, particularly medicinal products, within their terri-

tory by means of distance contracts, with due regard for the Treaty.

## Article 15
### Implementation

1. Member States shall bring into force the laws, regulations and administrative provisions necessary to comply with this Directive no later than three years after it enters into force. They shall forthwith inform the Commission thereof.

2. When Member States adopt the measures referred to in paragraph 1, these shall contain a reference to this Directive or shall be accompanied by such reference on the occasion of their official publication. The procedure for such reference shall be laid down by Member States.

3. Member States shall communicate to the Commission the text of the provisions of national law which they adopt in the field governed by this Directive.

4. No later than four years after the entry into force of this Directive the Commission shall submit a report to the European Parliament and the Council on the implementation of this Directive, accompanied if appropriate by a proposal for the revision thereof.

## Article 16
### Consumer information

Member States shall take appropriate measures to inform the consumer of the national law transposing this Directive and shall encourage, where appropriate, professional organisations to inform consumers of their codes of practice.

## Article 17
### Complaints systems

The Commission shall study the feasibility of establishing effective means to deal with consumers' complaints in respect of distance selling. Within two years after the entry into force of this Directive the Commission shall submit a report to the European Parliament and the Council on the results of the studies, accompanied if appropriate by proposals.

## Article 18

This Directive shall enter into force on the day of its publication in the Official Journal of the European Communities.

Article 19

This Directive is addressed to the Member States.

Done at Brussels, 20 May 1997.

For the European Parliament
The President
J.M. GIL-ROBLES

For the Council
The President
J. VAN AARTSEN

ANNEX I

Means of communication covered by Article 2 (4)
- Unaddressed printed matter
- Addressed printed matter
- Standard letter
- Press advertising with order form
- Catalogue
- Telephone with human intervention
- Telephone without human intervention (automatic calling machine, audiotext)
- Radio
- Videophone (telephone with screen)
- Videotex (microcomputer and television screen) with keyboard or touch screen
- Electronic mail
- Facsimile machine (fax)
- Television (teleshopping).

ANNEX II

Financial services within the meaning of Article 3 (1)
- Investment services
- Insurance and reinsurance operations
- Banking services
- Operations relating to dealings in futures or options.
Such services include in particular:
- investment services referred to in the Annex to Directive 93/22/EEC[11]; services of collective investment undertakings,
- services covered by the activities subject to mutual recognition referred to in the Annex to

---

Directive 89/646/EEC[12];
- operations covered by the insurance and reinsurance activities referred to in:
- Article 1 of Directive 73/239/EEC[13],
- the Annex to Directive 79/267/EEC[14],
- Directive 64/225/EEC[15],
- Directives 92/49/EEC[16] and 92/96/EEC[17].

Statement by the Council and the Parliament re Article 6 (1)
The Council and the Parliament note that the Commission will examine the possibility and desirability of harmonising the method of calculating the cooling-off period under existing consumer-protection legislation, notably Directive 85/577/EEC of 20 December 1985 on the protection of consumers in respect of contracts negotiated away from commercial establishments ('door-to-door sales')[18].

Statement by the Commission re Article 3 (1), first indent
The Commission recognises the importance of protecting consumers in respect of distance contracts concerning financial services and has published a Green Paper entitled 'Financial services: meeting consumers' expectations'. In the light of reactions to the Green Paper the Commission will examine ways of incorporating consumer protection into the policy on financial services and the possible legislative implications and, if need be, will submit appropriate proposals.

---

[11] OJ No L 141, 11.6.1993, p. 27.

[12] OJ No L 386, 30. 12. 1989, p. 1. Directive as amended by Directive 92/30/EEC (OJ No L 110, 28.4.1992, p. 52).
[13] OJ No L 228, 16. 8. 1973, p. 3. Directive as last amended by Directive 92/49/EEC (OJ No L 228, 11.8.1992, p. 1).
[14] OJ No L 63, 13. 3. 1979, p. 1. Directive as last amended by Directive 90/619/EEC (OJ No L 330, 29.11.1990, p. 50).
[15] OJ No 56, 4. 4. 1964, p. 878/64. Directive as amended by the 1973 Act of Accession.
[16] OJ No L 228, 11.8.1992, p. 1.
[17] OJ No L 360, 9.12.1992, p. 1.
[18] OJ No L 372, 31.12.1985, p. 31.

# Appendix 2

### Directive 1999/93/EC of the European Parliament and of the Council
### of 13 December 1999
### on a Community framework for electronic signatures

THE EUROPEAN PARLIAMENT AND THE COUNCIL OF THE EUROPEAN UNION,

Having regard to the Treaty establishing the European Community, and in particular Articles 47(2), 55 and 95 thereof,

Having regard to the proposal from the Commission[19],

Having regard to the opinion of the Economic and Social Committee[20],

Having regard to the opinion of the Committee of the Regions[21],

Acting in accordance with the procedure laid down in Article 251 of the Treaty[22],

Whereas:

(1) On 16 April 1997 the Commission presented to the European Parliament, the Council, the Economic and Social Committee and the Committee of the Regions a Communication on a European Initiative in Electronic Commerce;

(2) On 8 October 1997 the Commission presented to the European Parliament, the Council, the Economic and Social Committee and the Committee of the Regions a Communication on ensuring security and trust in electronic communication - towards a European framework for digital signatures and encryption;

(3) On 1 December 1997 the Council invited the Commission to submit as soon as possible a proposal for a Directive of the European Parliament and of the Council on digital signatures;

(4) Electronic communication and commerce necessitate " electronic signatures" and related services allowing data authentication; divergent rules with respect to legal recognition of electronic signatures and the accreditation of certification-service providers in the Member States may create a significant barrier to the use of electronic communications and electronic commerce; on the other hand, a clear Community framework regarding the conditions applying to electronic signatures will strengthen confidence in, and general acceptance of, the new technologies; legislation in the Member States should not hinder the free movement of goods and services in the internal market;

(5) The interoperability of electronic-signature products should be promoted; in accordance with Article 14 of the Treaty, the internal market comprises an area without internal frontiers in which the free movement of goods is ensured; essential requirements specific to electronic-signature products must be met in order to ensure free movement within the internal market and to build trust in electronic signatures, without prejudice to Council Regulation (EC) No 3381/94 of 19 December 1994 setting up a Community regime for the control of exports of dual-use goods[23] and Council Decision 94/942/CFSP of 19 December 1994 on the joint action adopted by the Council concerning the control of exports of dual-use goods[24];

---

[19] OJ C 325, 23.10.1998, p. 5.

[20] OJ C 40, 15.2.1999, p. 29.

[21] OJ C 93, 6.4.1999, p. 33.

[22] Opinion of the European Parliament of 13 January 1999 (OJ C 104, 14.4.1999, p. 49), Council Common Position of 28 June 1999 (OJ C 243, 27.8.1999, p. 33) and Decision of the European Parliament of 27 October 1999 (not yet published in the Official Journal). Council Decision of 30 November 1999.

[23] OJ L 367, 31.12.1994, p. 1. Regulation as amended by Regulation (EC) No 837/95 (OJ L 90, 21.4.1995, p. 1).

[24] OJ L 367, 31.12.1994, p. 8. Decision as last amended by Decision 99/193/CFSP (OJ L 73, 19.3.1999, p. 1).

*A.R. Lodder and H.W.K. Kaspersen (eds.),*
*eDirectives: Guide to European Union Law on E-Commerce, 155–164.*
© 2002 *Kluwer Law International. Printed in the Netherlands.*

(6) This Directive does not harmonise the provision of services with respect to the confidentiality of information where they are covered by national provisions concerned with public policy or public security;

(7) The internal market ensures the free movement of persons, as a result of which citizens and residents of the European Union increasingly need to deal with authorities in Member States other than the one in which they reside; the availability of electronic communication could be of great service in this respect;

(8) Rapid technological development and the global character of the Internet necessitate an approach which is open to various technologies and services capable of authenticating data electronically;

(9) Electronic signatures will be used in a large variety of circumstances and applications, resulting in a wide range of new services and products related to or using electronic signatures; the definition of such products and services should not be limited to the issuance and management of certificates, but should also encompass any other service and product using, or ancillary to, electronic signatures, such as registration services, time-stamping services, directory services, computing services or consultancy services related to electronic signatures;

(10) The internal market enables certification-service-providers to develop their cross-border activities with a view to increasing their competitiveness, and thus to offer consumers and businesses new opportunities to exchange information and trade electronically in a secure way, regardless of frontiers; in order to stimulate the Community-wide provision of certification services over open networks, certification-service-providers should be free to provide their services without prior authorisation; prior authorisation means not only any permission whereby the certification-service-provider concerned has to obtain a decision by national authorities before being allowed to provide its certification services, but also any other measures having the same effect;

(11) Voluntary accreditation schemes aiming at an enhanced level of service-provision may offer certification-service-providers the appropriate framework for developing further their services towards the levels of trust, security and quality demanded by the evolving market; such schemes should encourage the development of best practice among certification-service-providers; certification-service-providers should be left free to adhere to and benefit from such accreditation schemes;

(12) Certification services can be offered either by a public entity or a legal or natural person, when it is established in accordance with the national law; whereas Member States should not prohibit certification-service-providers from operating outside voluntary accreditation schemes; it should be ensured that such accreditation schemes do not reduce competition for certification services;

(13) Member States may decide how they ensure the supervision of compliance with the provisions laid down in this Directive; this Directive does not preclude the establishment of private-sector-based supervision systems; this Directive does not oblige certification-service-providers to apply to be supervised under any applicable accreditation scheme;

(14) It is important to strike a balance between consumer and business needs;

(15) Annex III covers requirements for secure signature-creation devices to ensure the functionality of advanced electronic signatures; it does not cover the entire system environment in which such devices operate; the functioning of the internal market requires the Commission and the Member States to act swiftly to enable the bodies charged with the conformity assessment of secure signature devices with Annex III to be designated; in order to meet market needs conformity assessment must be timely and efficient;

(16) This Directive contributes to the use and legal recognition of electronic signatures within the Community; a regulatory framework is not needed for electronic signatures exclusively used within systems, which are based on voluntary agreements under private law between a specified number of participants; the freedom of parties to agree among themselves the terms and conditions under which they accept electronically signed data should be respected to the extent allowed by national law; the legal effectiveness of electronic signatures used in such systems and their admissibility as evi-

dence in legal proceedings should be recognised;

(17) This Directive does not seek to harmonise national rules concerning contract law, particularly the formation and performance of contracts, or other formalities of a non-contractual nature concerning signatures; for this reason the provisions concerning the legal effect of electronic signatures should be without prejudice to requirements regarding form laid down in national law with regard to the conclusion of contracts or the rules determining where a contract is concluded;

(18) The storage and copying of signature-creation data could cause a threat to the legal validity of electronic signatures;

(19) Electronic signatures will be used in the public sector within national and Community administrations and in communications between such administrations and with citizens and economic operators, for example in the public procurement, taxation, social security, health and justice systems;

(20) Harmonised criteria relating to the legal effects of electronic signatures will preserve a coherent legal framework across the Community; national law lays down different requirements for the legal validity of hand-written signatures; whereas certificates can be used to confirm the identity of a person signing electronically; advanced electronic signatures based on qualified certificates aim at a higher level of security; advanced electronic signatures which are based on a qualified certificate and which are created by a secure-signature-creation device can be regarded as legally equivalent to hand-written signatures only if the requirements for hand-written signatures are fulfilled;

(21) In order to contribute to the general acceptance of electronic authentication methods it has to be ensured that electronic signatures can be used as evidence in legal proceedings in all Member States; the legal recognition of electronic signatures should be based upon objective criteria and not be linked to authorisation of the certification-service-provider involved; national law governs the legal spheres in which electronic documents and electronic signatures may be used; this Directive is without prejudice to the power of a national court to make a ruling regarding conformity with the require-

ments of this Directive and does not affect national rules regarding the unfettered judicial consideration of evidence;

(22) Certification-service-providers providing certification-services to the public are subject to national rules regarding liability;

(23) The development of international electronic commerce requires cross-border arrangements involving third countries; in order to ensure interoperability at a global level, agreements on multilateral rules with third countries on mutual recognition of certification services could be beneficial;

(24) In order to increase user confidence in electronic communication and electronic commerce, certification-service-providers must observe data protection legislation and individual privacy;

(25) Provisions on the use of pseudonyms in certificates should not prevent Member States from requiring identification of persons pursuant to Community or national law;

(26) The measures necessary for the implementation of this Directive are to be adopted in accordance with Council Decision 1999/468/EC of 28 June 1999 laying down the procedures for the exercise of implementing powers conferred on the Commission[25];

(27) Two years after its implementation the Commission will carry out a review of this Directive so as, inter alia, to ensure that the advance of technology or changes in the legal environment have not created barriers to achieving the aims stated in this Directive; it should examine the implications of associated technical areas and submit a report to the European Parliament and the Council on this subject;

(28) In accordance with the principles of subsidiarity and proportionality as set out in Article 5 of the Treaty, the objective of creating a harmonised legal framework for the provision of electronic signatures and related services cannot be sufficiently achieved by the Member States and can therefore be better achieved by the Community; this Directive does not go beyond what is necessary to achieve that objective,

---

[25] OJ L 184, 17.7.1999, p. 23.

HAVE ADOPTED THIS DIRECTIVE:

## Article 1
### Scope

The purpose of this Directive is to facilitate the use of electronic signatures and to contribute to their legal recognition. It establishes a legal framework for electronic signatures and certain certification-services in order to ensure the proper functioning of the internal market.

It does not cover aspects related to the conclusion and validity of contracts or other legal obligations where there are requirements as regards form prescribed by national or Community law nor does it affect rules and limits, contained in national or Community law, governing the use of documents.

## Article 2
### Definitions

For the purpose of this Directive:

1. "electronic signature" means data in electronic form which are attached to or logically associated with other electronic data and which serve as a method of authentication;

2. "advanced electronic signature" means an electronic signature which meets the following requirements:
(a) it is uniquely linked to the signatory;
(b) it is capable of identifying the signatory;
(c) it is created using means that the signatory can maintain under his sole control; and
(d) it is linked to the data to which it relates in such a manner that any subsequent change of the data is detectable;

3. "signatory" means a person who holds a signature-creation device and acts either on his own behalf or on behalf of the natural or legal person or entity he represents;

4. "signature-creation data" means unique data, such as codes or private cryptographic keys, which are used by the signatory to create an electronic signature;

5. "signature-creation device" means configured software or hardware used to implement the signature-creation data;

6. "secure-signature-creation device" means a signature-creation device which meets the requirements laid down in Annex III;

7. "signature-verification-data" means data, such as codes or public cryptographic keys, which are used for the purpose of verifying an electronic signature;

8. "signature-verification device" means configured software or hardware used to implement the signature-verification-data;

9. "certificate" means an electronic attestation which links signature-verification data to a person and confirms the identity of that person;

10. "qualified certificate" means a certificate which meets the requirements laid down in Annex I and is provided by a certification-service-provider who fulfils the requirements laid down in Annex II;

11. "certification-service-provider" means an entity or a legal or natural person who issues certificates or provides other services related to electronic signatures;

12. "electronic-signature product" means hardware or software, or relevant components thereof, which are intended to be used by a certification-service-provider for the provision of electronic-signature services or are intended to be used for the creation or verification of electronic signatures;

13. "voluntary accreditation" means any permission, setting out rights and obligations specific to the provision of certification services, to be granted upon request by the certification-service-provider concerned, by the public or private body charged with the elaboration of, and supervision of compliance with, such rights and obligations, where the certification-service-provider is not entitled to exercise the rights stemming from the permission until it has received the decision by the body.

## Article 3
### Market access

1. Member States shall not make the provision of certification services subject to prior authorisation.

2. Without prejudice to the provisions of paragraph 1, Member States may introduce or maintain voluntary accreditation schemes aiming at enhanced levels of certification-service provision. All conditions related to such schemes must be objective, transparent, proportionate and non-discriminatory. Member States may not limit the number of accredited certification-service-providers for reasons which fall within the scope of this Directive.

3. Each Member State shall ensure the establishment of an appropriate system that allows for supervision of certification-service-providers which are established on its territory and issue qualified certificates to the public.

4. The conformity of secure signature-creation-devices with the requirements laid down in Annex III shall be determined by appropriate public or private bodies designated by Member States. The Commission shall, pursuant to the procedure laid down in Article 9, establish criteria for Member States to determine whether a body should be designated. A determination of conformity with the requirements laid down in Annex III made by the bodies referred to in the first subparagraph shall be recognised by all Member States.

5. The Commission may, in accordance with the procedure laid down in Article 9, establish and publish reference numbers of generally recognised standards for electronic-signature products in the Official Journal of the European Communities. Member States shall presume that there is compliance with the requirements laid down in Annex II, point (f), and Annex III when an electronic signature product meets those standards.

6. Member States and the Commission shall work together to promote the development and use of signature-verification devices in the light of the recommendations for secure signature-verification laid down in Annex IV and in the interests of the consumer.

7. Member States may make the use of electronic signatures in the public sector subject to possible additional requirements. Such requirements shall be objective, transparent, proportionate and non-discriminatory and shall relate only to the specific characteristics of the application concerned. Such requirements may not constitute an obstacle to cross-border services for citizens.

## Article 4
### Internal market principles

1. Each Member State shall apply the national provisions which it adopts pursuant to this Directive to certification-service-providers established on its territory and to the services which they provide. Member States may not restrict the provision of certification-services

originating in another Member State in the fields covered by this Directive.

2. Member States shall ensure that electronic-signature products which comply with this Directive are permitted to circulate freely in the internal market.

## Article 5
### Legal effects of electronic signatures

1. Member States shall ensure that advanced electronic signatures which are based on a qualified certificate and which are created by a secure-signature-creation device:

(a) satisfy the legal requirements of a signature in relation to data in electronic form in the same manner as a handwritten signature satisfies those requirements in relation to paper-based data; and

(b) are admissible as evidence in legal proceedings.

2. Member States shall ensure that an electronic signature is not denied legal effectiveness and admissibility as evidence in legal proceedings solely on the grounds that it is:

- in electronic form, or

- not based upon a qualified certificate, or

- not based upon a qualified certificate issued by an accredited certification-service-provider, or

- not created by a secure signature-creation device.

## Article 6
### Liability

1. As a minimum, Member States shall ensure that by issuing a certificate as a qualified certificate to the public or by guaranteeing such a certificate to the public a certification-service-provider is liable for damage caused to any entity or legal or natural person who reasonably relies on that certificate:

(a) as regards the accuracy at the time of issuance of all information contained in the qualified certificate and as regards the fact that the certificate contains all the details prescribed for a qualified certificate;

(b) for assurance that at the time of the issuance of the certificate, the signatory identified in the qualified certificate held the signature-creation data corresponding to the signature-verification data given or identified in the certificate;

(c) for assurance that the signature-creation data and the signature-verification data can be used in a complementary manner in cases where the certification-service-provider generates them both;

unless the certification-service-provider proves that he has not acted negligently.

2. As a minimum Member States shall ensure that a certification-service-provider who has issued a certificate as a qualified certificate to the public is liable for damage caused to any entity or legal or natural person who reasonably relies on the certificate for failure to register revocation of the certificate unless the certification-service-provider proves that he has not acted negligently.

3. Member States shall ensure that a certification-service-provider may indicate in a qualified certificate limitations on the use of that certificate. provided that the limitations are recognisable to third parties. The certification-service-provider shall not be liable for damage arising from use of a qualified certificate which exceeds the limitations placed on it.

4. Member States shall ensure that a certification-service-provider may indicate in the qualified certificate a limit on the value of transactions for which the certificate can be used, provided that the limit is recognisable to third parties.

The certification-service-provider shall not be liable for damage resulting from this maximum limit being exceeded.

5. The provisions of paragraphs 1 to 4 shall be without prejudice to Council Directive 93/13/EEC of 5 April 1993 on unfair terms in consumer contracts[26].

## Article 7
### International aspects

1. Member States shall ensure that certificates which are issued as qualified certificates to the public by a certification-service-provider established in a third country are recognised as legally equivalent to certificates issued by a certification-service-provider established within the Community if:

(a) the certification-service-provider fulfils the requirements laid down in this Directive and has been accredited under a voluntary accreditation scheme established in a Member State; or

(b) a certification-service-provider established within the Community which fulfils the requirements laid down in this Directive guarantees the certificate; or

(c) the certificate or the certification-service-provider is recognised under a bilateral or multilateral agreement between the Community and third countries or international organisations.

2. In order to facilitate cross-border certification services with third countries and legal recognition of advanced electronic signatures originating in third countries, the Commission shall make proposals, where appropriate, to achieve the effective implementation of standards and international agreements applicable to certification services. In particular, and where necessary, it shall submit proposals to the Council for appropriate mandates for the negotiation of bilateral and multilateral agreements with third countries and international organisations. The Council shall decide by qualified majority.

3. Whenever the Commission is informed of any difficulties encountered by Community undertakings with respect to market access in third countries, it may, if necessary, submit proposals to the Council for an appropriate mandate for the negotiation of comparable rights for Community undertakings in these third countries. The Council shall decide by qualified majority.

Measures taken pursuant to this paragraph shall be without prejudice to the obligations of the Community and of the Member States under relevant international agreements.

## Article 8
### Data protection

1. Member States shall ensure that certification-service-providers and national bodies responsible for accreditation or supervision comply with the requirements laid down in Directive 95/46/EC of the European Parliament and of the Council of 24 October 1995 on tile protection of individuals with regard to the processing

---

[26] OJ L 95, 21.4.1993, p. 29.

of personal data and on the free movement of such data[27].

2. Member States shall ensure that a certification-service-provider which issues certificates to the public may collect personal data only directly from the data subject, or after the explicit consent of the data subject, and only insofar as it is necessary for the purposes of issuing and maintaining the certificate. The data may not be collected or processed for any other purposes without the explicit consent of the data subject.

3. Without prejudice to the legal effect given to pseudonyms under national law, Member States shall not prevent certification service providers from indicating in the certificate a pseudonym instead of the signatory's name.

## Article 9
### Committee

1. The Commission shall be assisted by an "Electronic-Signature Committee", hereinafter referred to as "the committee".

2. Where reference is made to this paragraph, Articles 4 and 7 of Decision 1999/468/EC shall apply, having regard to the provisions of Article 8 thereof.

The period laid down in Article 4(3) of Decision 1999/468/EC shall be set at three months.

3. The Committee shall adopt its own rules of procedure.

## Article 10
### Tasks of the committee

The committee shall clarify the requirements laid down in the Annexes of this Directive, the criteria referred to in Article 3(4) and the generally recognised standards for electronic signature products established and published pursuant to Article 3(5), in accordance with the procedure laid down in Article 9(2).

## Article 11
### Notification

1. Member States shall notify to the Commission and the other Member States the following:

(a) information on national voluntary accredi-

tation schemes, including any additional requirements pursuant to Article 3(7);

(b) the names and addresses of the national bodies responsible for accreditation and supervision as well as of the bodies referred to in Article 3(4);

(c) the names and addresses of all accredited national certification service providers.

2. Any information supplied under paragraph 1 and changes in respect of that information shall be notified by the Member States as soon as possible.

## Article 12
### Review

1. The Commission shall review the operation of this Directive and report thereon to the European Parliament and to the Council by 19 July 2003 at the latest.

2. The review shall inter alia assess whether the scope of this Directive should be modified, taking account of technological, market and legal developments. The report shall in particular include an assessment, on the basis of experience gained, of aspects of harmonisation. The report shall be accompanied, where appropriate, by legislative proposals.

## Article 13
### Implementation

1. Member States shall bring into force the laws, regulations and administrative provisions necessary to comply with this Directive before 19 July 2001. They shall forthwith inform the Commission thereof.

When Member States adopt these measures, they shall contain a reference to this Directive or shall be accompanied by such a reference on the occasion of their official publication. The methods of making such reference shall be laid down by the Member States.

2. Member States shall communicate to the Commission the text of the main provisions of domestic law which they adopt in the field governed by this Directive.

## Article 14
### Entry into force

This Directive shall enter into force on the day of its publication in the Official Journal of the European Communities

---

[27] OJ L 281, 23.11.1995, p. 31.

Article 15

Addressees

This Directive is addressed to the Member States.

Done at Brussels, 13 December 1999.

For the European Parliament
The President
N. FONTAINE

For the Council
The President
S. HASSI

ANNEX I

Requirements for qualified certificates

Qualified certificates must contain:

(a) an indication that the certificate is issued as a qualified certificate;

(b) the identification of the certification-service-provider and the State in which it is established;

(c) the name of the signatory or a pseudonym, which shall be identified as such;

(d) provision for a specific attribute of the signatory to be included if relevant, depending on the purpose for which the certificate is intended;

(e) signature-verification data which correspond to signature-creation data under the control of the signatory;

(f) an indication of the beginning and end of the period of validity of the certificate;

(g) the identity code of the certificate;

(h) the advanced electronic signature of the certification-service-provider issuing it;

(i) limitations on the scope of use of the certificate, if applicable; and

(j) limits on the value of transactions for which the certificate can be used, if applicable.

## ANNEX II

Requirements for certification-service-providers issuing qualified certificates

Certification-service-providers must:

(a) demonstrate the reliability necessary for providing certification services;

(b) ensure the operation of a prompt and secure directory and a secure and immediate revocation service;

(c) ensure that the date and time when a certificate is issued or revoked can be determined precisely;

(d) verify, by appropriate means in accordance with national law, the identity and, if applicable, any specific attributes of the person to which a qualified certificate is issued;

(e) employ personnel who possess the expert knowledge, experience, and qualifications necessary for the services provided, in particular competence at managerial level, expertise in electronic signature techology and familiarity with proper security procedures; they must also apply administrative and management procedures which are adequate and correspond to recognised standards;

(f) use trustworthy systems and products which are protected against modification and ensure the technical and cryptographic security of the process supported by them;

(g) take measures against forgery of certificates, and, in cases where the certification-service-provider generates signature-creation data, guarantee confidentiality during the process of generating such data;

(h) maintain sufficient financial resources to operate in conformity with the requirements laid down in the Directive, in particular to bear the risk of liability for damages, for example, by obtaining appropriate insurance;

(i) record all relevant information concerning a qualified certificate for an appropriate period of time, in particular for the purpose of providing evidence of certification for the purposes of legal proceedings. Such recording may be done electronically;

(j) not store or copy signature-creation data of the person to whom the certification-service-provider provided key management services;

(k) before entering into a contractual relationship with a person seeking a certificate to support his electronic signature inform that person by a durable means of communication of the precise terms and conditions regarding the use of the certificate, including any limitations on its use, the existence of a voluntary accreditation scheme and procedures for complaints and dispute settlement. Such information, which may be transmitted electronically, must be in writing and in redily understandable language. Relevant parts of this information must also be made available on request to third-parties relying on the certificate;

(l) use trustworthy systems to store certificates in a verifiable form so that:

- only authorised persons can make entries and changes,

- information can be checked for authenticity,

- certificates are publicly available for retrieval in only those cases for which the certificate-holder's consent has been obtained, and

- any technical changes compromising these security requirements are apparent to the operator.

## ANNEX III

Requirements for secure signature-creation devices

1. Secure signature-creation devices must, by appropriate technical and procedural means, ensure at the least that:

(a) the signature-creation-data used for signature generation can practically occur only once, and that their secrecy is reasonably assured;

(b) the signature-creation-data used for signature generation cannot, with reasonable assurance, be derived and the signature is protected against forgery using currently available technology;

(c) the signature-creation-data used for signature generation can be reliably protected by the legitimate signatory against the use of others.

2. Secure signature-creation devices must not alter the data to be signed or prevent such data from being presented to the signatory prior to the signature process.

## ANNEX IV

Recommendations for secure signature verification

During the signature-verification process it should be ensured with reasonable certainty that:

(a) the data used for verifying the signature correspond to the data displayed to the verifier;

(b) the signature is reliably verified and the result of that verification is correctly displayed;

(c) the verifier can, as necessary, reliably establish the contents of the signed data;

(d) the authenticity and validity of the certificate required at the time of signature verification are reliably verified;

(e) the result of verification and the signatory's identity are correctly displayed;

(f) the use of a pseudonym is clearly indicated; and

(g) any security-relevant changes can be detected.

# Appendix 3

**Directive 2000/31/EC of the European Parliament and of the Council
of 8 June 2000
on certain legal aspects of information society services, in particular electronic commerce,
in the Internal Market (Directive on electronic commerce)**

THE EUROPEAN PARLIAMENT AND THE COUNCIL OF THE EUROPEAN UNION,

Having regard to the Treaty establishing the European Community, and in particular Articles 47(2), 55 and 95 thereof,

Having regard to the proposal from the Commission[28],

Having regard to the opinion of the Economic and Social Committee[29],

Acting in accordance with the procedure laid down in Article 251 of the Treaty[30],

Whereas:

(1) The European Union is seeking to forge ever closer links between the States and peoples of Europe, to ensure economic and social progress; in accordance with Article 14(2) of the Treaty, the internal market comprises an area without internal frontiers in which the free movements of goods, services and the freedom of establishment are ensured; the development of information society services within the area without internal frontiers is vital to eliminating the barriers which divide the European peoples.

(2) The development of electronic commerce within the information society offers significant employment opportunities in the Community, particularly in small and medium-sized enterprises, and will stimulate economic growth and investment in innovation by European companies, and can also enhance the competitiveness of European industry, provided that everyone has access to the Internet.

(3) Community law and the characteristics of the Community legal order are a vital asset to enable European citizens and operators to take full advantage, without consideration of borders, of the opportunities afforded by electronic commerce; this Directive therefore has the purpose of ensuring a high level of Community legal integration in order to establish a real area without internal borders for information society services.

(4) It is important to ensure that electronic commerce could fully benefit from the internal market and therefore that, as with Council Directive 89/552/EEC of 3 October 1989 on the coordination of certain provisions laid down by law, regulation or administrative action in Member States concerning the pursuit of television broadcasting activities[31], a high level of Community integration is achieved.

(5) The development of information society services within the Community is hampered by a number of legal obstacles to the proper functioning of the internal market which make less attractive the exercise of the freedom of establishment and the freedom to provide services; these obstacles arise from divergences in legislation and from the legal uncertainty as to which national rules apply to such services; in the absence of coordination and adjustment of legislation in the relevant areas, obstacles might be justified in the light of the case-law of the Court of Justice of the European Communities; legal uncertainty exists with regard to the extent to which Member States may control services originating from another Member State.

---

[28] OJ C 30, 5.2.1999, p. 4.

[29] OJ C 169, 16.6.1999, p. 36.

[30] Opinion of the European Parliament of 6 May 1999 (OJ C 279, 1.10.1999, p. 389), Council common position of 28 February 2000 (OJ C 128, 8.5.2000, p. 32) and Decision of the European Parliament of 4 May 2000 (not yet published in the Official Journal).

[31] OJ L 298, 17.10.1989, p. 23. Directive as amended by Directive 97/36/EC of the European Parliament and of the Council (OJ L 202, 30.7.1997, p. 60).

*A.R. Lodder and H.W.K. Kaspersen (eds.),*
*eDirectives: Guide to European Union Law on E-Commerce, 165–181.*
© 2002 *Kluwer Law International. Printed in the Netherlands.*

(6) In the light of Community objectives, of Articles 43 and 49 of the Treaty and of secondary Community law, these obstacles should be eliminated by coordinating certain national laws and by clarifying certain legal concepts at Community level to the extent necessary for the proper functioning of the internal market; by dealing only with certain specific matters which give rise to problems for the internal market, this Directive is fully consistent with the need to respect the principle of subsidiarity as set out in Article 5 of the Treaty.

(7) In order to ensure legal certainty and consumer confidence, this Directive must lay down a clear and general framework to cover certain legal aspects of electronic commerce in the internal market.

(8) The objective of this Directive is to create a legal framework to ensure the free movement of information society services between Member States and not to harmonise the field of criminal law as such.

(9) The free movement of information society services can in many cases be a specific reflection in Community law of a more general principle, namely freedom of expression as enshrined in Article 10(1) of the Convention for the Protection of Human Rights and Fundamental Freedoms, which has been ratified by all the Member States; for this reason, directives covering the supply of information society services must ensure that this activity may be engaged in freely in the light of that Article, subject only to the restrictions laid down in paragraph 2 of that Article and in Article 46(1) of the Treaty; this Directive is not intended to affect national fundamental rules and principles relating to freedom of expression.

(10) In accordance with the principle of proportionality, the measures provided for in this Directive are strictly limited to the minimum needed to achieve the objective of the proper functioning of the internal market; where action at Community level is necessary, and in order to guarantee an area which is truly without internal frontiers as far as electronic commerce is concerned, the Directive must ensure a high level of protection of objectives of general interest, in particular the protection of minors and human dignity, consumer protection and the protection of public health; according to

Article 152 of the Treaty, the protection of public health is an essential component of other Community policies.

(11) This Directive is without prejudice to the level of protection for, in particular, public health and consumer interests, as established by Community acts; amongst others, Council Directive 93/13/EEC of 5 April 1993 on unfair terms in consumer contracts[32] and Directive 97/7/EC of the European Parliament and of the Council of 20 May 1997 on the protection of consumers in respect of distance contracts[33] form a vital element for protecting consumers in contractual matters; those Directives also apply in their entirety to information society services; that same Community acquis, which is fully applicable to information society services, also embraces in particular Council Directive 84/450/EEC of 10 September 1984 concerning misleading and comparative advertising[34], Council Directive 87/102/EEC of 22 December 1986 for the approximation of the laws, regulations and administrative provisions of the Member States concerning consumer credit[35], Council Directive 93/22/EEC of 10 May 1993 on investment services in the securities field[36], Council Directive 90/314/EEC of 13 June 1990 on package travel, package holidays and package tours[37]), Directive 98/6/EC of the European Parliament and of the Council of 16 February 1998 on consumer production in the indication of prices of products offered to consumers[38], Council Directive 92/59/EEC of 29 June 1992 on general product safety[39], Directive 94/47/EC of the European Parliament

---

[32] OJ L 95, 21.4.1993, p. 29.

[33] OJ L 144, 4.6.1999, p. 19.

[34] OJ L 250, 19.9.1984, p. 17. Directive as amended by Directive 97/55/EC of the European Parliament and of the Council (OJ L 290, 23.10.1997, p. 18).

[35] OJ L 42, 12.2.1987, p. 48. Directive as last amended by Directive 98/7/EC of the European Parliament and of the Council (OJ L 101, 1.4.1998, p. 17).

[36] OJ L 141, 11.6.1993, p. 27. Directive as last amended by Directive 97/9/EC of the European Parliament and of the Council (OJ L 84, 26.3.1997, p. 22).

[37] OJ L 158, 23.6.1990, p. 59.

[38] OJ L 80, 18.3.1998, p. 27.

[39] OJ L 228, 11.8.1992, p. 24.

and of the Council of 26 October 1994 on the protection of purchasers in respect of certain aspects on contracts relating to the purchase of the right to use immovable properties on a timeshare basis[40], Directive 98/27/EC of the European Parliament and of the Council of 19 May 1998 on injunctions for the protection of consumers' interests[41], Council Directive 85/374/EEC of 25 July 1985 on the approximation of the laws, regulations and administrative provisions concerning liability for defective products[42], Directive 1999/44/EC of the European Parliament and of the Council of 25 May 1999 on certain aspects of the sale of consumer goods and associated guarantees[43], the future Directive of the European Parliament and of the Council concerning the distance marketing of consumer financial services and Council Directive 92/28/EEC of 31 March 1992 on the advertising of medicinal products[44]; this Directive should be without prejudice to Directive 98/43/EC of the European Parliament and of the Council of 6 July 1998 on the approximation of the laws, regulations and administrative provisions of the Member States relating to the advertising and sponsorship of tobacco products[45] adopted within the framework of the internal market, or to directives on the protection of public health; this Directive complements information requirements established by the abovementioned Directives and in particular Directive 97/7/EC.

(12) It is necessary to exclude certain activities from the scope of this Directive, on the grounds that the freedom to provide services in these fields cannot, at this stage, be guaranteed under the Treaty or existing secondary legislation; excluding these activities does not preclude any instruments which might prove necessary for the proper functioning of the internal market;

taxation, particularly value added tax imposed on a large number of the services covered by this Directive, must be excluded form the scope of this Directive.

(13) This Directive does not aim to establish rules on fiscal obligations nor does it pre-empt the drawing up of Community instruments concerning fiscal aspects of electronic commerce.

(14) The protection of individuals with regard to the processing of personal data is solely governed by Directive 95/46/EC of the European Parliament and of the Council of 24 October 1995 on the protection of individuals with regard to the processing of personal data and on the free movement of such data[46] and Directive 97/66/EC of the European Parliament and of the Council of 15 December 1997 concerning the processing of personal data and the protection of privacy in the telecommunications sector[47] which are fully applicable to information society services; these Directives already establish a Community legal framework in the field of personal data and therefore it is not necessary to cover this issue in this Directive in order to ensure the smooth functioning of the internal market, in particular the free movement of personal data between Member States; the implementation and application of this Directive should be made in full compliance with the principles relating to the protection of personal data, in particular as regards unsolicited commercial communication and the liability of intermediaries; this Directive cannot prevent the anonymous use of open networks such as the Internet.

(15) The confidentiality of communications is guaranteed by Article 5 Directive 97/66/EC; in accordance with that Directive, Member States must prohibit any kind of interception or surveillance of such communications by others than the senders and receivers, except when legally authorised.

(16) The exclusion of gambling activities from the scope of application of this Directive covers only games of chance, lotteries and betting transactions, which involve wagering a stake with monetary value; this does not cover pro-

---

[40] OJ L 280, 29.10.1994, p. 83.

[41] OJ L 166, 11.6.1998, p. 51. Directive as amended by Directive 1999/44/EC (OJ L 171, 7.7.1999, p. 12).

[42] OJ L 210, 7.8.1985, p. 29. Directive as amended by Directive 1999/34/EC (OJ L 141, 4.6.1999, p. 20).

[43] OJ L 171, 7.7.1999, p. 12.

[44] OJ L 113, 30.4.1992, p. 13.

[45] OJ L 213, 30.7.1998, p. 9.

[46] OJ L 281, 23.11.1995, p. 31.

[47] OJ L 24, 30.1.1998, p. 1.

motional competitions or games where the purpose is to encourage the sale of goods or services and where payments, if they arise, serve only to acquire the promoted goods or services.

(17) The definition of information society services already exists in Community law in Directive 98/34/EC of the European Parliament and of the Council of 22 June 1998 laying down a procedure for the provision of information in the field of technical standards and regulations and of rules on information society services[48] and in Directive 98/84/EC of the European Parliament and of the Council of 20 November 1998 on the legal protection of services based on, or consisting of, conditional access[49]; this definition covers any service normally provided for remuneration, at a distance, by means of electronic equipment for the processing (including digital compression) and storage of data, and at the individual request of a recipient of a service; those services referred to in the indicative list in Annex V to Directive 98/34/EC which do not imply data processing and storage are not covered by this definition.

(18) Information society services span a wide range of economic activities which take place on-line; these activities can, in particular, consist of selling goods on-line; activities such as the delivery of goods as such or the provision of services off-line are not covered; information society services are not solely restricted to services giving rise to on-line contracting but also, in so far as they represent an economic activity, extend to services which are not remunerated by those who receive them, such as those offering on-line information or commercial communications, or those providing tools allowing for search, access and retrieval of data; information society services also include services consisting of the transmission of information via a communication network, in providing access to a communication network or in hosting information provided by a recipient of the service; television broadcasting within the meaning of Directive EEC/89/552 and radio broadcasting are not information

society services because they are not provided at individual request; by contrast, services which are transmitted point to point, such as video-on-demand or the provision of commercial communications by electronic mail are information society services; the use of electronic mail or equivalent individual communications for instance by natural persons acting outside their trade, business or profession including their use for the conclusion of contracts between such persons is not an information society service; the contractual relationship between an employee and his employer is not an information society service; activities which by their very nature cannot be carried out at a distance and by electronic means, such as the statutory auditing of company accounts or medical advice requiring the physical examination of a patient are not information society services.

(19) The place at which a service provider is established should be determined in conformity with the case-law of the Court of Justice according to which the concept of establishment involves the actual pursuit of an economic activity through a fixed establishment for an indefinite period; this requirement is also fulfilled where a company is constituted for a given period; the place of establishment of a company providing services via an Internet website is not the place at which the technology supporting its website is located or the place at which its website is accessible but the place where it pursues its economic activity; in cases where a provider has several places of establishment it is important to determine from which place of establishment the service concerned is provided; in cases where it is difficult to determine from which of several places of establishment a given service is provided, this is the place where the provider has the centre of his activities relating to this particular service.

(20) The definition of "recipient of a service" covers all types of usage of information society services, both by persons who provide information on open networks such as the Internet and by persons who seek information on the Internet for private or professional reasons.

(21) The scope of the coordinated field is without prejudice to future Community harmonisation relating to information society services and

---

[48] OJ L 204, 21.7.1998, p. 37. Directive as amended by Directive 98/48/EC (OJ L 217, 5.8.1998, p. 18).
[49] OJ L 320, 28.11.1998, p. 54.

to future legislation adopted at national level in accordance with Community law; the coordinated field covers only requirements relating to on-line activities such as on-line information, on-line advertising, on-line shopping, on-line contracting and does not concern Member States' legal requirements relating to goods such as safety standards, labelling obligations, or liability for goods, or Member States' requirements relating to the delivery or the transport of goods, including the distribution of medicinal products; the coordinated field does not cover the exercise of rights of pre-emption by public authorities concerning certain goods such as works of art.

(22) Information society services should be supervised at the source of the activity, in order to ensure an effective protection of public interest objectives; to that end, it is necessary to ensure that the competent authority provides such protection not only for the citizens of its own country but for all Community citizens; in order to improve mutual trust between Member States, it is essential to state clearly this responsibility on the part of the Member State where the services originate; moreover, in order to effectively guarantee freedom to provide services and legal certainty for suppliers and recipients of services, such information society services should in principle be subject to the law of the Member State in which the service provider is established.

(23) This Directive neither aims to establish additional rules on private international law relating to conflicts of law nor does it deal with the jurisdiction of Courts; provisions of the applicable law designated by rules of private international law must not restrict the freedom to provide information society services as established in this Directive.

(24) In the context of this Directive, notwithstanding the rule on the control at source of information society services, it is legitimate under the conditions established in this Directive for Member States to take measures to restrict the free movement of information society services.

(25) National courts, including civil courts, dealing with private law disputes can take measures to derogate from the freedom to provide information society services in conformity with conditions established in this Directive.

(26) Member States, in conformity with conditions established in this Directive, may apply their national rules on criminal law and criminal proceedings with a view to taking all investigative and other measures necessary for the detection and prosecution of criminal offences, without there being a need to notify such measures to the Commission.

(27) This Directive, together with the future Directive of the European Parliament and of the Council concerning the distance marketing of consumer financial services, contributes to the creating of a legal framework for the on-line provision of financial services; this Directive does not pre-empt future initiatives in the area of financial services in particular with regard to the harmonisation of rules of conduct in this field; the possibility for Member States, established in this Directive, under certain circumstances of restricting the freedom to provide information society services in order to protect consumers also covers measures in the area of financial services in particular measures aiming at protecting investors.

(28) The Member States' obligation not to subject access to the activity of an information society service provider to prior authorisation does not concern postal services covered by Directive 97/67/EC of the European Parliament and of the Council of 15 December 1997 on common rules for the development of the internal market of Community postal services and the improvement of quality of service[50] consisting of the physical delivery of a printed electronic mail message and does not affect voluntary accreditation systems, in particular for providers of electronic signature certification service.

(29) Commercial communications are essential for the financing of information society services and for developing a wide variety of new, charge-free services; in the interests of consumer protection and fair trading, commercial communications, including discounts, promotional offers and promotional competitions or games, must meet a number of transparency

---

[50] OJ L 15, 21.1.1998, p. 14.

requirements; these requirements are without prejudice to Directive 97/7/EC; this Directive should not affect existing Directives on commercial communications, in particular Directive 98/43/EC.

(30) The sending of unsolicited commercial communications by electronic mail may be undesirable for consumers and information society service providers and may disrupt the smooth functioning of interactive networks; the question of consent by recipient of certain forms of unsolicited commercial communications is not addressed by this Directive, but has already been addressed, in particular, by Directive 97/7/EC and by Directive 97/66/EC; in Member States which authorise unsolicited commercial communications by electronic mail, the setting up of appropriate industry filtering initiatives should be encouraged and facilitated; in addition it is necessary that in any event unsolicited commercial communities are clearly identifiable as such in order to improve transparency and to facilitate the functioning of such industry initiatives; unsolicited commercial communications by electronic mail should not result in additional communication costs for the recipient.

(31) Member States which allow the sending of unsolicited commercial communications by electronic mail without prior consent of the recipient by service providers established in their territory have to ensure that the service providers consult regularly and respect the opt-out registers in which natural persons not wishing to receive such commercial communications can register themselves.

(32) In order to remove barriers to the development of cross-border services within the Community which members of the regulated professions might offer on the Internet, it is necessary that compliance be guaranteed at Community level with professional rules aiming, in particular, to protect consumers or public health; codes of conduct at Community level would be the best means of determining the rules on professional ethics applicable to commercial communication; the drawing-up or, where appropriate, the adaptation of such rules should be encouraged without prejudice to the autonomy of professional bodies and associations.

(33) This Directive complements Community law and national law relating to regulated professions maintaining a coherent set of applicable rules in this field.

(34) Each Member State is to amend its legislation containing requirements, and in particular requirements as to form, which are likely to curb the use of contracts by electronic means; the examination of the legislation requiring such adjustment should be systematic and should cover all the necessary stages and acts of the contractual process, including the filing of the contract; the result of this amendment should be to make contracts concluded electronically workable; the legal effect of electronic signatures is dealt with by Directive 1999/93/EC of the European Parliament and of the Council of 13 December 1999 on a Community framework for electronic signatures[51]; the acknowledgement of receipt by a service provider may take the form of the on-line provision of the service paid for.

(35) This Directive does not affect Member States' possibility of maintaining or establishing general or specific legal requirements for contracts which can be fulfilled by electronic means, in particular requirements concerning secure electronic signatures.

(36) Member States may maintain restrictions for the use of electronic contracts with regard to contracts requiring by law the involvement of courts, public authorities, or professions exercising public authority; this possibility also covers contracts which require the involvement of courts, public authorities, or professions exercising public authority in order to have an effect with regard to third parties as well as contracts requiring by law certification or attestation by a notary.

(37) Member States' obligation to remove obstacles to the use of electronic contracts concerns only obstacles resulting from legal requirements and not practical obstacles resulting from the impossibility of using electronic means in certain cases.

(38) Member States' obligation to remove obstacles to the use of electronic contracts is to be implemented in conformity with legal re-

---

[51] OJ L 13, 19.1.2000, p. 12.

quirements for contracts enshrined in Community law.

(39) The exceptions to the provisions concerning the contracts concluded exclusively by electronic mail or by equivalent individual communications provided for by this Directive, in relation to information to be provided and the placing of orders, should not enable, as a result, the by-passing of those provisions by providers of information society services.

(40) Both existing and emerging disparities in Member States' legislation and case-law concerning liability of service providers acting as intermediaries prevent the smooth functioning of the internal market, in particular by impairing the development of cross-border services and producing distortions of competition; service providers have a duty to act, under certain circumstances, with a view to preventing or stopping illegal activities; this Directive should constitute the appropriate basis for the development of rapid and reliable procedures for removing and disabling access to illegal information; such mechanisms could be developed on the basis of voluntary agreements between all parties concerned and should be encouraged by Member States; it is in the interest of all parties involved in the provision of information society services to adopt and implement such procedures; the provisions of this Directive relating to liability should not preclude the development and effective operation, by the different interested parties, of technical systems of protection and identification and of technical surveillance instruments made possible by digital technology within the limits laid down by Directives 95/46/EC and 97/66/EC.

(41) This Directive strikes a balance between the different interests at stake and establishes principles upon which industry agreements and standards can be based.

(42) The exemptions from liability established in this Directive cover only cases where the activity of the information society service provider is limited to the technical process of operating and giving access to a communication network over which information made available by third parties is transmitted or temporarily stored, for the sole purpose of making the transmission more efficient; this activity is of a mere technical, automatic and passive nature, which implies that the information society service provider has neither knowledge of nor control over the information which is transmitted or stored.

(43) A service provider can benefit from the exemptions for "mere conduit" and for "caching" when he is in no way involved with the information transmitted; this requires among other things that he does not modify the information that he transmits; this requirement does not cover manipulations of a technical nature which take place in the course of the transmission as they do not alter the integrity of the information contained in the transmission.

(44) A service provider who deliberately collaborates with one of the recipients of his service in order to undertake illegal acts goes beyond the activities of "mere conduit" or "caching" and as a result cannot benefit from the liability exemptions established for these activities.

(45) The limitations of the liability of intermediary service providers established in this Directive do not affect the possibility of injunctions of different kinds; such injunctions can in particular consist of orders by courts or administrative authorities requiring the termination or prevention of any infringement, including the removal of illegal information or the disabling of access to it.

(46) In order to benefit from a limitation of liability, the provider of an information society service, consisting of the storage of information, upon obtaining actual knowledge or awareness of illegal activities has to act expeditiously to remove or to disable access to the information concerned; the removal or disabling of access has to be undertaken in the observance of the principle of freedom of expression and of procedures established for this purpose at national level; this Directive does not affect Member States' possibility of establishing specific requirements which must be fulfilled expeditiously prior to the removal or disabling of information.

(47) Member States are prevented from imposing a monitoring obligation on service providers only with respect to obligations of a general nature; this does not concern monitoring obligations in a specific case and, in par-

ticular, does not affect orders by national authorities in accordance with national legislation.

(48) This Directive does not affect the possibility for Member States of requiring service providers, who host information provided by recipients of their service, to apply duties of care, which can reasonably be expected from them and which are specified by national law, in order to detect and prevent certain types of illegal activities.

(49) Member States and the Commission are to encourage the drawing-up of codes of conduct; this is not to impair the voluntary nature of such codes and the possibility for interested parties of deciding freely whether to adhere to such codes.

(50) It is important that the proposed directive on the harmonisation of certain aspects of copyright and related rights in the information society and this Directive come into force within a similar time scale with a view to establishing a clear framework of rules relevant to the issue of liability of intermediaries for copyright and relating rights infringements at Community level.

(51) Each Member State should be required, where necessary, to amend any legislation which is liable to hamper the use of schemes for the out-of-court settlement of disputes through electronic channels; the result of this amendment must be to make the functioning of such schemes genuinely and effectively possible in law and in practice, even across borders.

(52) The effective exercise of the freedoms of the internal market makes it necessary to guarantee victims effective access to means of settling disputes; damage which may arise in connection with information society services is characterised both by its rapidity and by its geographical extent; in view of this specific character and the need to ensure that national authorities do not endanger the mutual confidence which they should have in one another, this Directive requests Member States to ensure that appropriate court actions are available; Member States should examine the need to provide access to judicial procedures by appropriate electronic means.

(53) Directive 98/27/EC, which is applicable to information society services, provides a mechanism relating to actions for an injunction aimed at the protection of the collective interests of consumers; this mechanism will contribute to the free movement of information society services by ensuring a high level of consumer protection.

(54) The sanctions provided for under this Directive are without prejudice to any other sanction or remedy provided under national law; Member States are not obliged to provide criminal sanctions for infringement of national provisions adopted pursuant to this Directive.

(55) This Directive does not affect the law applicable to contractual obligations relating to consumer contracts; accordingly, this Directive cannot have the result of depriving the consumer of the protection afforded to him by the mandatory rules relating to contractual obligations of the law of the Member State in which he has his habitual residence.

(56) As regards the derogation contained in this Directive regarding contractual obligations concerning contracts concluded by consumers, those obligations should be interpreted as including information on the essential elements of the content of the contract, including consumer rights, which have a determining influence on the decision to contract.

(57) The Court of Justice has consistently held that a Member State retains the right to take measures against a service provider that is established in another Member State but directs all or most of his activity to the territory of the first Member State if the choice of establishment was made with a view to evading the legislation that would have applied to the provider had he been established on the territory of the first Member State.

(58) This Directive should not apply to services supplied by service providers established in a third country; in view of the global dimension of electronic commerce, it is, however, appropriate to ensure that the Community rules are consistent with international rules; this Directive is without prejudice to the results of discussions within international organisations (amongst others WTO, OECD, Uncitral) on legal issues.

(59) Despite the global nature of electronic communications, coordination of national regulatory measures at European Union level is

necessary in order to avoid fragmentation of the internal market, and for the establishment of an appropriate European regulatory framework; such coordination should also contribute to the establishment of a common and strong negotiating position in international forums.

(60) In order to allow the unhampered development of electronic commerce, the legal framework must be clear and simple, predictable and consistent with the rules applicable at international level so that it does not adversely affect the competitiveness of European industry or impede innovation in that sector.

(61) If the market is actually to operate by electronic means in the context of globalisation, the European Union and the major non-European areas need to consult each other with a view to making laws and procedures compatible.

(62) Cooperation with third countries should be strengthened in the area of electronic commerce, in particular with applicant countries, the developing countries and the European Union's other trading partners.

(63) The adoption of this Directive will not prevent the Member States from taking into account the various social, societal and cultural implications which are inherent in the advent of the information society; in particular it should not hinder measures which Member States might adopt in conformity with Community law to achieve social, cultural and democratic goals taking into account their linguistic diversity, national and regional specificities as well as their cultural heritage, and to ensure and maintain public access to the widest possible range of information society services; in any case, the development of the information society is to ensure that Community citizens can have access to the cultural European heritage provided in the digital environment.

(64) Electronic communication offers the Member States an excellent means of providing public services in the cultural, educational and linguistic fields.

(65) The Council, in its resolution of 19 January 1999 on the consumer dimension of the information society[52], stressed that the protection of consumers deserved special attention in

this field; the Commission will examine the degree to which existing consumer protection rules provide insufficient protection in the context of the information society and will identify, where necessary, the deficiencies of this legislation and those issues which could require additional measures; if need be, the Commission should make specific additional proposals to resolve such deficiencies that will thereby have been identified,

HAVE ADOPTED THIS DIRECTIVE:

## CHAPTER I GENERAL PROVISIONS
### Article 1
### Objective and scope

1. This Directive seeks to contribute to the proper functioning of the internal market by ensuring the free movement of information society services between the Member States.

2. This Directive approximates, to the extent necessary for the achievement of the objective set out in paragraph 1, certain national provisions on information society services relating to the internal market, the establishment of service providers, commercial communications, electronic contracts, the liability of intermediaries, codes of conduct, out-of-court dispute settlements, court actions and cooperation between Member States.

3. This Directive complements Community law applicable to information society services without prejudice to the level of protection for, in particular, public health and consumer interests, as established by Community acts and national legislation implementing them in so far as this does not restrict the freedom to provide information society services.

4. This Directive does not establish additional rules on private international law nor does it deal with the jurisdiction of Courts.

5. This Directive shall not apply to:

(a) the field of taxation;

(b) questions relating to information society services covered by Directives 95/46/EC and 97/66/EC;

(c) questions relating to agreements or practices governed by cartel law;

(d) the following activities of information society services:

---

[52] OJ C 23, 28.1.1999, p. 1.

- the activities of notaries or equivalent professions to the extent that they involve a direct and specific connection with the exercise of public authority,
- the representation of a client and defence of his interests before the courts,
- gambling activities which involve wagering a stake with monetary value in games of chance, including lotteries and betting transactions.
6. This Directive does not affect measures taken at Community or national level, in the respect of Community law, in order to promote cultural and linguistic diversity and to ensure the defence of pluralism.

## Article 2
## Definitions

For the purpose of this Directive, the following terms shall bear the following meanings:
(a) "information society services": services within the meaning of Article 1(2) of Directive 98/34/EC as amended by Directive 98/48/EC;
(b) "service provider": any natural or legal person providing an information society service;
(c) "established service provider": a service provider who effectively pursues an economic activity using a fixed establishment for an indefinite period. The presence and use of the technical means and technologies required to provide the service do not, in themselves, constitute an establishment of the provider;
(d) "recipient of the service": any natural or legal person who, for professional ends or otherwise, uses an information society service, in particular for the purposes of seeking information or making it accessible;
(e) "consumer": any natural person who is acting for purposes which are outside his or her trade, business or profession;
(f) "commercial communication": any form of communication designed to promote, directly or indirectly, the goods, services or image of a company, organisation or person pursuing a commercial, industrial or craft activity or exercising a regulated profession. The following do not in themselves constitute commercial communications:
- information allowing direct access to the activity of the company, organisation or person, in particular a domain name or an electronic-mail address,
- communications relating to the goods, services or image of the company, organisation or person compiled in an independent manner, particularly when this is without financial consideration;
(g) "regulated profession": any profession within the meaning of either Article 1(d) of Council Directive 89/48/EEC of 21 December 1988 on a general system for the recognition of higher-education diplomas awarded on completion of professional education and training of at least three-years' duration[53] or of Article 1(f) of Council Directive 92/51/EEC of 18 June 1992 on a second general system for the recognition of professional education and training to supplement Directive 89/48/EEC[54];
(h) "coordinated field": requirements laid down in Member States' legal systems applicable to information society service providers or information society services, regardless of whether they are of a general nature or specifically designed for them.
(i) The coordinated field concerns requirements with which the service provider has to comply in respect of:
- the taking up of the activity of an information society service, such as requirements concerning qualifications, authorisation or notification,
- the pursuit of the activity of an information society service, such as requirements concerning the behaviour of the service provider, requirements regarding the quality or content of the service including those applicable to advertising and contracts, or requirements concerning the liability of the service provider;
(ii) The coordinated field does not cover requirements such as:
- requirements applicable to goods as such,
- requirements applicable to the delivery of goods,
- requirements applicable to services not provided by electronic means.

---

[53] OJ L 19, 24.1.1989, p. 16.
[54] OJ L 209, 24.7.1992, p. 25. Directive as last amended by Commission Directive 97/38/EC (OJ L 184, 12.7.1997, p. 31).

## Article 3
### Internal market

1. Each Member State shall ensure that the information society services provided by a service provider established on its territory comply with the national provisions applicable in the Member State in question which fall within the coordinated field.

2. Member States may not, for reasons falling within the coordinated field, restrict the freedom to provide information society services from another Member State.

3. Paragraphs 1 and 2 shall not apply to the fields referred to in the Annex.

4. Member States may take measures to derogate from paragraph 2 in respect of a given information society service if the following conditions are fulfilled:

(a) the measures shall be:

(i) necessary for one of the following reasons:

- public policy, in particular the prevention, investigation, detection and prosecution of criminal offences, including the protection of minors and the fight against any incitement to hatred on grounds of race, sex, religion or nationality, and violations of human dignity concerning individual persons,

- the protection of public health,

- public security, including the safeguarding of national security and defence,

- the protection of consumers, including investors;

(ii) taken against a given information society service which prejudices the objectives referred to in point (i) or which presents a serious and grave risk of prejudice to those objectives;

(iii) proportionate to those objectives;

(b) before taking the measures in question and without prejudice to court proceedings, including preliminary proceedings and acts carried out in the framework of a criminal investigation, the Member State has:

- asked the Member State referred to in paragraph 1 to take measures and the latter did not take such measures, or they were inadequate,

- notified the Commission and the Member State referred to in paragraph 1 of its intention to take such measures.

5. Member States may, in the case of urgency, derogate from the conditions stipulated in paragraph 4(b). Where this is the case, the measures shall be notified in the shortest possible time to the Commission and to the Member State referred to in paragraph 1, indicating the reasons for which the Member State considers that there is urgency.

6. Without prejudice to the Member State's possibility of proceeding with the measures in question, the Commission shall examine the compatibility of the notified measures with Community law in the shortest possible time; where it comes to the conclusion that the measure is incompatible with Community law, the Commission shall ask the Member State in question to refrain from taking any proposed measures or urgently to put an end to the measures in question.

## CHAPTER II PRINCIPLES
### Section 1: Establishment and information requirements
### Article 4
### Principle excluding prior authorisation

1. Member States shall ensure that the taking up and pursuit of the activity of an information society service provider may not be made subject to prior authorisation or any other requirement having equivalent effect.

2. Paragraph 1 shall be without prejudice to authorisation schemes which are not specifically and exclusively targeted at information society services, or which are covered by Directive 97/13/EC of the European Parliament and of the Council of 10 April 1997 on a common framework for general authorisations and individual licences in the field of telecommunications services[55].

## Article 5
### General information to be provided

1. In addition to other information requirements established by Community law, Member States shall ensure that the service provider shall render easily, directly and permanently accessible to the recipients of the service and competent authorities, at least the following information:

(a) the name of the service provider;

(b) the geographic address at which the service provider is established;

---

[55] OJ L 117, 7.5.1997, p. 15.

(c) the details of the service provider, including his electronic mail address, which allow him to be contacted rapidly and communicated with in a direct and effective manner;

(d) where the service provider is registered in a trade or similar public register, the trade register in which the service provider is entered and his registration number, or equivalent means of identification in that register;

(e) where the activity is subject to an authorisation scheme, the particulars of the relevant supervisory authority;

(f) as concerns the regulated professions:

- any professional body or similar institution with which the service provider is registered,

- the professional title and the Member State where it has been granted,

- a reference to the applicable professional rules in the Member State of establishment and the means to access them;

(g) where the service provider undertakes an activity that is subject to VAT, the identification number referred to in Article 22(1) of the sixth Council Directive 77/388/EEC of 17 May 1977 on the harmonisation of the laws of the Member States relating to turnover taxes - Common system of value added tax: uniform basis of assessment[56].

2. In addition to other information requirements established by Community law, Member States shall at least ensure that, where information society services refer to prices, these are to be indicated clearly and unambiguously and, in particular, must indicate whether they are inclusive of tax and delivery costs.

## Section 2: Commercial communications
## Article 6
### Information to be provided

In addition to other information requirements established by Community law, Member States shall ensure that commercial communications which are part of, or constitute, an information society service comply at least with the following conditions:

(a) the commercial communication shall be clearly identifiable as such;

(b) the natural or legal person on whose behalf the commercial communication is made shall be clearly identifiable;

(c) promotional offers, such as discounts, premiums and gifts, where permitted in the Member State where the service provider is established, shall be clearly identifiable as such, and the conditions which are to be met to qualify for them shall be easily accessible and be presented clearly and unambiguously;

(d) promotional competitions or games, where permitted in the Member State where the service provider is established, shall be clearly identifiable as such, and the conditions for participation shall be easily accessible and be presented clearly and unambiguously.

## Article 7
### Unsolicited commercial communication

1. In addition to other requirements established by Community law, Member States which permit unsolicited commercial communication by electronic mail shall ensure that such commercial communication by a service provider established in their territory shall be identifiable clearly and unambiguously as such as soon as it is received by the recipient.

2. Without prejudice to Directive 97/7/EC and Directive 97/66/EC, Member States shall take measures to ensure that service providers undertaking unsolicited commercial communications by electronic mail consult regularly and respect the opt-out registers in which natural persons not wishing to receive such commercial communications can register themselves.

## Article 8
### Regulated professions

1. Member States shall ensure that the use of commercial communications which are part of, or constitute, an information society service provided by a member of a regulated profession is permitted subject to compliance with the professional rules regarding, in particular, the independence, dignity and honour of the profession, professional secrecy and fairness towards clients and other members of the profession.

---

[56] OJ L 145, 13.6.1977, p. 1. Directive as last amended by Directive 1999/85/EC (OJ L 277, 28.10.1999, p. 34).

2. Without prejudice to the autonomy of professional bodies and associations, Member States and the Commission shall encourage professional associations and bodies to establish codes of conduct at Community level in order to determine the types of information that can be given for the purposes of commercial communication in conformity with the rules referred to in paragraph 1

3. When drawing up proposals for Community initiatives which may become necessary to ensure the proper functioning of the Internal Market with regard to the information referred to in paragraph 2, the Commission shall take due account of codes of conduct applicable at Community level and shall act in close cooperation with the relevant professional associations and bodies.

4. This Directive shall apply in addition to Community Directives concerning access to, and the exercise of, activities of the regulated professions.

### Section 3: Contracts concluded by electronic means
### Article 9
### Treatment of contracts

1. Member States shall ensure that their legal system allows contracts to be concluded by electronic means. Member States shall in particular ensure that the legal requirements applicable to the contractual process neither create obstacles for the use of electronic contracts nor result in such contracts being deprived of legal effectiveness and validity on account of their having been made by electronic means.

2. Member States may lay down that paragraph 1 shall not apply to all or certain contracts falling into one of the following categories:

(a) contracts that create or transfer rights in real estate, except for rental rights;

(b) contracts requiring by law the involvement of courts, public authorities or professions exercising public authority;

(c) contracts of suretyship granted and on collateral securities furnished by persons acting for purposes outside their trade, business or profession;

(d) contracts governed by family law or by the law of succession.

3. Member States shall indicate to the Commission the categories referred to in paragraph 2 to which they do not apply paragraph 1. Member States shall submit to the Commission every five years a report on the application of paragraph 2 explaining the reasons why they consider it necessary to maintain the category referred to in paragraph 2(b) to which they do not apply paragraph 1.

### Article 10
### Information to be provided

1. In addition to other information requirements established by Community law, Member States shall ensure, except when otherwise agreed by parties who are not consumers, that at least the following information is given by the service provider clearly, comprehensibly and unambiguously and prior to the order being placed by the recipient of the service:

(a) the different technical steps to follow to conclude the contract;

(b) whether or not the concluded contract will be filed by the service provider and whether it will be accessible;

(c) the technical means for identifying and correcting input errors prior to the placing of the order;

(d) the languages offered for the conclusion of the contract.

2. Member States shall ensure that, except when otherwise agreed by parties who are not consumers, the service provider indicates any relevant codes of conduct to which he subscribes and information on how those codes can be consulted electronically.

3. Contract terms and general conditions provided to the recipient must be made available in a way that allows him to store and reproduce them.

4. Paragraphs 1 and 2 shall not apply to contracts concluded exclusively by exchange of electronic mail or by equivalent individual communications.

### Article 11
### Placing of the order

1. Member States shall ensure, except when otherwise agreed by parties who are not consumers, that in cases where the recipient of the

service places his order through technological means, the following principles apply:

- the service provider has to acknowledge the receipt of the recipient's order without undue delay and by electronic means,
- the order and the acknowledgement of receipt are deemed to be received when the parties to whom they are addressed are able to access them.

2. Member States shall ensure that, except when otherwise agreed by parties who are not consumers, the service provider makes available to the recipient of the service appropriate, effective and accessible technical means allowing him to identify and correct input errors, prior to the placing of the order.

3. Paragraph 1, first indent, and paragraph 2 shall not apply to contracts concluded exclusively by exchange of electronic mail or by equivalent individual communications.

### Section 4: Liability of intermediary service providers
### Article 12
### "Mere conduit"

1. Where an information society service is provided that consists of the transmission in a communication network of information provided by a recipient of the service, or the provision of access to a communication network, Member States shall ensure that the service provider is not liable for the information transmitted, on condition that the provider:

(a) does not initiate the transmission;
(b) does not select the receiver of the transmission; and
(c) does not select or modify the information contained in the transmission.

2. The acts of transmission and of provision of access referred to in paragraph 1 include the automatic, intermediate and transient storage of the information transmitted in so far as this takes place for the sole purpose of carrying out the transmission in the communication network, and provided that the information is not stored for any period longer than is reasonably necessary for the transmission.

3. This Article shall not affect the possibility for a court or administrative authority, in accordance with Member States' legal systems, of

requiring the service provider to terminate or prevent an infringement.

### Article 13
### "Caching"

1. Where an information society service is provided that consists of the transmission in a communication network of information provided by a recipient of the service, Member States shall ensure that the service provider is not liable for the automatic, intermediate and temporary storage of that information, performed for the sole purpose of making more efficient the information's onward transmission to other recipients of the service upon their request, on condition that:

(a) the provider does not modify the information;
(b) the provider complies with conditions on access to the information;
(c) the provider complies with rules regarding the updating of the information, specified in a manner widely recognised and used by industry;
(d) the provider does not interfere with the lawful use of technology, widely recognised and used by industry, to obtain data on the use of the information; and
(e) the provider acts expeditiously to remove or to disable access to the information it has stored upon obtaining actual knowledge of the fact that the information at the initial source of the transmission has been removed from the network, or access to it has been disabled, or that a court or an administrative authority has ordered such removal or disablement.

2. This Article shall not affect the possibility for a court or administrative authority, in accordance with Member States' legal systems, of requiring the service provider to terminate or prevent an infringement.

### Article 14
### Hosting

1. Where an information society service is provided that consists of the storage of information provided by a recipient of the service, Member States shall ensure that the service provider is not liable for the information stored at the request of a recipient of the service, on condition that:

(a) the provider does not have actual knowledge of illegal activity or information and, as regards claims for damages, is not aware of facts or circumstances from which the illegal activity or information is apparent; or

(b) the provider, upon obtaining such knowledge or awareness, acts expeditiously to remove or to disable access to the information.

2. Paragraph 1 shall not apply when the recipient of the service is acting under the authority or the control of the provider.

3. This Article shall not affect the possibility for a court or administrative authority, in accordance with Member States' legal systems, of requiring the service provider to terminate or prevent an infringement, nor does it affect the possibility for Member States of establishing procedures governing the removal or disabling of access to information.

### Article 15
### No general obligation to monitor

1. Member States shall not impose a general obligation on providers, when providing the services covered by Articles 12, 13 and 14, to monitor the information which they transmit or store, nor a general obligation actively to seek facts or circumstances indicating illegal activity.

2. Member States may establish obligations for information society service providers promptly to inform the competent public authorities of alleged illegal activities undertaken or information provided by recipients of their service or obligations to communicate to the competent authorities, at their request, information enabling the identification of recipients of their service with whom they have storage agreements.

### CHAPTER III IMPLEMENTATION
### Article 16
### Codes of conduct

1. Member States and the Commission shall encourage:

(a) the drawing up of codes of conduct at Community level, by trade, professional and consumer associations or organisations, designed to contribute to the proper implementation of Articles 5 to 15;

(b) the voluntary transmission of draft codes of conduct at national or Community level to the Commission;

(c) the accessibility of these codes of conduct in the Community languages by electronic means;

(d) the communication to the Member States and the Commission, by trade, professional and consumer associations or organisations, of their assessment of the application of their codes of conduct and their impact upon practices, habits or customs relating to electronic commerce;

(e) the drawing up of codes of conduct regarding the protection of minors and human dignity.

2. Member States and the Commission shall encourage the involvement of associations or organisations representing consumers in the drafting and implementation of codes of conduct affecting their interests and drawn up in accordance with paragraph 1(a). Where appropriate, to take account of their specific needs, associations representing the visually impaired and disabled should be consulted.

### Article 17
### Out-of-court dispute settlement

1. Member States shall ensure that, in the event of disagreement between an information society service provider and the recipient of the service, their legislation does not hamper the use of out-of-court schemes, available under national law, for dispute settlement, including appropriate electronic means.

2. Member States shall encourage bodies responsible for the out-of-court settlement of, in particular, consumer disputes to operate in a way which provides adequate procedural guarantees for the parties concerned.

3. Member States shall encourage bodies responsible for out-of-court dispute settlement to inform the Commission of the significant decisions they take regarding information society services and to transmit any other information on the practices, usages or customs relating to electronic commerce.

### Article 18
### Court actions

1. Member States shall ensure that court actions available under national law concerning information society services' activities allow for the

rapid adoption of measures, including interim measures, designed to terminate any alleged infringement and to prevent any further impairment of the interests involved.

2. The Annex to Directive 98/27/EC shall be supplemented as follows:

"11. Directive 2000/31/EC of the European Parliament and of the Council of 8 June 2000 on certain legal aspects on information society services, in particular electronic commerce, in the internal market (Directive on electronic commerce) (OJ L 178, 17.7.2000, p. 1)."

## Article 19
### Cooperation

1. Member States shall have adequate means of supervision and investigation necessary to implement this Directive effectively and shall ensure that service providers supply them with the requisite information.

2. Member States shall cooperate with other Member States; they shall, to that end, appoint one or several contact points, whose details they shall communicate to the other Member States and to the Commission.

3. Member States shall, as quickly as possible, and in conformity with national law, provide the assistance and information requested by other Member States or by the Commission, including by appropriate electronic means.

4. Member States shall establish contact points which shall be accessible at least by electronic means and from which recipients and service providers may:

(a) obtain general information on contractual rights and obligations as well as on the complaint and redress mechanisms available in the event of disputes, including practical aspects involved in the use of such mechanisms;

(b) obtain the details of authorities, associations or organisations from which they may obtain further information or practical assistance.

5. Member States shall encourage the communication to the Commission of any significant administrative or judicial decisions taken in their territory regarding disputes relating to information society services and practices, usages and customs relating to electronic commerce. The Commission shall communicate these decisions to the other Member States.

## Article 20
### Sanctions

Member States shall determine the sanctions applicable to infringements of national provisions adopted pursuant to this Directive and shall take all measures necessary to ensure that they are enforced. The sanctions they provide for shall be effective, proportionate and dissuasive.

## CHAPTER IV FINAL PROVISIONS
### Article 21
### Re-examination

1. Before 17 July 2003, and thereafter every two years, the Commission shall submit to the European Parliament, the Council and the Economic and Social Committee a report on the application of this Directive, accompanied, where necessary, by proposals for adapting it to legal, technical and economic developments in the field of information society services, in particular with respect to crime prevention, the protection of minors, consumer protection and to the proper functioning of the internal market.

2. In examining the need for an adaptation of this Directive, the report shall in particular analyse the need for proposals concerning the liability of providers of hyperlinks and location tool services, "notice and take down" procedures and the attribution of liability following the taking down of content. The report shall also analyse the need for additional conditions for the exemption from liability, provided for in Articles 12 and 13, in the light of technical developments, and the possibility of applying the internal market principles to unsolicited commercial communications by electronic mail.

## Article 22
### Transposition

1. Member States shall bring into force the laws, regulations and administrative provisions necessary to comply with this Directive before 17 January 2002. They shall forthwith inform the Commission thereof.

2. When Member States adopt the measures referred to in paragraph 1, these shall contain a reference to this Directive or shall be accompanied by such reference at the time of their official publication. The methods of making

such reference shall be laid down by Member States.

## Article 23
### Entry into force
This Directive shall enter into force on the day of its publication in the Official Journal of the European Communities.

## Article 24
### Addressees
This Directive is addressed to the Member States.

Done at Luxemburg, 8 June 2000.

For the European Parliament
The President
N. Fontaine

For the Council
The President
G. d'Oliveira Martins

## ANNEX
### DEROGATIONS FROM ARTICLE 3
As provided for in Article 3(3), Article 3(1) and (2) do not apply to:
- copyright, neighbouring rights, rights referred to in Directive 87/54/EEC[57] and Directive 96/9/EC[58] as well as industrial property rights,
- the emission of electronic money by institutions in respect of which Member States have applied one of the derogations provided for in Article 8(1) of Directive 2000/46/EC[59],
- Article 44(2) of Directive 85/611/EEC[60],
- Article 30 and Title IV of Directive 92/49/EEC[61], Title IV of Directive 92/96/EEC[62], Articles 7 and 8 of Directive 88/357/EEC[63] and Article 4 of Directive 90/619/EEC[64],
- the freedom of the parties to choose the law applicable to their contract,
- contractual obligations concerning consumer contacts,
- formal validity of contracts creating or transferring rights in real estate where such contracts are subject to mandatory formal requirements of the law of the Member State where the real estate is situated,
- the permissibility of unsolicited commercial communications by electronic mail

---

[57] OJ L 24, 27.1.1987, p. 36.
[58] OJ L 77, 27.3.1996, p. 20.
[59] Not yet published in the Official Journal.
[60] OJ L 375, 31.12.1985, p. 3. Directive as last amended by Directive 95/26/EC (OJ L 168, 18.7.1995, p. 7).
[61] OJ L 228, 11.8.1992, p. 1. Directive as last amended by Directive 95/26/EC.
[62] OJ L 360, 9.12.1992, p. 2. Directive as last amended by Directive 95/26/EC.
[63] OJ L 172, 4.7.1988, p. 1. Directive as last amended by Directive 92/49/EC.
[64] OJ L 330, 29.11.1990, p. 50. Directive as last amended by Directive 92/96/EC.

# Appendix 4

**Directive 2001/29/EC of the European Parliament and of the Council
of 22 May 2001
on the harmonisation of certain aspects of copyright and related rights
in the information society**

THE EUROPEAN PARLIAMENT AND THE COUNCIL OF THE EUROPEAN UNION,
Having regard to the Treaty establishing the European Community, and in particular Articles 47(2), 55 and 95 thereof,
Having regard to the proposal from the Commission[65],
Having regard to the opinion of the Economic and Social Committee[66],
Acting in accordance with the procedure laid down in Article 251 of the Treaty[67],

Whereas:

(1) The Treaty provides for the establishment of an internal market and the institution of a system ensuring that competition in the internal market is not distorted. Harmonisation of the laws of the Member States on copyright and related rights contributes to the achievement of these objectives.

(2) The European Council, meeting at Corfu on 24 and 25 June 1994, stressed the need to create a general and flexible legal framework at Community level in order to foster the development of the information society in Europe. This requires, inter alia, the existence of an internal market for new products and services. Important Community legislation to ensure such a regulatory framework is already in place

or its adoption is well under way. Copyright and related rights play an important role in this context as they protect and stimulate the development and marketing of new products and services and the creation and exploitation of their creative content.

(3) The proposed harmonisation will help to implement the four freedoms of the internal market and relates to compliance with the fundamental principles of law and especially of property, including intellectual property, and freedom of expression and the public interest.

(4) A harmonised legal framework on copyright and related rights, through increased legal certainty and while providing for a high level of protection of intellectual property, will foster substantial investment in creativity and innovation, including network infrastructure, and lead in turn to growth and increased competitiveness of European industry, both in the area of content provision and information technology and more generally across a wide range of industrial and cultural sectors. This will safeguard employment and encourage new job creation.

(5) Technological development has multiplied and diversified the vectors for creation, production and exploitation. While no new concepts for the protection of intellectual property are needed, the current law on copyright and related rights should be adapted and supplemented to respond adequately to economic realities such as new forms of exploitation.

(6) Without harmonisation at Community level, legislative activities at national level which have already been initiated in a number of Member States in order to respond to the technological challenges might result in significant differences in protection and thereby in restrictions on the free movement of services and products incorporating, or based on, intellectual

---

[65] OJ C 108, 7.4.1998, p. 6 and OJ C 180, 25.6.1999, p. 6.

[66] OJ C 407, 28.12.1998, p. 30.

[67] Opinion of the European Parliament of 10 February 1999 (OJ C 150, 28.5.1999, p. 171), Council Common Position of 28 September 2000 (OJ C 344, 1.12.2000, p. 1) and Decision of the European Parliament of 14 February 2001 (not yet published in the Official Journal). Council Decision of 9 April 2001.

*A.R. Lodder and H.W.K. Kaspersen (eds.),*
*eDirectives: Guide to European Union Law on E-Commerce, 183–196.*
© 2002 *Kluwer Law International. Printed in the Netherlands.*

property, leading to a refragmentation of the internal market and legislative inconsistency. The impact of such legislative differences and uncertainties will become more significant with the further development of the information society, which has already greatly increased transborder exploitation of intellectual property. This development will and should further increase. Significant legal differences and uncertainties in protection may hinder economies of scale for new products and services containing copyright and related rights.

(7) The Community legal framework for the protection of copyright and related rights must, therefore, also be adapted and supplemented as far as is necessary for the smooth functioning of the internal market. To that end, those national provisions on copyright and related rights which vary considerably from one Member State to another or which cause legal uncertainties hindering the smooth functioning of the internal market and the proper development of the information society in Europe should be adjusted, and inconsistent national responses to the technological developments should be avoided, whilst differences not adversely affecting the functioning of the internal market need not be removed or prevented.

(8) The various social, societal and cultural implications of the information society require that account be taken of the specific features of the content of products and services.

(9) Any harmonisation of copyright and related rights must take as a basis a high level of protection, since such rights are crucial to intellectual creation. Their protection helps to ensure the maintenance and development of creativity in the interests of authors, performers, producers, consumers, culture, industry and the public at large. Intellectual property has therefore been recognised as an integral part of property.

(10) If authors or performers are to continue their creative and artistic work, they have to receive an appropriate reward for the use of their work, as must producers in order to be able to finance this work. The investment required to produce products such as phonograms, films or multimedia products, and services such as "on-demand" services, is considerable. Adequate legal protection of intellectual property rights is necessary in order to guarantee the availability of such a reward and provide the opportunity for satisfactory returns on this investment.

(11) A rigorous, effective system for the protection of copyright and related rights is one of the main ways of ensuring that European cultural creativity and production receive the necessary resources and of safeguarding the independence and dignity of artistic creators and performers.

(12) Adequate protection of copyright works and subject-matter of related rights is also of great importance from a cultural standpoint. Article 151 of the Treaty requires the Community to take cultural aspects into account in its action.

(13) A common search for, and consistent application at European level of, technical measures to protect works and other subject-matter and to provide the necessary information on rights are essential insofar as the ultimate aim of these measures is to give effect to the principles and guarantees laid down in law.

(14) This Directive should seek to promote learning and culture by protecting works and other subject-matter while permitting exceptions or limitations in the public interest for the purpose of education and teaching.

(15) The Diplomatic Conference held under the auspices of the World Intellectual Property Organisation (WIPO) in December 1996 led to the adoption of two new Treaties, the "WIPO Copyright Treaty" and the "WIPO Performances and Phonograms Treaty", dealing respectively with the protection of authors and the protection of performers and phonogram producers. Those Treaties update the international protection for copyright and related rights significantly, not least with regard to the so-called "digital agenda", and improve the means to fight piracy world-wide. The Community and a majority of Member States have already signed the Treaties and the process of making arrangements for the ratification of the Treaties by the Community and the Member States is under way. This Directive also serves to implement a number of the new international obligations.

(16) Liability for activities in the network environment concerns not only copyright and

related rights but also other areas, such as defamation, misleading advertising, or infringement of trademarks, and is addressed horizontally in Directive 2000/31/EC of the European Parliament and of the Council of 8 June 2000 on certain legal aspects of information society services, in particular electronic commerce, in the internal market ("Directive on electronic commerce")[68], which clarifies and harmonises various legal issues relating to information society services including electronic commerce. This Directive should be implemented within a timescale similar to that for the implementation of the Directive on electronic commerce, since that Directive provides a harmonised framework of principles and provisions relevant inter alia to important parts of this Directive. This Directive is without prejudice to provisions relating to liability in that Directive.

(17) It is necessary, especially in the light of the requirements arising out of the digital environment, to ensure that collecting societies achieve a higher level of rationalisation and transparency with regard to compliance with competition rules.

(18) This Directive is without prejudice to the arrangements in the Member States concerning the management of rights such as extended collective licences.

(19) The moral rights of rightholders should be exercised according to the legislation of the Member States and the provisions of the Berne Convention for the Protection of Literary and Artistic Works, of the WIPO Copyright Treaty and of the WIPO Performances and Phonograms Treaty. Such moral rights remain outside the scope of this Directive.

(20) This Directive is based on principles and rules already laid down in the Directives currently in force in this area, in particular Directives 91/250/EEC[69], 92/100/EEC[70],

93/83/EEC[71], 93/98/EEC[72] and 96/9/EC[73], and it develops those principles and rules and places them in the context of the information society. The provisions of this Directive should be without prejudice to the provisions of those Directives, unless otherwise provided in this Directive.

(21) This Directive should define the scope of the acts covered by the reproduction right with regard to the different beneficiaries. This should be done in conformity with the acquis communautaire. A broad definition of these acts is needed to ensure legal certainty within the internal market.

(22) The objective of proper support for the dissemination of culture must not be achieved by sacrificing strict protection of rights or by tolerating illegal forms of distribution of counterfeited or pirated works.

(23) This Directive should harmonise further the author's right of communication to the public. This right should be understood in a broad sense covering all communication to the public not present at the place where the communication originates. This right should cover any such transmission or retransmission of a work to the public by wire or wireless means, including broadcasting. This right should not cover any other acts.

(24) The right to make available to the public subject-matter referred to in Article 3(2) should be understood as covering all acts of making available such subject-matter to members of the public not present at the place where the act of making available originates, and as not covering any other acts.

---

[68] OJ L 178, 17.7.2000, p. 1.

[69] Council Directive 91/250/EEC of 14 May 1991 on the legal protection of computer programs (OJ L 122, 17.5.1991, p. 42). Directive as amended by Directive 93/98/EEC.

[70] Council Directive 92/100/EEC of 19 November 1992 on rental right and lending right and on certain rights related to copyright in the field of intel-

lectual property (OJ L 346, 27.11.1992, p. 61). Directive as amended by Directive 93/98/EEC.

[71] Council Directive 93/83/EEC of 27 September 1993 on the coordination of certain rules concerning copyright and rights related to copyright applicable to satellite broadcasting and cable retransmission (OJ L 248, 6.10.1993, p. 15).

[72] Council Directive 93/98/EEC of 29 October 1993 harmonising the term of protection of copyright and certain related rights (OJ L 290, 24.11.1993, p. 9).

[73] Directive 96/9/EC of the European Parliament and of the Council of 11 March 1996 on the legal protection of databases (OJ L 77, 27.3.1996, p. 20).

(25) The legal uncertainty regarding the nature and the level of protection of acts of on-demand transmission of copyright works and subject-matter protected by related rights over networks should be overcome by providing for harmonised protection at Community level. It should be made clear that all rightholders recognised by this Directive should have an exclusive right to make available to the public copyright works or any other subject-matter by way of interactive on-demand transmissions. Such interactive on-demand transmissions are characterised by the fact that members of the public may access them from a place and at a time individually chosen by them.

(26) With regard to the making available in on-demand services by broadcasters of their radio or television productions incorporating music from commercial phonograms as an integral part thereof, collective licensing arrangements are to be encouraged in order to facilitate the clearance of the rights concerned.

(27) The mere provision of physical facilities for enabling or making a communication does not in itself amount to communication within the meaning of this Directive.

(28) Copyright protection under this Directive includes the exclusive right to control distribution of the work incorporated in a tangible article. The first sale in the Community of the original of a work or copies thereof by the rightholder or with his consent exhausts the right to control resale of that object in the Community. This right should not be exhausted in respect of the original or of copies thereof sold by the rightholder or with his consent outside the Community. Rental and lending rights for authors have been established in Directive 92/100/EEC. The distribution right provided for in this Directive is without prejudice to the provisions relating to the rental and lending rights contained in Chapter I of that Directive.

(29) The question of exhaustion does not arise in the case of services and on-line services in particular. This also applies with regard to a material copy of a work or other subject-matter made by a user of such a service with the consent of the rightholder. Therefore, the same applies to rental and lending of the original and copies of works or other subject-matter which are services by nature. Unlike CD-ROM or CD-I, where the intellectual property is incorporated in a material medium, namely an item of goods, every on-line service is in fact an act which should be subject to authorisation where the copyright or related right so provides.

(30) The rights referred to in this Directive may be transferred, assigned or subject to the granting of contractual licences, without prejudice to the relevant national legislation on copyright and related rights.

(31) A fair balance of rights and interests between the different categories of rightholders, as well as between the different categories of rightholders and users of protected subject-matter must be safeguarded. The existing exceptions and limitations to the rights as set out by the Member States have to be reassessed in the light of the new electronic environment. Existing differences in the exceptions and limitations to certain restricted acts have direct negative effects on the functioning of the internal market of copyright and related rights. Such differences could well become more pronounced in view of the further development of transborder exploitation of works and cross-border activities. In order to ensure the proper functioning of the internal market, such exceptions and limitations should be defined more harmoniously. The degree of their harmonisation should be based on their impact on the smooth functioning of the internal market.

(32) This Directive provides for an exhaustive enumeration of exceptions and limitations to the reproduction right and the right of communication to the public. Some exceptions or limitations only apply to the reproduction right, where appropriate. This list takes due account of the different legal traditions in Member States, while, at the same time, aiming to ensure a functioning internal market. Member States should arrive at a coherent application of these exceptions and limitations, which will be assessed when reviewing implementing legislation in the future.

(33) The exclusive right of reproduction should be subject to an exception to allow certain acts of temporary reproduction, which are transient or incidental reproductions, forming an integral and essential part of a technological process and carried out for the sole purpose of enabling

either efficient transmission in a network between third parties by an intermediary, or a lawful use of a work or other subject-matter to be made. The acts of reproduction concerned should have no separate economic value on their own. To the extent that they meet these conditions, this exception should include acts which enable browsing as well as acts of caching to take place, including those which enable transmission systems to function efficiently, provided that the intermediary does not modify the information and does not interfere with the lawful use of technology, widely recognised and used by industry, to obtain data on the use of the information. A use should be considered lawful where it is authorised by the rightholder or not restricted by law.

(34) Member States should be given the option of providing for certain exceptions or limitations for cases such as educational and scientific purposes, for the benefit of public institutions such as libraries and archives, for purposes of news reporting, for quotations, for use by people with disabilities, for public security uses and for uses in administrative and judicial proceedings.

(35) In certain cases of exceptions or limitations, rightholders should receive fair compensation to compensate them adequately for the use made of their protected works or other subject-matter. When determining the form, detailed arrangements and possible level of such fair compensation, account should be taken of the particular circumstances of each case. When evaluating these circumstances, a valuable criterion would be the possible harm to the rightholders resulting from the act in question. In cases where rightholders have already received payment in some other form, for instance as part of a licence fee, no specific or separate payment may be due. The level of fair compensation should take full account of the degree of use of technological protection measures referred to in this Directive. In certain situations where the prejudice to the rightholder would be minimal, no obligation for payment may arise.

(36) The Member States may provide for fair compensation for rightholders also when applying the optional provisions on exceptions or limitations which do not require such compensation.

(37) Existing national schemes on reprography, where they exist, do not create major barriers to the internal market. Member States should be allowed to provide for an exception or limitation in respect of reprography.

(38) Member States should be allowed to provide for an exception or limitation to the reproduction right for certain types of reproduction of audio, visual and audio-visual material for private use, accompanied by fair compensation. This may include the introduction or continuation of remuneration schemes to compensate for the prejudice to rightholders. Although differences between those remuneration schemes affect the functioning of the internal market, those differences, with respect to analogue private reproduction, should not have a significant impact on the development of the information society. Digital private copying is likely to be more widespread and have a greater economic impact. Due account should therefore be taken of the differences between digital and analogue private copying and a distinction should be made in certain respects between them.

(39) When applying the exception or limitation on private copying, Member States should take due account of technological and economic developments, in particular with respect to digital private copying and remuneration schemes, when effective technological protection measures are available. Such exceptions or limitations should not inhibit the use of technological measures or their enforcement against circumvention.

(40) Member States may provide for an exception or limitation for the benefit of certain non-profit making establishments, such as publicly accessible libraries and equivalent institutions, as well as archives. However, this should be limited to certain special cases covered by the reproduction right. Such an exception or limitation should not cover uses made in the context of on-line delivery of protected works or other subject-matter. This Directive should be without prejudice to the Member States' option to derogate from the exclusive public lending right in accordance with Article 5 of Directive 92/100/EEC. Therefore, specific contracts or licences should be promoted which, without

creating imbalances, favour such establishments and the disseminative purposes they serve.

(41) When applying the exception or limitation in respect of ephemeral recordings made by broadcasting organisations it is understood that a broadcaster's own facilities include those of a person acting on behalf of and under the responsibility of the broadcasting organisation.

(42) When applying the exception or limitation for non-commercial educational and scientific research purposes, including distance learning, the non-commercial nature of the activity in question should be determined by that activity as such. The organisational structure and the means of funding of the establishment concerned are not the decisive factors in this respect.

(43) It is in any case important for the Member States to adopt all necessary measures to facilitate access to works by persons suffering from a disability which constitutes an obstacle to the use of the works themselves, and to pay particular attention to accessible formats.

(44) When applying the exceptions and limitations provided for in this Directive, they should be exercised in accordance with international obligations. Such exceptions and limitations may not be applied in a way which prejudices the legitimate interests of the rightholder or which conflicts with the normal exploitation of his work or other subject-matter. The provision of such exceptions or limitations by Member States should, in particular, duly reflect the increased economic impact that such exceptions or limitations may have in the context of the new electronic environment. Therefore, the scope of certain exceptions or limitations may have to be even more limited when it comes to certain new uses of copyright works and other subject-matter.

(45) The exceptions and limitations referred to in Article 5(2), (3) and (4) should not, however, prevent the definition of contractual relations designed to ensure fair compensation for the rightholders insofar as permitted by national law.

(46) Recourse to mediation could help users and rightholders to settle disputes. The Commission, in cooperation with the Member States within the Contact Committee, should undertake a study to consider new legal ways of settling disputes concerning copyright and related rights.

(47) Technological development will allow rightholders to make use of technological measures designed to prevent or restrict acts not authorised by the rightholders of any copyright, rights related to copyright or the sui generis right in databases. The danger, however, exists that illegal activities might be carried out in order to enable or facilitate the circumvention of the technical protection provided by these measures. In order to avoid fragmented legal approaches that could potentially hinder the functioning of the internal market, there is a need to provide for harmonised legal protection against circumvention of effective technological measures and against provision of devices and products or services to this effect.

(48) Such legal protection should be provided in respect of technological measures that effectively restrict acts not authorised by the rightholders of any copyright, rights related to copyright or the sui generis right in databases without, however, preventing the normal operation of electronic equipment and its technological development. Such legal protection implies no obligation to design devices, products, components or services to correspond to technological measures, so long as such device, product, component or service does not otherwise fall under the prohibition of Article 6. Such legal protection should respect proportionality and should not prohibit those devices or activities which have a commercially significant purpose or use other than to circumvent the technical protection. In particular, this protection should not hinder research into cryptography.

(49) The legal protection of technological measures is without prejudice to the application of any national provisions which may prohibit the private possession of devices, products or components for the circumvention of technological measures.

(50) Such a harmonised legal protection does not affect the specific provisions on protection provided for by Directive 91/250/EEC. In particular, it should not apply to the protection of technological measures used in connection

with computer programs, which is exclusively addressed in that Directive. It should neither inhibit nor prevent the development or use of any means of circumventing a technological measure that is necessary to enable acts to be undertaken in accordance with the terms of Article 5(3) or Article 6 of Directive 91/250/EEC. Articles 5 and 6 of that Directive exclusively determine exceptions to the exclusive rights applicable to computer programs.

(51) The legal protection of technological measures applies without prejudice to public policy, as reflected in Article 5, or public security. Member States should promote voluntary measures taken by rightholders, including the conclusion and implementation of agreements between rightholders and other parties concerned, to accommodate achieving the objectives of certain exceptions or limitations provided for in national law in accordance with this Directive. In the absence of such voluntary measures or agreements within a reasonable period of time, Member States should take appropriate measures to ensure that rightholders provide beneficiaries of such exceptions or limitations with appropriate means of benefiting from them, by modifying an implemented technological measure or by other means. However, in order to prevent abuse of such measures taken by rightholders, including within the framework of agreements, or taken by a Member State, any technological measures applied in implementation of such measures should enjoy legal protection.

(52) When implementing an exception or limitation for private copying in accordance with Article 5(2)(b), Member States should likewise promote the use of voluntary measures to accommodate achieving the objectives of such exception or limitation. If, within a reasonable period of time, no such voluntary measures to make reproduction for private use possible have been taken, Member States may take measures to enable beneficiaries of the exception or limitation concerned to benefit from it. Voluntary measures taken by rightholders, including agreements between rightholders and other parties concerned, as well as measures taken by Member States, do not prevent rightholders from using technological measures which are consistent with the exceptions or

limitations on private copying in national law in accordance with Article 5(2)(b), taking account of the condition of fair compensation under that provision and the possible differentiation between various conditions of use in accordance with Article 5(5), such as controlling the number of reproductions. In order to prevent abuse of such measures, any technological measures applied in their implementation should enjoy legal protection.

(53) The protection of technological measures should ensure a secure environment for the provision of interactive on-demand services, in such a way that members of the public may access works or other subject-matter from a place and at a time individually chosen by them. Where such services are governed by contractual arrangements, the first and second subparagraphs of Article 6(4) should not apply. Non-interactive forms of online use should remain subject to those provisions.

(54) Important progress has been made in the international standardisation of technical systems of identification of works and protected subject-matter in digital format. In an increasingly networked environment, differences between technological measures could lead to an incompatibility of systems within the Community. Compatibility and interoperability of the different systems should be encouraged. It would be highly desirable to encourage the development of global systems.

(55) Technological development will facilitate the distribution of works, notably on networks, and this will entail the need for rightholders to identify better the work or other subject-matter, the author or any other rightholder, and to provide information about the terms and conditions of use of the work or other subject-matter in order to render easier the management of rights attached to them. Rightholders should be encouraged to use markings indicating, in addition to the information referred to above, inter alia their authorisation when putting works or other subject-matter on networks.

(56) There is, however, the danger that illegal activities might be carried out in order to remove or alter the electronic copyright-management information attached to it, or otherwise to distribute, import for distribution, broadcast, communicate to the public or make

available to the public works or other protected subject-matter from which such information has been removed without authority. In order to avoid fragmented legal approaches that could potentially hinder the functioning of the internal market, there is a need to provide for harmonised legal protection against any of these activities.

(57) Any such rights-management information systems referred to above may, depending on their design, at the same time process personal data about the consumption patterns of protected subject-matter by individuals and allow for tracing of on-line behaviour. These technical means, in their technical functions, should incorporate privacy safeguards in accordance with Directive 95/46/EC of the European Parliament and of the Council of 24 October 1995 on the protection of individuals with regard to the processing of personal data and the free movement of such data[74].

(58) Member States should provide for effective sanctions and remedies for infringements of rights and obligations as set out in this Directive. They should take all the measures necessary to ensure that those sanctions and remedies are applied. The sanctions thus provided for should be effective, proportionate and dissuasive and should include the possibility of seeking damages and/or injunctive relief and, where appropriate, of applying for seizure of infringing material.

(59) In the digital environment, in particular, the services of intermediaries may increasingly be used by third parties for infringing activities. In many cases such intermediaries are best placed to bring such infringing activities to an end. Therefore, without prejudice to any other sanctions and remedies available, rightholders should have the possibility of applying for an injunction against an intermediary who carries a third party's infringement of a protected work or other subject-matter in a network. This possibility should be available even where the acts carried out by the intermediary are exempted under Article 5. The conditions and modalities relating to such injunctions should be left to the national law of the Member States.

(60) The protection provided under this Directive should be without prejudice to national or Community legal provisions in other areas, such as industrial property, data protection, conditional access, access to public documents, and the rule of media exploitation chronology, which may affect the protection of copyright or related rights.

(61) In order to comply with the WIPO Performances and Phonograms Treaty, Directives 92/100/EEC and 93/98/EEC should be amended,

HAVE ADOPTED THIS DIRECTIVE:

CHAPTER I
OBJECTIVE AND SCOPE
Article 1
Scope

1. This Directive concerns the legal protection of copyright and related rights in the framework of the internal market, with particular emphasis on the information society.

2. Except in the cases referred to in Article 11, this Directive shall leave intact and shall in no way affect existing Community provisions relating to:

(a) the legal protection of computer programs;

(b) rental right, lending right and certain rights related to copyright in the field of intellectual property;

(c) copyright and related rights applicable to broadcasting of programmes by satellite and cable retransmission;

(d) the term of protection of copyright and certain related rights;

(e) the legal protection of databases.

CHAPTER II
RIGHTS AND EXCEPTIONS
Article 2
Reproduction right

Member States shall provide for the exclusive right to authorise or prohibit direct or indirect, temporary or permanent reproduction by any means and in any form, in whole or in part:

(a) for authors, of their works;

(b) for performers, of fixations of their performances;

(c) for phonogram producers, of their phonograms;

---

[74] OJ L 281, 23.11.1995, p. 31.

(d) for the producers of the first fixations of films, in respect of the original and copies of their films;

(e) for broadcasting organisations, of fixations of their broadcasts, whether those broadcasts are transmitted by wire or over the air, including by cable or satellite.

## Article 3
### Right of communication to the public of works and right of making available to the public other subject-matter

1. Member States shall provide authors with the exclusive right to authorise or prohibit any communication to the public of their works, by wire or wireless means, including the making available to the public of their works in such a way that members of the public may access them from a place and at a time individually chosen by them.

2. Member States shall provide for the exclusive right to authorise or prohibit the making available to the public, by wire or wireless means, in such a way that members of the public may access them from a place and at a time individually chosen by them:

(a) for performers, of fixations of their performances;

(b) for phonogram producers, of their phonograms;

(c) for the producers of the first fixations of films, of the original and copies of their films;

(d) for broadcasting organisations, of fixations of their broadcasts, whether these broadcasts are transmitted by wire or over the air, including by cable or satellite.

3. The rights referred to in paragraphs 1 and 2 shall not be exhausted by any act of communication to the public or making available to the public as set out in this Article.

## Article 4
### Distribution right

1. Member States shall provide for authors, in respect of the original of their works or of copies thereof, the exclusive right to authorise or prohibit any form of distribution to the public by sale or otherwise.

2. The distribution right shall not be exhausted within the Community in respect of the original or copies of the work, except where the first sale or other transfer of ownership in the Community of that object is made by the rightholder or with his consent.

## Article 5
### Exceptions and limitations

1. Temporary acts of reproduction referred to in Article 2, which are transient or incidental [and] an integral and essential part of a technological process and whose sole purpose is to enable:

(a) a transmission in a network between third parties by an intermediary, or

(b) a lawful use of a work or other subject-matter to be made, and which have no independent economic significance, shall be exempted from the reproduction right provided for in Article 2.

2. Member States may provide for exceptions or limitations to the reproduction right provided for in Article 2 in the following cases:

(a) in respect of reproductions on paper or any similar medium, effected by the use of any kind of photographic technique or by some other process having similar effects, with the exception of sheet music, provided that the rightholders receive fair compensation;

(b) in respect of reproductions on any medium made by a natural person for private use and for ends that are neither directly nor indirectly commercial, on condition that the rightholders receive fair compensation which takes account of the application or non-application of technological measures referred to in Article 6 to the work or subject-matter concerned;

(c) in respect of specific acts of reproduction made by publicly accessible libraries, educational establishments or museums, or by archives, which are not for direct or indirect economic or commercial advantage;

(d) in respect of ephemeral recordings of works made by broadcasting organisations by means of their own facilities and for their own broadcasts; the preservation of these recordings in official archives may, on the grounds of their exceptional documentary character, be permitted;

(e) in respect of reproductions of broadcasts made by social institutions pursuing non-commercial purposes, such as hospitals or prisons, on condition that the rightholders receive fair compensation.

3. Member States may provide for exceptions or limitations to the rights provided for in Articles 2 and 3 in the following cases:

(a) use for the sole purpose of illustration for teaching or scientific research, as long as the source, including the author's name, is indicated, unless this turns out to be impossible and to the extent justified by the non-commercial purpose to be achieved;

(b) uses, for the benefit of people with a disability, which are directly related to the disability and of a non-commercial nature, to the extent required by the specific disability;

(c) reproduction by the press, communication to the public or making available of published articles on current economic, political or religious topics or of broadcast works or other subject-matter of the same character, in cases where such use is not expressly reserved, and as long as the source, including the author's name, is indicated, or use of works or other subject-matter in connection with the reporting of current events, to the extent justified by the informatory purpose and as long as the source, including the author's name, is indicated, unless this turns out to be impossible;

(d) quotations for purposes such as criticism or review, provided that they relate to a work or other subject-matter which has already been lawfully made available to the public, that, unless this turns out to be impossible, the source, including the author's name, is indicated, and that their use is in accordance with fair practice, and to the extent required by the specific purpose;

(e) use for the purposes of public security or to ensure the proper performance or reporting of administrative, parliamentary or judicial proceedings;

(f) use of political speeches as well as extracts of public lectures or similar works or subject-matter to the extent justified by the informatory purpose and provided that the source, including the author's name, is indicated, except where this turns out to be impossible;

(g) use during religious celebrations or official celebrations organised by a public authority;

(h) use of works, such as works of architecture or sculpture, made to be located permanently in public places;

(i) incidental inclusion of a work or other subject-matter in other material;

(j) use for the purpose of advertising the public exhibition or sale of artistic works, to the extent necessary to promote the event, excluding any other commercial use;

(k) use for the purpose of caricature, parody or pastiche;

(l) use in connection with the demonstration or repair of equipment;

(m) use of an artistic work in the form of a building or a drawing or plan of a building for the purposes of reconstructing the building;

(n) use by communication or making available, for the purpose of research or private study, to individual members of the public by dedicated terminals on the premises of establishments referred to in paragraph 2(c) of works and other subject-matter not subject to purchase or licensing terms which are contained in their collections;

(o) use in certain other cases of minor importance where exceptions or limitations already exist under national law, provided that they only concern analogue uses and do not affect the free circulation of goods and services within the Community, without prejudice to the other exceptions and limitations contained in this Article.

4. Where the Member States may provide for an exception or limitation to the right of reproduction pursuant to paragraphs 2 and 3, they may provide similarly for an exception or limitation to the right of distribution as referred to in Article 4 to the extent justified by the purpose of the authorised act of reproduction.

5. The exceptions and limitations provided for in paragraphs 1, 2, 3 and 4 shall only be applied in certain special cases which do not conflict with a normal exploitation of the work or other subject-matter and do not unreasonably prejudice the legitimate interests of the rightholder.

## CHAPTER III
## PROTECTION OF TECHNOLOGICAL MEASURES AND RIGHTS-MANAGEMENT INFORMATION
### Article 6
### Obligations as to technological measures

1. Member States shall provide adequate legal protection against the circumvention of any effective technological measures, which the person concerned carries out in the knowledge, or with reasonable grounds to know, that he or she is pursuing that objective.

2. Member States shall provide adequate legal protection against the manufacture, import, distribution, sale, rental, advertisement for sale or rental, or possession for commercial purposes of devices, products or components or the provision of services which:

(a) are promoted, advertised or marketed for the purpose of circumvention of, or

(b) have only a limited commercially significant purpose or use other than to circumvent, or

(c) are primarily designed, produced, adapted or performed for the purpose of enabling or facilitating the circumvention of, any effective technological measures.

3. For the purposes of this Directive, the expression "technological measures" means any technology, device or component that, in the normal course of its operation, is designed to prevent or restrict acts, in respect of works or other subject-matter, which are not authorised by the rightholder of any copyright or any right related to copyright as provided for by law or the sui generis right provided for in Chapter III of Directive 96/9/EC. Technological measures shall be deemed "effective" where the use of a protected work or other subject-matter is controlled by the rightholders through application of an access control or protection process, such as encryption, scrambling or other transformation of the work or other subject-matter or a copy control mechanism, which achieves the protection objective.

4. Notwithstanding the legal protection provided for in paragraph 1, in the absence of voluntary measures taken by rightholders, including agreements between rightholders and other parties concerned, Member States shall take appropriate measures to ensure that rightholders make available to the beneficiary of an exception or limitation provided for in national law in accordance with Article 5(2)(a), (2)(c), (2)(d), (2)(e), (3)(a), (3)(b) or (3)(e) the means of benefiting from that exception or limitation, to the extent necessary to benefit from that exception or limitation and where that beneficiary has legal access to the protected work or subject-matter concerned.

A Member State may also take such measures in respect of a beneficiary of an exception or limitation provided for in accordance with Article 5(2)(b), unless reproduction for private use has already been made possible by rightholders to the extent necessary to benefit from the exception or limitation concerned and in accordance with the provisions of Article 5(2)(b) and (5), without preventing rightholders from adopting adequate measures regarding the number of reproductions in accordance with these provisions.

The technological measures applied voluntarily by rightholders, including those applied in implementation of voluntary agreements, and technological measures applied in implementation of the measures taken by Member States, shall enjoy the legal protection provided for in paragraph 1.

The provisions of the first and second subparagraphs shall not apply to works or other subject-matter made available to the public on agreed contractual terms in such a way that members of the public may access them from a place and at a time individually chosen by them.

When this Article is applied in the context of Directives 92/100/EEC and 96/9/EC, this paragraph shall apply mutatis mutandis.

### Article 7
### Obligations concerning rights-management information

1. Member States shall provide for adequate legal protection against any person knowingly performing without authority any of the following acts:

(a) the removal or alteration of any electronic rights-management information;

(b) the distribution, importation for distribution, broadcasting, communication or making available to the public of works or other subject-matter protected under this Directive or under

Chapter III of Directive 96/9/EC from which electronic rights-management information has been removed or altered without authority, if such person knows, or has reasonable grounds to know, that by so doing he is inducing, enabling, facilitating or concealing an infringement of any copyright or any rights related to copyright as provided by law, or of the sui generis right provided for in Chapter III of Directive 96/9/EC.

2. For the purposes of this Directive, the expression "rights-management information" means any information provided by rightholders which identifies the work or other subject-matter referred to in this Directive or covered by the sui generis right provided for in Chapter III of Directive 96/9/EC, the author or any other rightholder, or information about the terms and conditions of use of the work or other subject-matter, and any numbers or codes that represent such information.

The first subparagraph shall apply when any of these items of information is associated with a copy of, or appears in connection with the communication to the public of, a work or other subjectmatter referred to in this Directive or covered by the sui generis right provided for in Chapter III of Directive 96/9/EC.

## CHAPTER IV
## COMMON PROVISIONS
### Article 8
### Sanctions and remedies

1. Member States shall provide appropriate sanctions and remedies in respect of infringements of the rights and obligations set out in this Directive and shall take all the measures necessary to ensure that those sanctions and remedies are applied. The sanctions thus provided for shall be effective, proportionate and dissuasive.

2. Each Member State shall take the measures necessary to ensure that rightholders whose interests are affected by an infringing activity carried out on its territory can bring an action for damages and/or apply for an injunction and, where appropriate, for the seizure of infringing material as well as of devices, products or components referred to in Article 6(2).

3. Member States shall ensure that rightholders are in a position to apply for an injunction against intermediaries whose services are used by a third party to infringe a copyright or related right.

### Article 9
### Continued application
### of other legal provisions

This Directive shall be without prejudice to provisions concerning in particular patent rights, trade marks, design rights, utility models, topographies of semi-conductor products, type faces, conditional access, access to cable of broadcasting services, protection of national treasures, legal deposit requirements, laws on restrictive practices and unfair competition, trade secrets, security, confidentiality, data protection and privacy, access to public documents, the law of contract.

### Article 10
### Application over time

1. The provisions of this Directive shall apply in respect of all works and other subject-matter referred to in this Directive which are, on 22 December 2002, protected by the Member States' legislation in the field of copyright and related rights, or which meet the criteria for protection under the provisions of this Directive or the provisions referred to in Article 1(2).

2. This Directive shall apply without prejudice to any acts concluded and rights acquired before 22 December 2002.

### Article 11
### Technical adaptations

1. Directive 92/100/EEC is hereby amended as follows:

(a) Article 7 shall be deleted;

(b) Article 10(3) shall be replaced by the following: "3. The limitations shall only be applied in certain special cases which do not conflict with a normal exploitation of the subject-matter and do not unreasonably prejudice the legitimate interests of the rightholder."

2. Article 3(2) of Directive 93/98/EEC shall be replaced by the following: "2. The rights of producers of phonograms shall expire 50 years after the fixation is made. However, if the phonogram has been lawfully published within this period, the said rights shall expire 50 years from the date of the first lawful publication. If

no lawful publication has taken place within the period mentioned in the first sentence, and if the phonogram has been lawfully communicated to the public within this period, the said rights shall expire 50 years from the date of the first lawful communication to the public. However, where through the expiry of the term of protection granted pursuant to this paragraph in its version before amendment by Directive 2001/29/EC of the European Parliament and of the Council of 22 May 2001 on the harmonisation of certain aspects of copyright and related rights in the information society[75] the rights of producers of phonograms are no longer protected on 22 December 2002, this paragraph shall not have the effect of protecting those rights anew."

### Article 12
### Final provisions

1. Not later than 22 December 2004 and every three years thereafter, the Commission shall submit to the European Parliament, the Council and the Economic and Social Committee a report on the application of this Directive, in which, inter alia, on the basis of specific information supplied by the Member States, it shall examine in particular the application of Articles 5, 6 and 8 in the light of the development of the digital market. In the case of Article 6, it shall examine in particular whether that Article confers a sufficient level of protection and whether acts which are permitted by law are being adversely affected by the use of effective technological measures. Where necessary, in particular to ensure the functioning of the internal market pursuant to Article 14 of the Treaty, it shall submit proposals for amendments to this Directive.

2. Protection of rights related to copyright under this Directive shall leave intact and shall in no way affect the protection of copyright.

3. A contact committee is hereby established. It shall be composed of representatives of the competent authorities of the Member States. It shall be chaired by a representative of the Commission and shall meet either on the initiative of the chairman or at the request of the delegation of a Member State.

4. The tasks of the committee shall be as follows:

(a) to examine the impact of this Directive on the functioning of the internal market, and to highlight any difficulties;

(b) to organise consultations on all questions deriving from the application of this Directive;

(c) to facilitate the exchange of information on relevant developments in legislation and case-law, as well as relevant economic, social, cultural and technological developments;

(d) to act as a forum for the assessment of the digital market in works and other items, including private copying and the use of technological measures.

### Article 13
### Implementation

1. Member States shall bring into force the laws, regulations and administrative provisions necessary to comply with this Directive before 22 December 2002. They shall forthwith inform the Commission thereof.

When Member States adopt these measures, they shall contain a reference to this Directive or shall be accompanied by such reference on the occasion of their official publication. The methods of making such reference shall be laid down by Member States.

2. Member States shall communicate to the Commission the text of the provisions of domestic law which they adopt in the field governed by this Directive.

### Article 14
### Entry into force

This Directive shall enter into force on the day of its publication in the Official Journal of the European Communities.

### Article 15
### Addressees

This Directive is addressed to the Member States.

---

[75] OJ L 167, 22.6.2001, p. 10.

Done at Brussels, 22 May 2001.

For the European Parliament
The President
N. Fontaine

For the Council
The President
M. Winberg

# The Authors

## DUMORTIER

Jos Dumortier graduated in Law at K.U.Leuven (1973). After postgraduate studies in Nancy (Centre Européen Universitaire, 1974) and Heidelberg (DAAD, 1975), he became research fellow at K.U.Leuven. In 1981 he finished his Ph.D in Law on a thesis about Private International Conflicts of Law in the area of Labour Relations.

In 1985 he became part-time lecturer and in 1993 full-time Professor in Law and IT at K.U.Leuven. In 1990 he was the co-founder of the Interdisciplinary Centre for Law and Information Technology of which he became the first Director.

Since 1991 he is active in lecturing, research and consultancy in the area of Law and IT and published several books and articles on this subject. He is a Board Member of several scientific and professional organisations such as the European Academy (Bad Neuenahr, Germany), BELTUG (Belgian Telecommunications Users Association) and SGOA (Mediation and Arbitration in IT Conflicts) and he participates in the editorial board of several national and international periodical publications.

Prof. Dumortier is the editor of the International Encyclopaedia of Cyberlaw (Kluwer International). He is an active member of several working groups in the Belgian Royal Academy of Sciences and an associate member of the American Bar Association. He is the chairman of the legal workgroup of EEMA (European Electronic Messaging Association).

Prof. Dumortier is regularly working as an expert for the Belgian federal government, the Flemish government, the European Commission and several national and international organisations on issues relating to Law and ICT.

## HÖRNLE

Julia Hörnle has been Research Assistant at the IT Law Unit, Centre for Commercial Law Studies, University of London, since May 2000. Her research areas are e-commerce, online dispute resolution/ADR, consumer protection, regulatory issues on the Internet, jurisdiction and conflict of law issues in e-commerce. She is the course head for the Unit's Internet Law Course and is participating in developing a distance learning module. Recent publications and research projects include: Article on European e-commerce legislation in JILT, Editor of the book *E-commerce Law and Practice in Europe* (collection of the research papers of the ECLIP I project), Overview of German E-commerce Legislation (for online portal), Phare Project Hungary: Report on the Implementation of the two Lawyers' Directives in Germany & Austria and several case reviews for Electronic Business Law. Julia Hörnle is a solicitor, previously working (1997- 2000) for the law firm of Eversheds in London and Brussels. She is a German national, and has studied at the Universities of Göttingen,

Leeds (LLB), the College of Europe, Hamburg (postgraduate) and the College of Law, Chester.

## KASPERSEN
After a career in the field of information technology Prof. dr. H.W.K. Kaspersen obtained his law degree at the University of Utrecht. In 1990 he defended his thesis at the Vrije Universiteit in Amsterdam on 'Computer Crime'. With regard to this subject he participated in the preparatory work of the governmental advisory committee on Computer Crime for the Dutch Computer Crime Act 1993. In 1991 he was appointed to professor and director of the Computer/Law Institute. Prof. Kaspersen chaired the expert committee of the Council of Europe that prepared the text of the Recommendation 1995 on Criminal Procedural issues in relation with computer-related crime. He is chairman of the expert-committee PC-CY of the Council of Europe which drafted the Cyber Crime Convention which has been adopted in November 2001. He now chairs the expert committee that drafts the first additional protocol to this Convention on racism. He is a member of the Legal Advisory Board of the European Commission. In 2000-2001, he participated at the national level in a governmental advisory committee on legal competences for law enforcement to gather electronic data.
Further he is the chief-editor of Dutch professional periodical *Computerrecht*, co-editor of the Dutch handbook on Computer/Law (*Recht & Computer*), member of the editorial board of *Privacy en Informatie* and editor-in-chief of the book series *Informaticarecht*.

## LODDER
Arno R. Lodder holds degrees in Computer/Law, Civil Law and Criminology. From 1992-1997 he did his Ph.D at the Universiteit Maastricht. Since 1998 he is lecturer at the Computer/Law Institute of the Vrije Universiteit Amsterdam. In 1999 appeared his 1998 dissertation *DiaLaw* in the Law and Philosophy Library of Kluwer Academic Publishers. Also in 1999 he edited with Anja Oskamp the Dutch handbook on legal informatics (*Informatietechnologie voor Juristen*). In 1999-2000 he was responsible for the electronic commerce module in Ian Lloyd's European ENLIST-project. In 2000 he participated in the governmental advisory committee on Information Technology & the Freedom of Information Act (*Wob & ICT*). In 2001 he co-edited *IT support in the judiciary in some European countries*.
His research interests lie both in AI & Law (in particular legal argumentation), and IT Law (E-commerce, Online Dispute Resolution). He is editor of the Dutch journal Law & Electronic Media, and treasurer of the Foundation of Knowledge-based systems JURIX.

## SUTTER
Gavin Sutter joined the IT Law Unit at the Centre for Commercial Law Studies, University of London, in February 1999, and has been working, amongst other things, on the ECLIP project and ENLIST (Internet distance learning project). He has also car-

ried out research into the interception of electronic communications for the purposes of criminal investigations. Presently he is part of the team working within ECLIPII towards the development of a new distance learning scheme. Gavin coordinates the IT Law course which the Unit offers as an option on the University of London LL.M.. He has also been involved in the Internet Law course, lecturing on online copy-protection and methods of internet content control. In his spare time, he is undertaking ongoing PhD research into the enforcement of internet regulation, with specific attention to censorship, free speech and ISP liability issues. He has also published a number of papers on subjects including electronic payment systems, internet censorship, interception regimes in the US & UK, and so on, in organs such as *Communications Law* and the *International Journal of Law and Information Technology*. He is a regular contributor to *Electronic Business Law*, and his views on the law in relation to computer pornography and sexual harassment in the workplace have been quoted in *Shine*, a glossy magazine marketed at women in their late 20s.

Gavin read Honours Law at the Queen's University of Belfast between 1994 and 1997. During 1997-98 he read for the LLM Degree of Computers & Law, graduating with a distinction in December 1998.

## VIVANT

Born in 1951, Michel Vivant is a professor at the University of Montpellier and he was the Dean for three years. He is also an honorary doctor (honoris causa) of the University of Heidelberg, associate professor of the University of Laval, Quebec (1992), invited professor of the National University of Mexico (1997), of the University of Tunis (1997 - 2000), of the University La Sagesse of Beirut (1996 - 2001), of the Lebanese University of Beirut (1999 - 2001), of the University Hassan II of Casablanca (2001) and of the Vargas Fondation of Rio (Brasil) (2001).

Member of the French *High Council of Industrial Property*, member of the Legal Advisory Board of DG *Information Society* of the European Commission and, within this group, a member of the Intellectual Property Rights Task Force, he is also an expert for several international organisations (in particular he was *scientific expert* for the Council of Europe: Committee of experts on Crime in Cyberspace) and French public authorities (Prime Minister, Minister of Industry, Minister of Research... which have recently charged him with a scientific research dealing with patentability in the fields of new technologies - 2001 -).

Director of the Research Team *Créations immatérielles et Droit* (Immaterial Creations and Law) (ERCIM), he is a specialist in intellectual property rights in general and the new technologies in particular, recognised within and outside Europe. He has published extensively on the following themes: patents, trade marks, copyright, computer law, communication, networks (internet),... in six languages in more than ten countries (from Argentina to Vietnam). Among others, he has published the *Code de la propriété intellectuelle annoté* - annotated Intellectual Property Code - (Litec), *Le droit des brevets* - Patent Law - (Dalloz), *Informatique et Réseaux* - Computer and Internet Law - (Lamy, re-published each year), *Les contrats du commerce électronique* - Contracts of e-commerce - (Litec).

He is called upon to be a national and international arbitrator (in particular he is member of the WIPO Arbitration Center) and is a regular consultant for lawyers and companies (Bouygues, Bouygues Télécom, Cegetel, EDF, Elf, IBM, L'Oréal, Pierre Fabre...).

**WALDEN**
Dr Ian Walden is Head of the IT Law Unit in the Centre for Commercial Law Studies, Queen Mary, University of London (www.ccls.edu/itlaw), and Director of QM's Computer-Related Crime Research Centre. He is editor of *EDI and the Law* (1989) and joint editor of *Information Technology and the Law* (1990), *EDI Audit and Control* (1993), *Cross-border Electronic Banking* (1995), *Telecommunications Law Handbook* (1997), *E-Commerce Law and Practice in Europe* (2001) and *Telecommunications Law* (2001). Ian is a member of the European Commission's Legal Advisory Board for the Information Market and is a consultant to the global law firm, Baker & McKenzie: www.bakernet.com. The IT Law Unit is part of the ECLIP network of academic institutions in Europe specialising in electronic commerce law: www.eclip.org

# Index

# Law and Electronic Commerce

1. V. Bekkers, B.-J. Koops and S. Nouwt (eds.): *Emerging Electronic Highways*. New Challenges for Politics and Law. 1996                    ISBN 90-411-0183-7
2. G.P. Jenkins (ed.): *Information Technology and Innovation in Tax Administration*. 1996                    ISBN 90-411-0966-8
3. A. Mitrakas: *Open EDI and Law in Europe*. A Regulatory Framework. 1997                    ISBN 90-411-0489-5
4. G.N. Yannopoulos: *Modelling the Legal Decision Process for Information Technology Applications in Law*. 1998                    ISBN 90-411-0540-9
5. K. Boele-Woelki and C. Kessedjian (eds.): *Internet*: Which Court Decides? Which Law Applies? Quel tribunal décide? Quel droit s'applique? 1998                    ISBN 90-411-1036-4
6. B.-J. Koops: *The Crypto Controversy*. A Key Conflict in the Information Society. 1999                    ISBN 90-411-1143-3
7. E. Schweighofer: *Legal Knowledge Representation*. Automatic Text Analysis in Public International and European Law. 1999                    ISBN 90-411-1148-4
8. L. Matthijssen: *Interfacing between Lawyers and Computers*. An Architecture for Knowledge-based Interfaces to Legal Databases. 1999                    ISBN 90-411-1181-6
9. K.W. Grewlich: *Governance in "Cyberspace"*. Access and Public Interest in Global Communications. 1999                    ISBN 90-411-1225-1
10. B.-J. Koops, C. Prins en H. Hijmans (eds.): *ICT Law and Internationalisation*. A Survey of Government Views. 2000                    ISBN Hb 90-411-1505-6; Pb 90-411-1506-4
11. C. Girot: *User Protection in IT Contracts*. A Comperative Study of the Protection of the User Against Defective Performance in Information Technology. 2001                    ISBN 90-411-1548-X
12. J.E.J. Prins (ed.): *Designing E-Government*. On the Crossroads of Technological Innovation and Institutional Change. 2001                    ISBN 90-411-1621-4
13. E. Lederman and R. Shapira (eds.): *Law, Information and Information Technology*. 2001                    ISBN 90-411-1675-3
14. A.R. Lodder and H.W.K. Kaspersen (eds.): *eDirectives: Guide to European Union Law on E-Commerce*. Commentary on the Directives on Distance Selling, Electronic Signatures, Electonic Commerce, Copyright in the Information Society, and Data Protection. 2002                    ISBN 90-411-1752-0

KLUWER LAW INTERNATIONAL – THE HAGUE / LONDON / BOSTON